HISTORICAL FIGURES

FAMOUS DISCOVERERS AND EXPLORERS OF AMERICA

HISTORICAL FIGURES

Additional books and e-books in this series can be found on Nova's website under the Series tab.

HISTORICAL FIGURES

FAMOUS DISCOVERERS AND EXPLORERS OF AMERICA

CHARLES H. L. JOHNSTON

Copyright © 2018 by Nova Science Publishers, Inc.

All rights reserved. No part of this book may be reproduced, stored in a retrieval system or transmitted in any form or by any means: electronic, electrostatic, magnetic, tape, mechanical photocopying, recording or otherwise without the written permission of the Publisher.

We have partnered with Copyright Clearance Center to make it easy for you to obtain permissions to reuse content from this publication. Simply navigate to this publication's page on Nova's website and locate the "Get Permission" button below the title description. This button is linked directly to the title's permission page on copyright.com. Alternatively, you can visit copyright.com and search by title, ISBN, or ISSN.

For further questions about using the service on copyright.com, please contact:
Copyright Clearance Center
Phone: +1-(978) 750-8400   Fax: +1-(978) 750-4470   E-mail: info@copyright.com.

NOTICE TO THE READER
The Publisher has taken reasonable care in the preparation of this book, but makes no expressed or implied warranty of any kind and assumes no responsibility for any errors or omissions. No liability is assumed for incidental or consequential damages in connection with or arising out of information contained in this book. The Publisher shall not be liable for any special, consequential, or exemplary damages resulting, in whole or in part, from the readers' use of, or reliance upon, this material. Any parts of this book based on government reports are so indicated and copyright is claimed for those parts to the extent applicable to compilations of such works.

Independent verification should be sought for any data, advice or recommendations contained in this book. In addition, no responsibility is assumed by the publisher for any injury and/or damage to persons or property arising from any methods, products, instructions, ideas or otherwise contained in this publication.

This publication is designed to provide accurate and authoritative information with regard to the subject matter covered herein. It is sold with the clear understanding that the Publisher is not engaged in rendering legal or any other professional services. If legal or any other expert assistance is required, the services of a competent person should be sought. FROM A DECLARATION OF PARTICIPANTS JOINTLY ADOPTED BY A COMMITTEE OF THE AMERICAN BAR ASSOCIATION AND A COMMITTEE OF PUBLISHERS.

Additional color graphics may be available in the e-book version of this book.

Library of Congress Cataloging-in-Publication Data

ISBN: 978-1-53614-457-4

Published by Nova Science Publishers, Inc. † New York

To the Great Brotherhood of the Clergy who, with self-sacrifice, devotion, and lack of personal profit, have consecrated their lives to the education and development of the youths of all English speaking countries.

CONTENTS

List of Illustrations		xi
Preface		xiii
The Voice		xv
Chapter 1	Leif Ericson	1
Chapter 2	Christopher Columbus	11
Chapter 3	Amerigo Vespucci	29
Chapter 4	Juan Ponce de Leon	41
Chapter 5	Vasco Nuñez de Balboa	57
Chapter 6	Hernando Cortés	73
Chapter 7	Ferdinand Magellan	127
Chapter 8	Giovanni Verrazano	139
Chapter 9	Francisco Pizarro	149
Chapter 10	Hernando de Soto	171
Chapter 11	Samuel de Champlain	187
Chapter 12	Henry Hudson	209

Chapter 13	Pierre-Esprit Radisson	233
Chapter 14	Father Marquette	249
Chapter 15	Robert de La Salle	265
Chapter 16	Robert Edwin Peary	283
Epilogue		295
Index		297

Figure 1. Amerigo Vespucci.

LIST OF ILLUSTRATIONS

Figure 1.	Amerigo Vespucci	ix
Figure 2.	Leif Ericson	6
Figure 3.	The Landing of Columbus	20
Figure 4.	Amerigo Vespucci off the Coast of Venezuela	32
Figure 5.	Juan Ponce de Leon at the Fountain of Youth	54
Figure 6.	Balboa Taking Possession of the Pacific Ocean in the Name of the King of Spain	64
Figure 7.	Capture by Cortés of the City of Mexico	122
Figure 8.	The Death of Magellan	137
Figure 9.	Giovanni Verrazano	142
Figure 10.	Execution of the Inca of Peru	168
Figure 11.	de Soto in the Florida Wilderness	176
Figure 12.	Champlain in the Indian Battle	196
Figure 13.	Henry Hudson in New York Harbor	218
Figure 13.	Marquette and Joliet Discovering the Mississippi River	253
Figure 14.	La Salle at the Mouth of the Mississippi River	274
Figure 15.	Robert Edwin Peary	286

PREFACE*

My Dear Boys:

It has seemed fitting to include in the Famous Leaders Series this volume upon the discoverers and explorers, not only of North America, but also of Central and South America.

It has been impossible to include them all in a volume of this character; but I have selected the most important, and have omitted such men as Sebastian Cabot, Jacques Cartier, Sir Francis Drake, Baffin, Verendrye, Robert Gray, Lewis and Clark, Pike, Franklin, Frémont, and many others.

This is no new subject. The lives and histories of these discoverers have been written by many another; but I have endeavored to bring before you a series of pictures of some of the most noted of these men of daring and grim determination, and, if I have succeeded in painting the canvas with colors which are agreeable, then, my dear boys, I shall feel that the moments occupied in the preparation of these pages have been well spent.

Believe me,
Yours very affectionately,
Charles H. L. Johnston.
Chevy Chase,
Maryland. August, 1917

---

* This is an edited, reformatted, and augmented version of *Famous Discovers and Explorers of America,* by Charles H.L. Johnston, as it was originally published in 1917. The views, opinions and nomenclature expressed in this book are those of the authors, and do not reflect the views of Nova Science Publishers Inc.

THE VOICE

A voice came from the westward, it whispered a message clear,
And the dripping fog banks parted as the clarion tones drew near;
It spoke of shores untrodden, and it sang of mountains bold,
Of shimmering sands in distant lands which were covered with glittering gold.
It sang of hemlock forests, where the moose roamed, and the bear,
Where the eider bred near the cascade's head, and the lucivee had his lair.
It praised the rushing water falls, it told of the salmon red,
Who swam in the spuming ripples by the rushing river's head.
It chanted its praise of the languorous days which lay 'neath the shimmering sun,
Of the birch canoe and the Indian, too, who trapped in the forests dun.
Yea, it told of the bars of silver, and it whispered of emeralds green,
Of topaz, sapphire, and amethyst, which shone with a dazzling sheen.
Of warriors red with feathered head, of buffalo, puma, and deer,
Of the coral strand in a palm-tree land, and of dizzying mountains sheer.
And the voice grew louder and louder, and it fell upon listening ears,
Of the men who had heard strange music which was moistened with women's tears.
Of the men who loved to wander, of the souls who cared to roam,

Whose bed was the hemlock's branches, who rejoiced in the forest's gloom.
Leif the Lucky, Magellan, deLeon and Cortés bold,
Cartier, Drake, and Franklin; Pizarro and Baffin, old;
Shackleton, Hudson, Roosevelt; brave Peary and gay Champlain,
Frémont, Lewis, Balboa; Verendrye, and the Cabots twain;
'Twas the voice that called them onward, 'twas the voice that is calling still,
And the voice will call 'till the end of it all, and the voice has a conquering will.

Chapter 1

LEIF ERICSON

THE FIRST EUROPEAN TO EXPLORE, AND SETTLE IN, AMERICA

"From Greenland's icy mountains; from Iceland's rocky shore,
We sailed the ship which forged ahead and ruddy oarsmen bore;
We found the wild grape growing; we scoured the river's bed,
And chased the moose whose horns were broad, whose blood was rich and red.
Our axes felled the wild-wood, our spears the Skraelings slew,
We sank their round skin-barges as the cutting North Winds blew,
Over the wild waves rolling, back to the fiords of home,
We safely came to anchor,—but we'll never cease to roam."

Saga of the Vikings, 1000 A.D.

On the shore of a great fiord, or estuary of the sea, in the far northern country of Greenland, stood a little boy. He was sturdy-limbed, blue-eyed, flaxen-haired, and he was looking out across the water at a great high-prowed Viking ship which lay bobbing upon the waves.

He stood there thinking,—thinking, until, as he gazed enraptured upon the scene before him, a tall, bearded Norwegian came up behind him. He smiled upon the little boy, and, laying his hand upon his head, said:

"Little one, what are you dreaming about?"

The youthful Norwegian looked around and also smiled.

"Good Lothair," he answered, "I am thinking of the time when I shall be able to sail far to the westward, with the older Vikings, and can have adventures of mine own."

The other laughed.

"Ah, ha, that time will not be far distant," said he, benignly. "You will wax tough and sinewy in this bracing air and by sailing in these blue fiords. And then, some day, one of the Vikings will want a stout fellow to man an oar. He will call upon Leif, little Leif. And I'll warrant that little Leif will then be ready."

"I will be."

"And would you go far to the westward, to the land of the setting sun?"

"Even so."

"And would you be willing to risk life and limb amidst ice and snow?"

"I'd be glad to do it."

Lothair laughed loud and long.

"You are a true Viking, my boy. You are, indeed, one of those whom Thor has smiled upon and whom the Valkyrias would love to assist in battle. Keep up your spirit, and, some day, you may be famous,—who knows?"

So saying he walked away, still laughing softly to himself.

And the little boy still kept on thinking, thinking, and looking out upon the great, blue sea which seemed to beckon to him, to nod to him, and to sigh: "Come on! Come on! I have marvelous things to reveal to you, little boy."

The youthful Viking turned around, went back to his home, and kept on working and sailing, and fishing, and playing, until a time came when he had waxed great in both strength and in stature, and, as he looked at himself in the polished surface of his shield he said: "Ah! Now, indeed, I am a true Viking. I am ready for great things."

This little boy was the son of Eric the Red, a strong man, and a bad man, also. Eric's father lived in Iceland, whither he had been forced to fly from Norway, for he had killed a man there and he would himself have been killed, had he not jumped into a boat, rowed to a Viking ship, and sailed to the westward. And Eric the Red seems to have inherited the traits of his father, for he, too, killed another. He had lent some of his furniture to a neighbor who would not restore it. Eric, therefore, carried off his goods and the other pursued him. They met, and hot words passed; so they had a struggle and Eric killed the fellow. He was thus made an outlaw, so he went sailing away to find some place where he could live in peace, far from his brother Vikings. He found a land, where he settled,—and called it Greenland, for, said he, "other Vikings will come here and settle, also, if I give this place a good name."

Eric the Red, had two children, of whom one was called Thorstein, and the other, Leif. The first developed into a thin youth with black hair and a sallow complexion, but the second was rosy- cheeked, fair-haired, blue-eyed, and sturdy-limbed. He was, in fact, the little boy to whom Lothair spoke as he stood upon the banks of the fiord, gazing far into the distance, determined, some day, to sail towards the West where he was certain that adventure and treasure, too, perhaps, were waiting for him.

One of the men who accompanied Eric, the murderer, to Greenland was named Herjulf. This bold and daring adventurer had a son named Bjarni, who roved the seas over, in search of adventure, for many, many years. Finally, in 986, he came home to Iceland in order to drink the Yuletide ale with his father. Finding that his parent had gone away, he weighed anchor and started after him to Greenland, but he encountered foggy weather, and thus sailed for many days by guess work, without seeing either the sun or the stars. When, at length, he sighted land, it was a shore without mountains. He saw, through the misty murk, only a small height covered with dense woods. So, without stopping in order to make explorations, he turned his prow to the north and kept on. He knew that this was not Greenland, and, so we may think it strange that he did not stop to examine the rugged coastline.

The sky was now fair and a brisk breeze was astern, so, after scudding along for nine or ten days, Bjarni saw the icy crags of Greenland looming up before him, and, after some further searching, found his way to his father's house. He had more than once sighted a heavily timbered shoreline, to the west, while steering for home, and, when he told of it, great curiosity was excited amongst the Norsemen.

Little Leif had now grown to be a man of size and strength. He had made many a journey to Norway, and, when there, in the year 998, found that Roman missionary priests were preaching up and down the land, and had converted the King, Olaf Tryggbesson, who had formerly worshiped the Gods Thor and Odin. Leif, himself, became a Christian and was baptized, so, when he returned to Greenland, he took several priests with him, who converted many of the people. Old Eric the Red, however, preferred to worship in the way of his fathers, and continued to believe in the mystical Valhalla, or hall of departed spirits, where the dead Vikings were supposed to drink huge cups of ale while feasting with their gods.

Upon a bright, warm day in the year 1000 a.d., a great Viking ship lay calmly upon the waters of the bay before the town of Bratthalid in Greenland, and on shore all was bustle and confusion. Leif Ericson, in fact, had determined to sail far to the westward, even as he had dreamed of doing when a little boy; and so, with thirty staunch adventurers, he was preparing to load his ship with sufficient provisions to last for the journey to that strange country of which Bjarni had brought news. It took several weeks to gather provisions and men, but at length everything was ready. The sail was hoisted, the great oaken oars were dipped into the water, and the sharp bow of the Viking ship was turned toward the open sea. "Huzzah! Huzzah!" shouted the Norsemen. "Huzzah!"

The Viking ship, which had a huge dragon's head at the prow, was such a tiny affair, when compared with the massive ocean liners of to-day, that one can well imagine how she must have been tossed about by the great, surging waves; but she kept on and on, ever steering westward, until a land was discovered which seemed to be filled with flat stones, so they called it Helluland, or flat-stone land. This was the Newfoundland of our maps, to-day.

Leaving this behind them, the Vikings kept on steering southward and westward, until they saw a low-lying and heavily wooded shore. This was Nova Scotia, and they coasted along it, for many days, occasionally coming to anchor in one of the deep bays, and heaving overboard their fishing lines, so as to catch some of the many fish which seemed to abound in these waters.

They sailed on towards the south, and at last reached a place where a beautiful river flowed through a sort of an inland lake into the sea. Many islands were near the mouth of this stream, and, as salmon seemed to abound in the waters of this blue and clear-flowing estuary of the Atlantic, Leif decided that this was a good place in which to spend the winter. So down went the anchor, the Viking ship was moored near the shore, and the men scrambled to the beach in order to erect huts in which to spend the cold season. Thus the dream of the little boy, as he had stood upon the shore of Greenland, years before, had come true, and Leif had reached a new world, to which he had been led by his daring and his love of adventure.

You see, that, although it was long supposed that Columbus was the first white man from Europe to ever set his foot upon the shore of America, such is not the case.

The real discoverer of America, of whom we have any definite record, was Bjarni, the son of Herjulf, who, in the midst of fog and murk, coasted along the shore of Nova Scotia in 986 a.d.

And the first European to make a settlement upon the shores of the new world was Leif Ericson, who sailed into that blue, salmon-filled river which flows "through a lake into the sea." So, if you look along the coast of New England, and try to find a river which answers this description, you will, I think, find but one. This is the river Charles, which, emptying into the Charles River Basin—a huge lake, if you wish—flows into the blue Atlantic. And, if you search the shore upon the Cambridge side near the hospital, you will find, to-day, the cellars of four houses,—the houses, no doubt, which Leif and his men erected in the year 1000 a.d.

Figure 2. Leif Ericson. (From the statue at Boston, Mass).

The Vikings built their huts, caught many salmon, and journeyed inland, where they found a profusion of wild grapes, so many, in fact, that they dried a great mass of them, loaded them into the hold, and called this land Vinland, the Good. They also found a race of people living in this country, who were ferocious in aspect, with ugly hair, big eyes, and broad cheeks. They were clad in the skins of the beaver, the lynx and the fox, and their weapons were bows and arrows, slings, and stone hatchets. As they screeched dismally when about to attack in battle, the Vikings called them Skraelings, or Screechers. It is apparent that the Skraelings were more like the Esquimaux, than like the Indians found by Columbus.

The Vikings spent a peaceful winter in Vinland and had no difficulty with the Skraelings, who left them alone. The Norsemen felled a great many trees and loaded their ship with lumber, with dried fish and grapes. Spring at last came and the ice and snow melted in the deep forests, the gray geese began to fly northward, and the robins chanted a melodious welcome from the budding thickets. The followers of Leif deserted their huts, clambered aboard their low-lying vessel, and, singing a song of thanksgiving, turned her prow towards the blue Atlantic. They coasted past the islands at the harbor-mouth, and, driven by a stout breeze, were soon careening over the waves upon their journey to Greenland.

But adventures were not entirely over, for, upon the way home, a dark spot appeared upon the horizon, and, upon sailing up to it, Leif and his seamen discovered a boat-load of sailors. These poor fellows had been out in a large vessel, but she had foundered, and had gone to the bottom in a squall. The castaways were rescued, were taken aboard the home-going Viking ship, and were carried along to Bratthalid, where Leif and his followers received a royal welcome, and great interest was taken in the story of their adventures. Leif was christened Leif the Lucky, and by that name he was to be known forever afterwards.

The daring navigator never again sailed to the pine-clad coast of Vinland, but other Norsemen made the journey and some left their bones to bleach upon the shores of New England. Thus in 1002, when Eric the Red died, and Leif the Lucky succeeded to his Earldom, Thorstein (Leif's brother) decided to explore the new-found country. So, with thirty or more men, he sailed to the westward, found the huts which the first adventurers had erected, and had the pleasure of spending the winter there. These voyagers stayed here for several years, for, in the spring of 1004, while some of the party were exploring, the ship was driven ashore in a storm, near a ness, or cape. They put a new keel into their damaged vessel and stuck the old one into the sand, calling the place Kjalarness, or Keel Cape. The cape was undoubtedly near the end of Cape Cod. Thorstein was subsequently slain in a battle with the Skraelings, but his men returned to Greenland, bringing lumber, dried fish, and many tales of this wonderful country; so that other Vikings longed to go and explore. Thus, in the summer of 1011, two ships set sail for Vinland, one with Leif's brother and sister, Thorwald and Freydis, and a crew of thirty men; the other with two brothers, Helgi and Finnibogi, and a crew of thirty-five. There were also a number of women.

Helgi and Finnibogi were the first to arrive at the huts which Leif had constructed, and had taken possession of them, when Freydis, arriving soon afterwards, ordered them to leave. Bad blood arose, and Freydis one day complained that Helgi had given her evil words and had struck her. She told Thorwald that he should avenge this insult, and taunted him so mercilessly, that, unable to bear her jeering words any longer, he was aroused to a deed of blood. Surrounded by his followers, he made a night attack upon the huts of Helgi and Finnibogi, seized and bound all the occupants, and killed them with cold steel. The peaceful shores of the river Charles witnessed such a murder as has never occurred again.

In 1012 the survivors sailed for Greenland in the vessel of the murdered brothers, which was the larger of the two. The evil woman, Freydis, who had caused all this trouble, pretended that the other party had been left in Vinland, and that ships had merely been exchanged. She threatened her men, that, if any told on her, they would be murdered, but words were let fall which came to the ears of Leif the Lucky. Three of those who had just returned were put to the torture, until they told the whole story of murder and death in the peaceful country of Vinland.

Leif was greatly affected by the news, but said with great show of magnanimity: "I have no heart to punish my wicked sister Freydis as she deserves. But this I do say to Freydis and Thorwald,—that their posterity will never thrive."

"And"—says an old Viking—"so it went that no one thought anything but evil of them from that time on."

This is the last that we hear of Leif the Lucky. That little rosy-cheeked boy, who dreamed that one day he would be a great adventurer, had accomplished his purpose. He had found a new country, he had lived to see it explored by other Vikings, and he had opened the eyes of Europeans to the fact that, far away there was a land which was richer in furs and in timber than anything which they had about them.

The citizens of Boston, Massachusetts, have erected a bronze statue to this navigator, upon Commonwealth Avenue; where, with hand shading his keen eyes, the staunch Norwegian is going out upon the Charles River;— that river, upon the banks of which in the year 1000 a.d., he and his followers spent a peaceful winter in the land of the Skraelings, the beaver, the bear, and the pink- fleshed salmon. Skoal, then, to Leif the Lucky! And remember that it was he, and not Columbus, who first trod upon the shores of America as an adventurer from the European world.

VINLAND

'Neath the scent of the green hemlock forests, near the sands of the storm-driven sea,
Lies a land which is good, filled with balsamy wood, and a voice there is calling to me;
There the grapes grow in reddening clusters, there the salmon jump clear of the falls,
And in crystalline splendor, the moon, in November, shines bright, as the lynx caterwauls.
From Moosehead the wild loon is screaming, from Rangely the trout jumps at play;
And from Kathadyn's bold peak, comes the osprey's fierce shriek, while the brown bear creeps near to its prey.
Oh! that is the land for the Vikings; yea, that is the kingdom of rest;
In the rude deer-skin boats, the warrior gloats, as the strangers press on to the West.
There is thunder for Thor and for Odin; there is silver for Tyr and Brogé,
In Jotunheim's palace, there is envy and malice; but nothing but love far away:
Come, Vikings, hoist up your rude anchors! Come, seamen, row hard, as ye should!

And steer to the West, where there's peace and there's rest; steer straightway to Vinland the Good.

Chapter 2

CHRISTOPHER COLUMBUS

RE-DISCOVERER OF AMERICA, WHO GAVE A NEW CONTINENT TO THE WORLD, (1436-1506)

> Great man, whose courage led you o'er
> The ocean's unknown length,
> A thousand voices thankfully
> Proclaim your power and strength.
> The treasures of the tropic isles,
> You found, but failed to gain.
> The honor that was due, was lost,
> You saw your subjects slain.
> Your plans for empire sailed away,
> Undone by other wills;
> And left but glorious memories,
> Which every seaman thrills.

The good and genial friar Juan Perez was working, one day, in front of the convent of La Rabida, which had been dedicated to Santa Maria de Rabida, near the pleasant city of Palos, in Spain. It was a lonely place, built upon beetling cliffs which overhung the blue ocean. The friar, with his brown cassock tucked up around his fat legs, was busily engaged in hoeing some beans, when he saw a man standing at the little wicket gate which was between himself and the roadway. The man was thin, care-worn, and cadaverous-looking. His hair was quite gray and he held a small boy by the hand.

"Kind priest," said he, "I am faint with hunger."

The good friar dropped his hoe and stood there smiling; for he had a warm heart, and the little boy, whom the stranger held by the hand, was very wistful.

"In God's name, my poor fellow," said Juan Perez, "come into the convent with me, and I will give you all that you wish, for I see that you are faint with hunger. And the little boy is surely very ill."

So the white-haired man and the little boy went into the convent of Santa Maria de Rabida, and there the priest fell into a long conversation with this traveler. He found out that the wanderer was named Christopher Columbus and that he had been born in Genoa, in Italy. The little boy was his son, Ferdinand.

The priest was a man of great learning and had been confessor to the Queen of Spain. He soon perceived that this Christopher Columbus was a man of considerable learning, also, and found out that he had been a sailor ever since he had been a boy of fourteen. Charmed and delighted with the conversation of this penniless mariner, he asked him to remain as a guest at the convent, for he saw that, within the lean body of this white-haired sailor, burned a spirit of adventure which was like a beacon light.

"Had I the money, the ships, and the men," said Columbus, "I could discover a new country lying far to the west. But, you see, I am a pauper."

"Yes," replied the good priest. "But I have powerful friends who have both money and ships. These will doubtless help you in your contemplated voyage. Stay with me for a few days. I will call them hither, so that you can discuss this matter with them."

Columbus was glad to have this prelate listen to his schemes for sailing far to the westward, for he had been endeavoring, for a long time, to get some one to give him the necessary financial assistance, so that he could fit out ships both with provisions and with men. In a day or two a physician arrived. He was a learned fellow, and his name was Garcia Fernandez. He was accompanied by a wealthy navigator, called Martin Alonzo Pinzon, who listened to the schemes of Columbus with great enthusiasm.

"I, myself, will lend you money for this voyage westward," said he. "And I will go in person upon this hazardous undertaking."

The good priest, Juan Perez, had become most enthusiastic over the scheme.

"Wait until I write to our gracious Queen Isabella," said he. "She, I know, will aid you in your contemplated journey. Be of good cheer, for she is the best of sovereigns, and cannot allow a Frenchman to have the honor of any discoveries in the West."

Christopher Columbus was quite willing to have this done, for he was sure that, could he but gain access to the ear of the great Queen, she, herself would see the righteousness of his cause and aid and abet in that which filled him with zeal and enthusiasm. So he waited patiently at the convent while a letter was dispatched to the kind-hearted Isabella, carried to the court by one Sebastian Rodriguez, a pilot of Lepe, and a man of considerable prominence. The Queen was at the military camp of Santa Fé, where she was directing her troops against the city of Granada, which was held by the Moors.

Fourteen days went by, and, at last, Rodriquez returned to the heights of Palos.

"The Queen is much interested in your mariner friend, Columbus," said he to Juan Perez. "She wishes greatly to add to the glory of Spain, and requests that you allow this sailor to travel to her military camp. But first she wishes to talk with you, good priest."

The friar was delighted. Quickly saddling his mule, he was soon upon his way to Santa Fé, where he was received with kindness and consideration. The Queen had a friend and companion called the Marchioness Moya who urged her to give aid to Columbus and thus bring much renown and glory both to herself and Spain. "This fellow has a great idea," she said. "Surely you will allow him, in the name of Spain, to find out what lies far to the westward."

Isabella was feeling particularly happy, just then, for her troops had nearly captured the city of Granada and the hated Moors were about to be driven from the soil of Spain. So she gave a great deal of money to the priest from Palos, in order that Christopher Columbus could buy a mule and sufficient clothing to appear at court. With smiles of satisfaction the good friar returned to the convent at La Rabida and the first link in the chain which led to the discovery of the West Indies by those of white complexion, had been forged.

The time had come when the schemes of western exploration, which for years had lain dormant in the breast of this penniless man from Genoa, were about to be put into execution. Columbus was now light-hearted, even merry, and, leaving his little son to the care of the good monks of Palos, he mounted a mule and journeyed to Santa Fé, accompanied by his friend Juan Perez.

It was a propitious moment. The Moorish leader had just handed over the keys of the city of Granada to Queen Isabella, who, mounted upon her horse and surrounded by a retinue of ladies- in-waiting and courtiers, joyfully received the keys, as evidence that the Moors were at last driven from the soil of Spain. Columbus soon was admitted to her presence and there told of his desire to sail westward toward the setting sun.

"But," said he, "if this voyage is a success, I must be made Admiral and Viceroy over the countries which I discover, and must also receive one-tenth of the revenues which come from these lands, either from trade or from agriculture."

These terms did not suit the Queen's counselors.

"It would be degrading to exalt an ordinary man to such high position," said Talavera, the Queen's foremost advisor. "The demands of this threadbare navigator are absurd."

More moderate terms were offered to Columbus, but he declined them.

"Good-by, Your Majesty," said he. "I will go to France, where the King will perhaps give me more advantageous offerings than you care to present."

So the good man mounted his mule—the very one which the Queen had presented him with—but he did not seem to mind using it, and, turning his back on Santa Fé, and the convent of La Rabida, he started for the Pyrenees Mountains in order to journey to France.

As soon as he had gone the Queen began to feel sorry that she had allowed him to depart. Her friends gathered around her and had a good deal to say.

"What an opportunity you are losing to enhance the glory of Spain," said several. "What a chance to make your own name forever great. If I were you, I would call this navigator back to court before he arrives upon the soil of France."

Her husband, King Ferdinand, looked coldly upon the project, for his treasury had been exhausted by the fighting with the Moors and he did not wish to spend any more money, just then. But the Queen had many jewels which she could pledge in order to raise money for ships and for supplies.

"Ferdinand," said she to her husband, "if you do not care to undertake this enterprise for the glory of the crown of Castile, I myself, will do so, and I will give all of my jewels as security for a loan to the navigator Columbus."

A courier was sent post haste after the sailor from Genoa, who was then ambling along upon his mule and was crossing the bridge of Pinos, some six miles from Granada.

"The Queen has changed her mind towards you," said the courier who had been sent to find the poor navigator. "Come back! You will now have funds with which to go upon your journey." Columbus hesitated a moment, for he feared that this was a lie, but, convinced of the truth of the statement, he turned about and whipped up his mule. They trotted along joyfully towards Santa Fé.

The Queen was now in a pleasant humor. Columbus was given all that he had asked for, but he was required to bear one-eighth of the expense of the journey. Papers to this effect were drawn up and signed on April the seventeenth, 1492, and, a month later, the joyful navigator set out for Palos in order to get ready the ships and provisions for the long-hoped-for voyage of discovery.

By the terms of the agreement between himself and the King and Queen he was to be called Viceroy and Governor of the new provinces which he wished to conquer in the rich territories of Asia, the country which he thought to be in the far west. He was to receive one-tenth of the pearls, precious stones, gold, silver, spices, and merchandise of whatever kind, which might be taken by his followers in the kingdoms which he expected to take possession of. Good terms these! Let us see how he fared!

Three caravels were now equipped for the journey at the port of Palos. It was difficult to find sailors to man them with. All were frightened at the enterprise and shuddered when they thought of a long sail into the unknown West. But the King said that he would pardon all those who had criminal charges hanging over them, should they join the expedition. In this way a sufficient number of sailors were secured.

The three ships were called the Gallega, the Pinta, and the Nina. The first was to be the flagship of Columbus, so he changed her name to the Santa Maria, as he was of a religious turn of mind. The Pinta was commanded by Martin Pinzon, and the Nina by his two brothers, Francis and Vincent.

On Friday, August 30th, 1492, the caravels headed out to sea and started upon this voyage of discovery. One hundred and twenty sailors had been secured, most of them with criminal records, so it was not to be expected that the Admiral, as Columbus was now called, would have an easy time with them. Some, in fact, were so anxious not to go that they purposely unshipped the rudder of the Pinta, when only a day from port, and the vessel had to be steered for the Canary Isles in order to repair the damage. Finally, after a three weeks' delay, during which another rudder was made, the expedition again hoisted canvas and headed for the blue horizon of the west. The hearts of the Spanish sailors now failed them and many cried like little children, for they were fearful of what lay before them; some, indeed, even thinking that they would come to a great hole and fall in. As for Columbus, he tried to comfort them with the prospect of gold and precious stones in India and Cathay which he was sure that they would discover.

"On, on, my men," said he. "On, and let us all be enriched by the treasures which we will soon come upon!"

But the ignorant sailors were constantly anxious and distrustful.

The bellying sails carried the three caravels ever to the westward. They sailed through vast masses of sea-weed on which small fish and crabs were hanging, and the sailors feared that they would be stranded upon this mass of vegetation. But when they threw lines into the water these did not touch the bottom, so they knew that they could go forward. The three vessels, in fact, were plowing through the Sargasso Sea, eight hundred miles from the Canary Isles. This is a mass of tangled sea-weed over two miles in depth, so it is no wonder that the lines did not touch anything when they let them down.

Now birds began to fly around the caravels, such as gannets and sea-swallows.

"Land must surely be near," cried many. "We have now been six weeks upon the water and Asia must certainly be before us."

But, in spite of the birds and the floating sea-weed, the boats kept on and on and still no land came to view.

Columbus, himself, never lost his confidence in the ultimate success of the journey.

"My men," said he, "land will eventually be sighted. You must bolster up your hearts and have great courage, for we will soon view the coast of Asia, where lives the mighty Khan."

And, each evening, he made the sailors chant a hymn to the Virgin. Cheered by the words of this heroic man, the Spaniards gained renewed hope and eagerly scanned the horizon for some signs of palm trees or tropic vegetation.

Before the expedition had set out, King Ferdinand had promised a reward of 10,000 maravédis, or 400 pounds sterling ($2,000), to the sailor who first discovered land. So, do you wonder that the mariners eagerly scanned the blue distance for a dark line of earth!

As the ships drowsed along with a gentle easterly wind in their rear, numerous large birds, petrels, man-of-war birds and damiers, flying in couples, were a sign that land must certainly be near, for otherwise how could these feathered sea-farers breed and lay their eggs? On, on, the mariners drifted, the sailors eager, depressed, even mutinous, but the courage of Columbus never wavered.

The month of October had now arrived and the Admiral announced to his crews that the ships had traveled 1,272 miles to the westward. In reality, they had sailed 2,100 miles; but Columbus hid the truth from his followers, for he knew them to be on the point of mutiny, and, should they learn how far they were from home, they would wish to return. On October the seventh the crews were much excited by hearing several musketry discharges from the Nina, the commander of which thought that he had discovered land. But this was an illusion; what he took to be land was but a patch of sea-weed, bobbing on the glassy waves.

A number of parroquets went flying by in a southwesterly direction, and, thinking that they were doubtless winging their way towards their homes, the Admiral was requested to steer more towards the south. This he did, and it is well that he so traveled, for, had the vessels kept due westward, they would doubtless have run aground upon the great Bahama Bank and would have been destroyed.

But why did not land appear?

Each evening the sun dipped down behind an interminable horizon of water. Sea-weed floated past, birds flew around upon every side, and still no land came to view. The Spaniards began to murmur loudly against Columbus.

"He is a Genoese, a foreigner," said some. "What does he care for Spaniards! He has enticed us from our own country only to drown us all. One thrust of a poniard and he will be out of the way forever!"

The Admiral heard of these remarks and knew that his sailors plotted his destruction, but his spirit never faltered, and, as the men still worked the ships, he kept courageously onward.

The eleventh of October had now come, and, as the bold navigator was looking over the side of the Santa Maria, he noticed a reed, still green, floating upon the top of a wave. His heart beat faster, for he realized that land must certainly be in the offing. Almost at the same time the men on board the Nina perceived the branch of a thorny tree, covered with blossoms, which bobbed upon the sprawling waves. All rejoiced exceedingly, for they knew that the coast of some strange country must be near. Night fell over the sea, and Columbus took up his position on the foremost part of his vessel, where he could watch until morning. About ten o'clock he thought that he saw a light in the distance and called to a sailor,

Pedro Gutierrez, a chamberlain in the King's service, who confirmed it. Once or twice, after this, the Admiral again saw the light, which looked as if some person were carrying a flambeau on shore, or in a boat, tossed by the waves.

Columbus spent a restless night. When morning broke, a sailor called Rodrigo de Triana, saw land from the deck of the Pinta, and a thrill of joy and thanksgiving ran through every heart. It was only two miles away, and the vessels quickly headed towards the low-lying shore. Every one eagerly crowded forward, with shouts and cries of joy, as the three caravels drew nearer and nearer to the sandy beach. The vessels anchored, and, crowding into the boats, Columbus, with his followers, rowed towards the breaking combers. All were eager to set foot upon the new-found territory.

Columbus had on a scarlet coat; and in one hand he held a cross, in the other a sword. When he reached the beach he knelt upon one knee and kissed the soil, while one of his followers held over his head the royal banner of gold, embroidered with crowns and with an F and I, the initials of Kind Ferdinand and Queen Isabella. He gave thanks to God; while all his crew of malcontents joined him in singing the Te Deum. His sailors gathered about him, embracing him with fervor, and begging his forgiveness for their mutinous spirit.

At this moment some naked savages appeared from behind the tropic foliage and came timidly towards the Spaniards. None of the men appeared to be over thirty years of age, and the women, too, were young. They were well made, their figures handsome, and their faces agreeable. Their hair, as coarse as the tail of a horse, hung down in front as far as their eyebrows, while behind it formed a long mass which was apparently never cut.

As they approached, the Spaniards greeted them kindly, and, when the voyageurs showed them their swords, the poor natives seized them in their hands so that they cut their fingers.

Figure 3. The Landing of Columbus.

The Spaniards roamed about for some time, glad indeed to stretch their legs, and then jumped into their long boats, in order to go back to the ships. Several of the natives plunged into the water and swam after them, crying out with apparent pleasure. Next day they came in crowds around the vessels, paddling themselves in enormous canoes shaped from the trunks of trees and guided by means of broad paddles, like a snow shovel. Several of the islanders wore little plates of gold hanging from their nostrils, which interested the Spaniards more than anything else. "Where did you get this?" they signaled to the chattering Indians. The natives pointed towards the south, when they understood what the mariners wished to know, and this made the voyageurs eager to get away, for gold was ever that which has lured the Spaniard onward.

Columbus named the island San Salvador, and believed that he had arrived upon the coast of Asia. The place was beautiful. Gray and yellow parroquets chattered and screamed from the trees, and brilliant tropic birds fluttered before them, as the Spaniards explored the interior. A small lake was in the center of the island, but there was no sign of gold or of gold mines. So the voyageurs turned away, disgusted, and determined to sail southward where the natives told them was a mighty monarch who possessed great vessels of gold, and immense riches.

The next morning, at day-break, Columbus gave orders to have the ships prepared for sea and all set sail towards the south, coasting along the western side of the island, while the natives, running down to the shore, offered the Spaniards water and cassava bread, made from the root of a plant called the "yucca." The Admiral landed upon the coast at different points and carried off some of the natives, so that he might exhibit them in Spain. Poor, ignorant islanders! Little did they guess that soon the white-skinned strangers would tear them from their country in order to sell them as slaves.

The Spaniards were really among the West Indies; but Columbus still had the idea that he was near China, the home of the mighty Khan, stories of whose wealth and possessions had already been brought to Spain. So, after the three caravels had left the island of Cuba, two emissaries were dispatched into the interior in order to take presents to the Khan. They soon returned, telling of the peaceful natives, beautiful groves of palm trees, but of no signs of the Asiatic potentate. They reported that both the native men and women smoked tobacco by means of a forked pipe, and that they had cotton houses made in the form of tents.

The crews now began to grow restless. They had come to find Asia or India, where were great hoards of gold. Instead of this they had found merely some tropic islands, populated by a race of naked savages who had no great treasures and knew nothing of gold mines. The Admiral sailed onward and kept discovering other islands, in all of which he found many articles of gold, but no particularly great city or town with riches and treasure. And there were no signs of the mighty Khan of Asia.

While exploring the coast of an island called Hayti, a young chief visited the caravels, attended by two hundred subjects. He spoke little, but gave the Admiral a curious belt and two pieces of gold, for which Columbus, in return, presented him with a piece of cloth, several amber beads, colored shoes, and a flask of orange water. In the evening the native was sent on shore with great ceremony and a salute was fired in his honor, which both surprised and interested him.

A short time after this a still greater chief, named Guacanagari, sent a messenger to the Admiral requesting him to come to his part of the island. The ships were therefore turned in the direction of this chief's home, and had sailed within a mile of his residence, when the Santa Maria ran upon a sand bank and quickly went to pieces. When news of this was brought to the native ruler, he sent his followers to unload the vessel and guard the contents, and his family to cheer the Spanish navigator and to assure him that everything which he possessed was at his disposal. All of the Spaniards went on board the Nina and were later entertained by the prince. So well, indeed, did Columbus like this island that he determined to erect a fort upon the coast, and to leave there a certain number of men with a year's provisions of bread, wine, and seed, also the long boat of the Santa Maria.

As a matter of fact the Spaniards were now eager to return to Spain, for, although they had discovered a new territory, they had not found the great quantities of gold. As for the mighty Khan, he was certainly not in the vicinity of these tropic isles, with their green paroquets screaming from the waving branches of the palm trees, and their naked savages with soft voices and hollowed canoes. The majority of the seamen thought that they had done quite sufficient exploring and were certainly ready to return to the bullfights and the crooked streets of old Seville.

"Back to Spain," they said to Columbus. "Back to Spain and let other adventurers come here if they wish. We have found the way for them. Let them explore and develop this territory."

Columbus was quite ready to set sail across the Atlantic, for he had found a new country for the Spanish Crown, and had added many square miles of territory to the possessions of King Ferdinand and Queen Isabella. It was now the month of January; the skies were blue and the weather was balmy; so all seemed propitious for a safe and speedy passage. Leaving thirty-nine men to garrison a fortress which he ordered to be constructed, and to search for gold until he could come back again from Spain, and naming one Rodrigo de Escovedo as their commander, the Admiral boarded the Nina, and, after fighting a mimic sham battle with his men, in order to amuse the Indians, he turned the prow of the little vessel toward the rising sun. The Pinta, under the command of Martin Pinzon, had been cruising to the south for some days; but she now returned, with the news that, although the natives had told of a great island to the south where there was much gold, none existed. The sailors were much distressed in mind, for they had certainly expected to find a quantity of gold and treasure in this tropic country.

It was now the seventh day of January and the boats lay to, in order to stop a leak which had sprung in the hold of the Nina. Columbus profited by the delay and explored a wide river which flowed from the base of a high mountain, called Monti Christi by some of the crew. The Admiral found the banks of this stream were full of gold-dust—so much, in fact, that he named it the Golden River. In spite of this discovery the Spanish sailors were still anxious to return and began to murmur against the authority of Columbus. Thus, on the ninth day of January, the two caravels set sail, and, steering towards the southeast, skirted the coast, en route for Spain.

As they swung lazily along, the natives sometimes followed them in their canoes. One day they began to shoot at the sailors with their arrows, so that discharge of musketry had to be resorted to, in order to drive them away. Two or three of the islanders were killed in this little affair, and thus, for the first time, the blood of an Indian flowed beneath the hand of a European.

Four of the natives were captured and taken on board so that they might be exhibited in Spain. They went unwillingly, but, when they endeavored to escape, were bound to the masts and were forced to join the Spanish adventurers. So, cruel even in this first expedition to the new world, just as they were ever afterwards, the Spanish navigators plowed eastward towards the land of Ferdinand and Isabella. The passage proved to be a quick one until the twelfth day of February, when the vessels encountered a fearful storm lasting three days.

The little caravels with their three-cornered sails were slapped around on the surging billows until all thought that they were lost, and the sailors swore on bended knee that they would go and pray in their shirts, and with naked feet, at the monastery of our Lady of Loretto, if a Kindly Heaven would only put an end to this fearful raging of the waters. Columbus seems to have given up all hope of ever reaching land, for he wrote out a description of his voyages, placed it inside a cask, and hurled it into the sea. This included a request that whoever should find this document would forward it to the King of Spain.

Luck, however, was with him, and the storm at length abated to such a degree that the two caravels cast anchor at the island of St. Mary, one of the Azores. The crew went ashore, and were immediately thrown into prison; but, after a period of five days, were allowed to leave by their Portuguese jailors. Again the two caravels headed for Spain, but again the winds blew vigorously, so that the Pinta was driven into the Bay of Biscay and the Nina had to take refuge at the mouth of the Tagus, in Portugal.

Here the Portuguese welcomed the Admiral in a kindly fashion, but he was anxious to return to Spain, and, as soon as the weather would permit, the Nina again set sail. Finally, on the fifteenth day of March, after seven months of navigation, she cast anchor at the port of Palos, that little harbor from which the man with a great idea had sailed with a half-hearted and distrusting crew. Columbus had guessed correctly. A new land did lie far to the westward across the blue Atlantic, and it was a land where was gold, that which every Spaniard prized the most. The Genoese mariner had discovered the islands of San Salvador, Conception, Great Exuma, Long Island, the Mucaras, Cuba, and San Domingo.

The first man to give him a welcoming pat on the back was the good old friar Juan Perez.

"You have done well, my good Columbus," said he. "How glad I am that I introduced you to the gracious Queen Isabella. You have indeed fulfilled the dreams that you dreamed in the convent of La Rabida."

Ferdinand and Isabella were then at Barcelona, and, hearing of the safe return of Columbus, a message was immediately dispatched to ask him to come at once to court. The Admiral landed, offered thanks to God for preserving him in all his trials, and, taking with him the Indian captives, started on his journey to the residence of his King. From all parts of the country the Spanish people ran to look at him as he passed. They threw their hats in their air, shouting: "Long live Columbus! Long live the discoverer of new countries! All honor to the Admiral!" He was preceded by a troop of cavalry and a band of music when he entered Barcelona, and flowers were strewn in his pathway.

Ferdinand and Isabella received him with great pomp at the Deputation. After hearing his story, told by him with graphic words, all knelt and chanted the Te Deum. Christopher Columbus was then ennobled by letters patent, and the King granted him a coat of arms bearing the device: "To Castile and Leon, Columbus gives a New World."

The fame of the poor navigator rang throughout all the then civilized world; the Indians were baptized in the presence of the whole court; and all tongues gave praise to this poor and unknown sailor who had dreamed a dream of conquest which had come true.

Strength of purpose and strength of will had won the day. Had the Genoese mariner given in to discouragement when his half-criminal sailors grew mutinous and wished to return to Spain after they had passed the Sargasso Sea, to some one else would have belonged the honor of the discovery of the West Indies. Had he not used a firm hand in dealing with them, they would have marooned him on one of the islands which he discovered and would have left him there to die. Had he not been sure that he would find what he was after, Queen Isabella would not have aided him to glory and renown. Great and valiant Sailor, you should indeed be remembered with reverence, for you knew how to triumph over doubt and discouragement and your faith was sublime! All honor then to Christopher Columbus!

The remaining adventures of this gallant soul can be briefly narrated. Upon a second voyage to the West Indies he found the men whom he had left behind him had all been murdered by the Indians. After Columbus had sailed to Spain the Spaniards had stolen some of the Indian women and had consequently stirred up the wrath of the great chief who lived in the interior of the island of Hayti, where they had been instructed to build a fort and live until the return of their companions. A row of graves under the swaying palm trees showed where once had been thirty- nine adventurous souls from Palos in Spain.

The Spaniards came over in numbers after this expedition, but, although they founded a city and attempted to settle in the new world, there were continual dissensions with the natives; fights; ambuscades; massacres. The men from Castile were lazy; greedy for gold; cruel to the natives; and treated them brutally when the poor Indians could not furnish them with the glittering metal which they so keenly desired. Then the more rapacious ones turned on Columbus himself, threw him in irons on one occasion, and continually derided him to the King of Spain, who, because the Indies did not produce the revenues which he had expected them to, turned coldly upon the mariner from Palos, and rather took the part of these malcontents against him. Like all persons who reach a certain pinnacle of greatness, Columbus could not remain a popular idol, for all men are human and he had the ambitions of others to contend with. There were fights with the natives; fights among the Colonists themselves; fights with the malaria, the yellow fever, and with other diseases.

Columbus himself fared badly. After the death of good Queen Isabella, Ferdinand would not aid him in the least. He had saved no money, after all these adventures, and, as his life drew to a close, had to live by borrowing. He did not even own a home in Spain, and had to reside at Inns and at boarding houses. Alone, neglected, miserable, poor, he finally passed to another and better world, on May the twentieth 1500. He was seventy years of age.

Buried in the convent of St. Francisco, at Valladolid, Spain, his body was removed to the monastery of Las Cuevas at Seville, and, still later, to the cathedral of San Domingo at Hispaniola. But again it was taken up, and transported by vessel to Havana, Cuba, that rich tropic isle which the great navigator himself had discovered. Here to-day it is lying, and the sad spirit of this strange man of destiny hovers over the richest of all the possessions which Spain held in the West Indies, until wrested from her feeble grasp by the people of the United States in the year 1898, and magnanimously presented to the Cuban people themselves, to govern as they wished.

Could the poor old mariner, as he lay dying at Valladolid, have but looked forward into the centuries and seen the New World which he had discovered, he would have indeed been well satisfied. Had he known that a great Exposition would have been held to his memory and fame, and could he have guessed that the children of the civilized world would ever afterwards be taught the history of his life, of his perseverance, his courage, and his faith, he would indeed have been cheered in those last cheerless and poverty-stricken days.

In the career of this poor Italian dreamer, studying in every moment of leisure, asking assistance year after year from crowned heads until he was fifty-six years of age, in order that he might make his immortal discoveries, is a lesson to all who feel that their lives have not been perhaps worth while as they near middle age. The lesson is:—keep on trying to win, and, even though you may not be appreciated during your lifetime, history will always give you a proper niche in the temple of fame. And do not believe that youth is the only time for adventurous discoveries. Columbus did not sail upon his epoch-making journey towards the West until after he had reached his fifty-sixth year. Middle age and perseverance, then, are good aids to place one within the halls of the immortals.

THE SONG OF THE ISLANDER

O brother, good brother, look out on the bay,
What's that that is nearing, so long and so gray?
'Tis a palm tree, I'll warrant, so large and so lean,
That it o'ershadows all palm trees that e'er I have seen.

O brother, good brother, it stops and is still;
White clouds are above it, they beckon and fill;
Two sticks running upward are covered with vines,
And a humming resounds like the wind when it whines.

O brother, good brother, a puff of white smoke
Rolls upward and onward—a voice surely spoke,

'Tis the speech of God Tezcal, he's calling aloud,
For the rest of the Gods to gather and crowd.

O brother, good brother, what's that to the rear?
A canoe is approaching, it fills me with fear,
For the white gods are paddling; they dress all in red,
And the skin of their hands looks like that of the dead.

O brother, good brother, bend low and keep still.
See the God in the bow, he is white-haired and ill.
Let us hide in the palms, ere they step on the shore,
Let us watch in the grass 'til this danger is o'er.

They jump to the beach, raise a cross-stick on high,
They speak a strange tongue and utter a cry.
O brother, good brother, what's that shines and gleams?
On their breasts, on their backs,—it glitters and beams.

Let us talk with these strangers, let us speak with these men,
There are hundreds of brothers behind in the glen,
They surely can't harm us, they come from the sky,
And they smile as they see us. Then let us draw nigh.
O brother, good brother, had I never been near,
These pale-visaged Gods who from Spain traveled here,
I'd be in the forest, not bound to the mast,
As the Nina rolls on and the shore flyeth past.

Good-bye, tropic islands! Good-bye, Salvador!
My spirit is crushed; my free life is o'er.
Farewell, beloved palm trees! Farewell and adieu!
My home is behind me and fades from my view.

Chapter 3

AMERIGO VESPUCCI

FLORENTINE NAVIGATOR FROM WHOM AMERICA HAS DERIVED ITS NAME, (1452-1512)

About the beginning of the thirteenth century a family called Vespucci established themselves in the City of Florence, Italy. Anastatio Vespucci was the head of the family in 1451 and lived in a stately mansion, now occupied as a hospital for the poor, near the gate of the city known as Porta del Prato. He was Secretary of the Senate, and, although he lived in a palatial dwelling, had little besides the salary attached to his high office. Upon March the ninth, 1451, the third son of this official was born, and, when three days of age, was duly christened Amerigo. He has since been called Americus.

Almost from his cradle the boy was destined to become a merchant. Yet he had a good schooling, too, and was educated at a private institution presided over by his father's brother, a monk of the Order of San Marco, who, before the birth of Americus, had become famous as a teacher of the noble youths of the city. Here the boy was taught mathematics, astronomy, geography, and the classics. He became especially interested in geography and was ambitious to excel as a geographer.

Amerigo, or Americus, seems to have remained a student under the direction of his uncle for a number of years, yet we have no record of when it was that he followed the wishes of his father and entered upon mercantile pursuits. At any rate, he never lost his early interest in geography. In spite of his days in a counting house, he eagerly studied maps and charts. He made a collection of them, and, for one map alone, paid a sum equivalent to five hundred and fifty-five dollars.

Americus had an elder brother, Geralamo, who had left home to seek his fortune in foreign climes and had established himself in business in Asia Minor. He became immensely wealthy, and all went well with him, until one day, while he was at church, thieves broke into his house and robbed him of all that he possessed. This greatly impoverished the family, so that Americus determined to leave Florence and journey to some other country where he could retrieve his brother's losses. He selected Spain as the scene of his future labors.

Just as Magellan deserted Portugal for Spain, so, also, Americus felt that here were fame and fortune awaiting him. Ferdinand and Isabella were then waging war upon the Moors who held the southern part of the peninsula, and, as this was regarded as a holy war, many of the young nobles from surrounding countries were in Spain fighting for the crown of Castile. The war created a demand for many articles of commerce, so Americus went to Spain as the agent for one of the Medici, a ruling family in Florence. At the beginning of the year 1492, when Columbus made his first journey of exploration to the West Indies, we find the young Italian associated with one Berardi, who, after the return of Columbus from his first voyage, was commissioned to furnish and equip four vessels to be sent to the New World at different intervals. Vespucci met Columbus, had lengthy conversations with him regarding the New World, and, from his letters, we can see that he had a very clear idea that Cuba was not the main land, as Columbus supposed it to be, but was an island.

Berardi died in December, 1495, and the management of all his affairs devolved upon the shoulders of Vespucci, who soon wearied of seeking the favors of fortune and determined to abandon mercantile life for something, "laudable and stable." He formed, in fact, a determination to visit the various parts of the world, a determination which he soon put into execution.

A navigator, called Ojeda, was about to set sail for the West Indies with four vessels and we find that Americus became one of his crew. According to some, he was to be one of the principal pilots; according to others he was to be an agent of the King and Queen, having a voice in the direction of the ships. On May 10th., 1497, the fleet left Cadiz, and, after reaching the Canary Islands, sailed so rapidly that, at the end of twenty-seven days, it came in sight of land. This was the coast of South America.

The Spaniards anchored and attempted to hold some intercourse with the natives, but the Indians were very shy and refused to come out to visit them. So, coasting along the shore, they came upon a village, which, much to their surprise, was built after the fashion of the city of Venice, Italy. The houses were placed upon piers in the water, and had entrances by means of drawbridges, so that the inhabitants, by leaving the bridges down, could traverse the whole town without difficulty. The explorers therefore called it Venezuela, a name which has endured to the present day.

The inhabitants, at first, shut themselves up in their houses and raised the drawbridges, and, as the ships came nearer, the savages embarked in their canoes and rowed out to sea. The Spaniards made every mark of friendship and invited the Indians to come to their ships, but the brown-skinned natives hastened away, making signs for the Spaniards to wait where they were, as they would return. They came back, bringing with them sixteen young girls, who beckoned to them and made signals of peace. The Castilians were much impressed by this; so much so, in fact, that their suspicions were not aroused by the sight of numerous natives who came swimming towards the ships. Suddenly they noticed that some of the women at the doors of the huts were wailing and tearing their hair, as if in great distress.

While wondering what this meant, suddenly all the girls sprang from their canoes, and the Spaniards saw that many men—who had been heretofore hidden by them—were armed with a bow and arrows. Each native in the water had a lance in his or her hand. Hardly had the white men perceived this before they were furiously attacked.

The Spaniards vigorously defended themselves with their muskets and then made a dash for the canoes in their long boats. They overturned several, killed about twenty of the South Americans, and took two of the girls and three men prisoners. Many of the natives were wounded. The Spaniards did not burn the town, but returned to their ships, where they placed the three men, whom they had captured, in irons. Then they sailed southward, but, when morning dawned, discovered that the natives had managed to wiggle out of their irons and had jumped overboard. Keeping their course continually along the coast, the explorers came to anchor about eighty miles from this new-world Venice, where they saw about four thousand persons gathered upon the shore. These set up a wild yelping, when the Spaniards let down their boats, and fled into the forest. The white men followed and found a camp where two natives were engaged in cooking iguanas, an animal which the early discoverers describe as a serpent. The two cooks fled, of course, but the whites disturbed nothing in the camp, in order to reassure the natives, and then leisurely returned to their boats.

Figure 4. Amerigo Vespucci off the Coast of Venezuela.

Upon the following day these Indians paddled to the ships, and when they saw the two girl prisoners whom the Spaniards had taken, they became suddenly very friendly, for these girls belonged to a tribe with which they were then at war.

"We have only come here for the fishing," said one of them, a chief. "We live far back in the country and wish you to journey to see us as our friends."

The invitation was received with great satisfaction by the whites.

"They importuned us so much," says Vespucci in his narrative of these events, published some years afterwards, "that, having taken counsel, twenty-three of us Christians concluded to go with them, well prepared, and with firm resolution to die manfully, if such was to be our fate."

So, the Spaniards journeyed inland, remained three days at the fishing camp, and then set out for the interior, where they visited so many villages that they were nine days on the journey, and their comrades on board the vessels grew very uneasy about them. The Indians, in fact, showed them great attention, and when they were about to return to the ships, insisted upon carrying them along in hammocks, slung upon the shoulders of strong and willing porters. When the explorers arrived at the shore, their boats were almost swamped by the numbers of savages who wished to accompany them, while swarms of natives who could not get into the boats, swam alongside to the ships. So many came aboard, that the mariners were quite troubled, fearing that they might make a sudden and unexpected attack. A cannon was fired off to impress the natives with the power of the explorers. At the explosion of the piece, many leaped into the sea, like frogs plunging into a marsh. Those who remained seemed to be unafraid and took leave of the mariners with many demonstrations of affection.

The Spaniards had now been thirteen months at sea, so their thoughts turned towards home. It was therefore decided to careen their vessels on the beach, in order to calk and pitch them anew, as they leaked badly, and then they would return to Spain. The Castilians made a breastwork of their boats and their casks, and placed their artillery so that it would play upon any enemies who might advance; then, having unloaded and lightened their ships, they hauled them on land to make much needed repairs.

No attack was made by the natives. Instead of this the South Americans brought them food, begging them to assist them in punishing a very cruel tribe of people who came to their country, every year, from the sea, and killed many of their warriors. They afterwards would eat them. Against these enemies they said that they were unable to defend themselves. When the Spaniards promised to march against the cannibals, no words could express their gratitude. Many wished to go with them, but the whites wisely rejected such offers, permitting only seven to accompany them.

The Spaniards sailed in a northeasterly direction for seven days, and then came upon some islands, many of which were peopled. They cast anchor before one of them and lowered the boats; but, as they did so, they saw about four hundred men and women gather on the beach; the men armed with bows, arrows, and lances, their naked bodies painted with various colors. As the Castilians approached to within bowshot of the shore, the savages sent a flight of arrows at them in an effort to prevent them from landing.

The cannon were therefore loaded and fired. As some of the Indians fell dead, the rest retreated. The Castilians, with a cheer, hastily landed and fell upon the savages, who put up a stiff fight. The battle raged for about two hours without a decisive victory upon either side; some of the Indians were killed and some of the whites were injured. At last, tired out, the explorers were glad enough to return to their vessels.

Next day the Spaniards landed again, and, under the leadership of Vespucci, had a bloody battle with the cannibals. The natives were at length badly worsted, were driven to their village, and this was burned to the ground. Only one of the explorers was killed, while twenty-two were wounded. Many of the Indians were burned in the ruins of their thatched huts.

Well satisfied with the outcome of this affair, the mariners now set sail for Spain, with the plaudits of the savages, whom they had assisted, ringing in their ears. They arrived in October, 1498, after an absence of about nineteen months, and were well received by the King and Queen, for they brought considerable gold, jewels, and skins of strange beasts and birds. Vespucci was highly pleased; he had been the first to visit the shore of South America and had really done something great in exploration,—his dream for many years.

Shortly after his return, a second expedition was prepared for a journey to this new-found country, headed by one Ojeda, a Spaniard of some wealth and influence. A fleet of four vessels was equipped, and the latter part of the Spring of 1499 saw them ready for sea. The reputation of Vespucci as a geographer was such as to make him the very man needed for this particular voyage, and, although at first disinclined to leave home at so early a date, he finally yielded to the entreaties of Ojeda, and joined the party.

They set sail from Cadiz in May, 1499, and twenty-four days later saw land. The shore was low and so densely covered with small aromatic trees that the explorers concluded to return to their ships and try some other spot. After coasting along in a southerly direction they came to the mouth of a great river, and, having manned their boats with twenty well-armed adventurers, entered the stream and ascended it for more than fifty miles. But the land was as low, up-stream, as it was at the mouth, so the reconnoitering party floated down-stream to the fleet again. Anchors were raised, the ships stood out to sea, and, sailing in a southerly direction, encountered the great equatorial current which sweeps along the coast of Brazil.

"We could scarcely make any headway against it," says Amerigo, in his description of this journey published some years later. "Seeing that we made no progress, or but very little, and also seeing the danger to which we were exposed, we determined to turn our prows to the northwest."

Ten degrees north of the equator, the explorers again saw land, and, drawing nearer, found that this was an island. Many of the inhabitants were gathered upon the shore; but, when the pale-faced strangers landed, they took fright and ran into the woods. Fortunately two were captured and acted as envoys, so, after a time, the rest allowed the Spaniards to approach and speak with them. They were cannibals, eating the bodies of all those whom they killed or captured in war, and had the heads and bones of those who had been eaten piled up in a big heap. Much disgusted at what they had seen, the Spaniards sailed away.

Drowsing along the coast of this island they came to another village of the same tribe, where they were hospitably received and were fed by the brown-skinned inhabitants. But they moved onward, sailed westward, and soon anchored near one of the mouths of the Orinoco River, where was a large village close to the sea, the inhabitants of which regaled the mariners with three different kinds of wine, and presented them with eleven large pearls, more than a hundred smaller ones, and a small quantity of gold. Here the navigators remained seventeen days, feasting upon fruits and the savory acorns with which the place abounded. Then they continued along the coast, stopping occasionally to hold intercourse with the natives.

These, for the most part, were unfriendly, and the Spaniards had many a battle with the South Americans.

Vespucci says: "Many times not more than sixteen of us fought with two thousand of them, and, in the end defeated them, killing many and robbing their houses. We were obliged to fight with a great many people, but we always had the victory."

Thus they progressed upon their way, fighting, trading, exploring, until their stock of provisions became so nearly exhausted that it was impossible for them to proceed further. Their ships, too, were sea-worn and leaky, so that the pumps could scarcely keep them free from water.

Other Spanish adventurers had founded a city called Hispaniola, not long before this, situated upon the eastern coast of Panama. The Ojeda expedition was now about three hundred and sixty miles from the point, but it was decided to sail thither in order to repair the ships and secure food, such as Europeans were accustomed to. After a voyage of several weeks, the Spanish caravels anchored in the harbor of the city founded by their countrymen, where they remained for two months.

Refreshed by their stay at Hispaniola, the Spaniards now cruised for some time among the numberless small islands north of Hayti, but the provisions which they had secured soon began to give out; they were reduced to six ounces of bread and three small measures of water a day for each man; and the ships began to leak again, in spite of all the caulking which had been done at Hispaniola. The leaders of the expedition, therefore, decided to capture some slaves for the purpose of selling to wealthy grandees in Spain, and to return home.

This harsh resolution was well carried out. Two hundred and thirty-two unfortunate natives were torn from their island home and their pleasant, indolent life, and were taken on board the ships. It was a dastardly thing to do, but men in these times were like the German invaders of Belgium in ours,—they were brutes. The prows of the four caravels were now turned towards Spain, and, after an uneventful voyage, they arrived at their place of departure, June 8th, 1500, after an absence of about thirteen months. Of the fifty-seven men who had set out upon the expedition, two had been killed by the Indians, the rest returned home. Thirty-two of the slaves died upon the journey across the Atlantic, the rest were sold to the Spanish grandees.

Amerigo wrote freely of the journey to South America and his letters had a wide circulation, for he was the first newspaper correspondent: the forerunner of the modern Richard Harding Davis and Frank G. Carpenters. By means of these epistles he gained a wide celebrity and his name became more closely connected with the New World than that of Columbus. Such being the case, it is no wonder that people began to call these new possessions after the man who wrote so graphically of what he had seen there. Amerigo Vespucci told of a land which came to be known as the land of Americus, or America. It should really have been called Columbia, after Christopher Columbus, but Columbus did not happen to have the facility for writing interesting letters.

Amerigo, greatly pleased with what he had accomplished, was resting quietly at Seville, when an invitation came from the King of Portugal to have him visit him, and, when he arrived at Lisbon, the King had much to say to him.

"Would he undertake another expedition to the new world under the Portuguese banner?" Yes, he would.

No sooner said than done. On May 13th, 1501, Vespucci left on another journey with three armed caravels. They ran south, touched at the

Canary Islands, and then, through fierce and violent tempests, plowed towards the coast of South America. This they reached at length, and, coasting southward, frequently landed on the shore, where they had intercourse with the natives, most of whom were cannibals.

Here the Spaniards remained for several months, then, having found no minerals of value in the country, although there was a great abundance of valuable woods of every kind, they decided to return to Portugal. All the vessels were stocked with food and with water for six months, their prows were turned eastward, and, bidding the cannibals of South America a fond adieu, the explorers headed for home. After a stormy passage, and, after a voyage of fifteen months, the adventurous navigators again sailed into the harbor of Lisbon, where they were received with much joy. Florence received the accounts of the discoveries of her illustrious son with much pride, and honors were bestowed upon those members of his family who lived in the city of the Arno. Amerigo Vespucci was now a popular idol. He had been the discoverer of the method of obtaining longitude at sea, by observing the conjunction of the moon with one of the planets, and his observations and enumeration of the stars in the southern heavens were of great value to mariners who came after him. He was far in advance of most other learned men of the age in his knowledge of the sciences of astronomy and geometry.

Believing that Amerigo would have reached India by way of the southwest, had not his last voyage been interrupted by the severe storm which he had encountered, the King of Portugal lost no time in fitting out another expedition. Six vessels were therefore prepared, Amerigo being placed in command of one of them, and recognized as the scientific authority of the squadron. The fleet set sail again for that country of which all Europe was talking and speculating.

This expedition was similar to those which preceded it. The vessels met with severe storms; saw cannibals, brightly plumaged birds, and islands of palm groves and chattering parrots. The Spaniards built a fortress upon one of the many harbors which they entered; then, as all but one ship had been lost by shipwreck, the vessel which Vespucci commanded sailed back to Lisbon, arriving on June 18th, 1504. He was received as one risen from the dead, for the whole city had given him up for lost.

Thus ended the last voyage of the famous Florentine. Perhaps disheartened by the unfortunate result of his cruise, he abandoned the idea of again going to sea, and devoted himself to writing an account of what he had already accomplished. Although younger by four years than Columbus, when the great Admiral had set sail upon his first voyage to the unknown West, Amerigo decided to rest upon laurels already won, and to never again tempt fame and fortune in an expedition to the shores of South America. He spent his declining years in writing a full and graphic account of his many expeditions to the New World, and, on February the twenty-second, 1512, the spirit of the astronomer and geographer passed to a better sphere.

For many years after its discovery there seems to have been no effort to give a name to the New World; indeed, it was so long supposed to be a part of Asia that this was thought to be unnecessary. In a Latin book, printed at Strassburg, Germany, in 1509—the work of an Italian called Ilacomilo—it was suggested that the country be called America, as it was discovered by Amerigo (Americus).

Not in the lifetime of the great Vespucci was this name so used. As late as the year 1550, North America was called Terra Florida on the Spanish maps, while Brazil was the name given to the coast of South America, where much dye-wood was obtained; the title coming from the Portuguese word braza, meaning live coal, or glowing fire. Both the names of America and Brazil were applied to the shore of South America, until, after a while, the second of these names was confined to that part of the coast where the valuable dye-wood was obtained, while the other name was attached to the part north and south of it. From this it was but a short step to speaking of all of the great southern peninsula as America, and gradually this name was given to the entire western continent.

Somewhere in Spain or Italy, Amerigo Vespucci sleeps in an unknown grave, but his epitaph is the name of a double continent: rich, populous, teeming with all things valuable.

Of noble thought, splendid mind, and facile pen, the memory of the great Florentine geographer should be revered and respected for all time.

Chapter 4

JUAN PONCE DE LEON

DREAMER AND SEARCHER FOR THE FOUNTAIN OF PERPETUAL YOUTH, (1460-1521)

The tropic breeze fanned a fairy tale, a tale of the sheltering palms,
Where the grimy sea cow sunned herself, in the bay where the ground-swell calms.
It sang a song of a fountain clear in the depth of the tropic glade,
Where the bubbles sparkle clear and cool, o'er the rocks of brown and jade.
It spoke of the waters healing, which to bathe in meant joyous youth,
To the gray-haired and decrepit, with wrinkles and hollowed tooth.
And the breeze came to the ears of men, who believed it to be no lie.
So the agéd de Leon chimeras chased, in the land where he was to die.

Once there lived in the island of Porto Rico, which became the property of the United States in 1898, a Spanish Knight who had fought against the Moors in Spain and who had helped to drive them from his native country. His name was Juan Ponce de Leon, and he was rich in slaves, in plantations, and in money.

The good knight was growing old. As he gazed in his mirror he saw that his once coal-black beard was now silvered with gray, that his head was not only bald, but also grizzled, and, as for his joints, well, he had strange rheumatic pains when he bent over, and he did not leap out of bed in the morning with the same spirit of enthusiasm that he had had twenty years before.

It is no wonder that this wrinkled soldier gave eager ear to the remarks of a native chieftain, Atamara, who one day said to the gray-haired veteran:

"I see, good sir, that you are nearing a time when you will have to bid farewell to all your earthly possessions, which will, I know, be far from pleasing to you. If you sail to the westward, you will find a fountain whose waters will restore the full vigor of youth. No matter how old you may be, should you but drink of this marvelous spring, you will be again twenty years of age. Your aches and pains will disappear, and you will enjoy life even as you did when a stripling."

Ponce de Leon pricked up his ears at this, and eagerly questioned the chief concerning the direction which the fountain lay from the Isle of Porto Rico.

"It lies towards the northwest," said the Indian. "Here a man and a woman, called Idona and Nomi, who had grown old together, came down to drink. Filling a pearly shell which lay near the water, first Nomi handed it to Idona, saying:

"'Drink, my love, that I may know thou wilt not part from me forever, for I have heard from the wind that this is a magic fountain where the water has the power of returning one's youth.'

"Idona drank, then turned and filled the cup for his mate. A marvel now came to pass. There stood Nomi, beautiful as in her youth; garlanded, too, with flowers as when Idona had first seen her, and facing her was her lover in all the glory of his young manhood.

"And, because these two had been so faithful to their pledges and had borne the pains of life so bravely together, the Spirit of the Earth led them to her own home, where they dwelt happily ever afterwards.

"But once in twelve moons they come to the fountain to drink together of its waters.

"This is the legend of the water," concluded Atamara, "as it has been known amongst us from a time so far away that our wise men cannot measure it."

Nowadays no one would give credence to such a legend, but those days were different from the present. For had not hundreds of Spaniards believed in the El Dorado, or Gilded Man, and had not they followed de Soto in order to view him? So the Knight of Spain asked many questions of Atamara concerning his knowledge of the land where was the Fountain of Youth, and he learned enough to satisfy himself that many unexplored islands and seas lay to the northward, which were only waiting for the eyes of some venturesome Castilian. He still had an iron constitution, built up by sound habits, military training, and temperate living; and he felt that he was not yet too old to use his good sword to carve out a greater dominion in new territories. On the other hand, he had reached the downward turn of life so that this tale of the Fountain of Youth appealed to him the more he pondered upon it; and he determined to go and seek for this mysterious water, even as de Soto had sought for the Gilded Man.

The King of Spain was quite ready to grant this knight permission to discover, explore, and colonize the fabled land of which de Leon now wrote him, and sent him a letter which ran as follows:

"To the Knight Don Juan Ponce de Leon. Inasmuch as you, Juan Ponce de Leon, have sent and asked permission to go and discover the Island of Bimini, in accordance with certain conditions herein stated, and in order to confer on you this favor:

> "We grant you that you may discover, explore, and colonize the said island, provided that it be not heretofore discovered and under the conditions herein stated, to wit:
>
> "First, that you, Juan Ponce de Leon, take with you such ships as you require for the discovery of the said island, and for the carrying out of such projects. We grant you a period of three years, dating from the day which you receive this document, with the understanding that you are to set out on this voyage of discovery the first year, also during your outward course you are privileged to touch at such islands, or mainlands in the ocean, as yet undiscovered, provided

they do not belong to the King of Portugal, our much beloved son. Nor can you take anything whatever save such articles as are required for your sustenance, and the equipment of your ships, paying for them according to value received.

"Moreover, to you, Ponce de Leon, in finding and discovering said island, we accord the Governorship, also the administration of justice, during your lifetime, and, to insure the privilege, we will make your authority extend to the civil and criminal jurisdiction, including every and all issues, and rights annexed.

"I order that the Indians be distributed among the people who make the first discoveries, as they should receive the most advantages.

"Dated at Burgos, January 22nd, 1512. " I, the King Fernando.

"Signed by the Bishop of Valencia."

De Leon overhauled his caravels, accumulated stores of arms, provisions, gifts, and trinkets of various kinds that would be suited to the tastes of the Indians whom he should find in these lands which he might discover, and arranged his home affairs. He had three caravels in all, and three hundred sailors and soldiers. Besides these, were several priests, for whose accommodation a chapel was built upon the after deck of the Dolores, the largest vessel. All things were now ready, and, bidding his good wife, the Doña Dolores, farewell, the Spanish adventurer turned the prow of his flagship towards the west, and sailed through azure seas, whose very fish were rainbow tinted, in quest of the Fountain of Youth.

The air was balmy, scented with the sweet odors of fruits and flowers, and fragrant with the spices of mango trees. The vessels drifted onward from one fairy-like islet to another, at all of which they made a brief stay, searching for that marvelous fountain of which the Indian had spoken.

Brown-skinned natives came from the forests, bearing gifts of precious stones, of fruit, and of beauteous flowers, for which they refused any recompense. White beaches glistened in the tropic sunlight as if their sands were polished grains of silver, and, as the caravels luffed under the lee of some of these palm-studded isles, the sailors saw quiet coves, shining like polished mirrors, into which crystal streams gurgled with murmurs almost human.

The Castilians were charmed with the beautiful scenery, and many said: "Surely in this land of peace and beauty there must be a Fountain of Perpetual Youth."

So they kept onward towards the north, ever looking for the marvellous water which was to turn their grizzled leader into a youth again.

The sailors gazed at the many birds which fluttered in the palms and sometimes hovered near their ships. There were white egrets, or herons, parroquets with green and yellow plumage, pink curlews, and flamingos with scarlet feathers and long curved bills. There were great sea turtles splashing in the shallows with huge, flabby feet, and gray sharks which whirled about amidst the foam in eager search for their prey.

Everywhere the natives were friendly, and, when asked if they knew aught of the Fountain of Youth, would shake their heads. Vainly the Spaniards drank of all the springs and the rivulets in these tropic isles, for none seemed to possess the wonderful healing properties for which they longed. The brown-skinned islanders knew little of Atamara's legend of the fountain, but they spoke of a great land lying far beyond, where perhaps the wondrous water might be spouting. It was a fine country, said they, called by the musical name of Florida.

One moonlight evening, as de Leon sat upon the high deck of his caravel, when his vessels threaded a channel between two shadowy islands upon the port and the starboard, suddenly, far, far in front of him he beheld a brownish gray strip of country. It was an hour when revery would take the form of dreams, and, fearing that the vision of coast and headland, gulf, bays, palm trees and ports-of-refuge might be some delusive vision of the brain, he turned to his companion, Perez de Esequera, saying:

"Is it true that I view the shadowy sea-coast of some undiscovered land? I see great bays, indentations, and projections. I believe, good Perez, that we are nearing a shore from which many Spains, nay, all of Europe might be carved and scarcely missed. Pray that the saints shall guide us to the land of Bimini and to that wondrous fountain of perpetual youth!"

"Indeed, good Knight," replied his companion. "I, also, see this vision. It may be a mirage, but I feel that soon we shall find this country of which the natives tell. Let us be optimistic!"

Next day the vessels were headed towards the north, and, with a stiff breeze filling the bellying canvas, made progress onward. During the night, the sailors of de Leon's caravel heard the distant booming of breakers, and awakened their leader. The good knight called to his sailing-master to make soundings, which showed that they were in shallow water. So the anchors were let go, the sails were furled, and the vessels lay waiting for the coming of the day.

Dawn reddened in the east, and, far to the north and south of the anchorage, stretched a multitude of sand dunes. The surging billows of the Atlantic threw white wisps of spray upon a long yellowish beach, beyond which was a background of dark green forests. From the masthead a sailor called out that he saw a winding river, coursing through grassy marshes, which grew broad and green-gray as it reached the ocean. It was Palm Sunday, March the 27th, 1512, so the Castilians sang the Te Deum and, with ringing cheers, gave voice to their pleasure in finding the fabled land of Florida.

When the vessels neared the beach, next day, the adventurers saw that there was little here but a succession of sand hills. So the Spaniards coasted along by the booming surf and at length reached a sheltered bay which they called the Bay of the Holy Cross. Many native canoes were seen disappearing into narrow creeks among the marshes, so it was apparent that the Indians had no desire to become acquainted with these strange mariners in the queer-shaped caravels. The ships anchored and that night de Leon called his captains and lieutenants on board his flag ship for counsel. It was decided that on the morning a landing should be made, in force, and that formal possession should be taken of this soil in the name of King Ferdinand of Spain.

The next morning was the second of April, a time when the foliage of Florida is at its best. As day crept on, boats were lowered along the sloping sides of the little caravels, which rapidly filled with armored men upon whose greaves and breastplates the sunlight flashed and gleamed with silvery reflections in the green-black water. Waving plumes and crimson scarfs tossed in the morning breeze, while high above all gleamed the golden cross borne by the Chaplain, good Father Antonio. The commander had decreed that all should appear in the best of armor and equipment so that the honor due the King of Spain by his followers should be ample and sufficient.

The tide being full, the boats landed high up on the shore, Ponce de Leon leading the way, and being the first to step upon the soil which would thenceforth be his by decree of his Sovereign. Halting, the cavalier waited for Father Antonio with his cross, before which, on bended knee, he gave thanks to God for his great mercy in bringing him safely to this goodly land.

Now all disembarked, and, while trumpets sounded and drums beat, formed a procession headed by the priests, the cross, and Ponce de Leon with his banner. Marching to the roll of drum and the blare of bugle, the cavalcade went some distance up the beach to a spot where the priests had erected the chapel altar, decorated with sacred emblems and votive offerings. This was in the square of an Indian village. The golden cross was placed in a position facing the morning sun and the soldiers knelt in a semi-circle around it, as service was held to commemorate this auspicious event.

Save for the deep booming of the sea, and the song of a mocking bird, there was silence. The Indians peered at the strange sight from behind trees and bushes in the neighboring forest, and, perceiving that the fair-skinned strangers were engaged in some ceremony or proceedings, they looked upon the crouching Spaniards with expressions of awe.

The mass was soon ended, and Ponce de Leon took formal possession of the country in the name of his sovereign, proclaiming himself, by virtue of the royal authority, Adelantodo of the Land of Florida. Then a fanfare of trumpets rent the air, mingled with the cheers of the soldiers.

A small stone pillar was now set up, which had been brought from Porto Rico for that purpose, and upon which was carved a cross, the royal arms, and an inscription reciting the discovery of Florida and its possession by the Crown of Spain.

Although de Leon felt that he was really the first Spaniard to find this country, such was really not the case, for the outline of the peninsula is plainly drawn in an old map published in the year 1502. To this discovery little attention seems to have been paid at the time, for it was a period when explorers were most anxious to find gold and pearls and there was nothing to fix particular attention to this new coast. Thus Ponce de Leon's vaunted first vision was really a rediscovery of what an earlier and equally valiant Castilian had seen.

The Spaniards, who had landed, it seems, not far from the site of St. Augustine, found, when they attempted to search for the Fountain of Perpetual Youth, that the natives did not have quite as good an opinion of their mission as they could wish.

After they had sailed from the Bay of the Holy Cross the wise men of the Indian village concluded that the stone pillar represented something inimical to their own rights of possession, so they had it taken to the deepest part of the bay and there thrown overboard. Previous to this they had vigorously protested against the invasion of their peaceful country. Yet no blows had been struck.

The caravels headed down the coast with fair wind behind them and, not far from the southern point of the island, which formed the seaward barrier of the Bay of the Holy Cross, they saw a curious spot upon the surface of the sea where the water boiled like a caldron, or as if some mighty fountain flowed upward from a hole in the bed of the ocean. This is a natural well in the Atlantic, quite similar to those on land, and can still be seen by sailors off the Florida coast. There were great schools of fish nearby, and many were captured in nets as the vessels drifted slowly upon their course.

The voyagers coasted along the low-lying shore, admiring the view, and finally saw a canoe approaching in which was a handsome youth, the messenger from a native chieftain Sannatowah. He bore a missive to the effect that, if the strangers came in peace, he was ready to meet them in the same spirit, also; but if they came not with such intent, it would be best for them to remain on board their floating houses, for there were as many warriors in the land as there were palm trees in the forests.

"How shall it be known whether we come in peace or in war?" asked Ponce de Leon.

"By this," answered the herald, touching the bow which was slung over his shoulder, "if it be war. Or this," laying his hand upon a green branch thrust in his girdle, "if it be peace. There are eagle eyes watching on yonder shore, and, whichever I hold up, the message goes straight to Sannatowah!"

"And if I let you make no sign nor go back, what then?"

"War!" was the answer.

A smile came to the serious countenance of the Spanish seeker for the Fountain of Youth as he said:

"I pray thee, then, young sea eagle, go to the prow of my ship and hold up the green bough of peace. I pledge you my sacred word that there shall be peace between thy people and mine as long as it is in my power to have it so. Tell me if there be any answer from the shore and if all is well. Tarry with us, so as to be our herald to your cacique."

As he ceased speaking, the youthful Indian went forward, and, standing upon the bowsprit, waved his green branch first towards the south, next to the north, and then towards the sky. This over, he came back to the after deck, saying:

"All is well. Sannatowah and his people will greet you as friends and as guests."

The Spaniards soon went ashore, greeted the Indian chieftain, and were told by him that, two days' easy journey to the westward, lay several great springs and a mighty river, the beginning and end of which was unknown to him. One of these springs, said he, was in the territory of a tribe with which they were now at war; but, when he was a youth, there had been peace, and he had often visited it. This spring was deemed to be sacred. It was a great fountain which welled up from the depths of the earth and was apparently bottomless. Its waters were as clear as azure, so that one could see far into the pearly depths.

"I drank not of it," he continued, "for the wise men of the tribe said that it was forbidden by the Great Spirit, except to one of the tribe in whose land it was. The fountain is in the country of Tegesta."

Ponce de Leon tarried quietly in the bay for several days; but finally landed his men, in order to travel to the place where lay this wondrous fountain. He had ten horses on the caravels and one mule. These were lowered overboard and swam ashore, which occasioned much surprise and astonishment among the natives, who viewed these strange animals with both fear and distrust. When Father Antonio's long-eared mule climbed from the ocean and struck the solid earth with his hoofs (the first of his kind to come to Florida) and then opened his mouth for one long, piercing bray, all the natives took to the woods in impulsive flight. It was some time before they dared to return.

Sannatowah was eager to befriend de Leon, and sent him guides to pilot him to the place where lay the great river and the crystal spring; and, although usually averse to such labor, a number of redskins went along as porters, agreeing of their own free will to go at least as far as their own boundaries. Everything was soon ready, the trumpets blared out their clarion notes of warning, and the march began.

Through forests of great oaks, magnolias and palm trees which hung with streamers of long, gray moss and matted vines, the Spaniards wended their way, startling many a shy deer from the leafy coverts and once or twice a great brown bear, which lumbered away, snorting with fear. Mocking birds trilled at them from leafy branches, and squirrels chattered and scolded from fallen tree trunks.

Carrying his helmet at his saddle-bow, so that he might feel the refreshing breeze, de Leon rode at the head of the little column of horse and foot until they came to a place in the forest where a great tree lay prostrate over the trail.

"This," said the native guides, "is the border of our lands. Beyond is Tegesta. We can go no farther, for, while the flower of peace[1] blooms, there is a truce between ourselves and those who live beyond."

So the Spaniards made camp, but next morning they pressed onward into the wilderness, and, passing around a great cypress swamp, suddenly came upon an Indian village named Colooza, near a large lake. They were

---

[1] A small star-like flower growing close to the ground and blooming through the planting season, when the redskins laid warfare aside.

met with a shower of arrows, but, clapping spurs to their horses, soon drove the redskins behind a rude stockade which surrounded their thatched huts.

De Leon flung himself from his horse, and, regardless of the arrows which were singing around him and were glancing from his steel breastplate, he led a charge upon the gate, with a wild cry of "St. Iago and at them!" With his battle-ax he swept an entrance to the palisade, and then, dashing in, followed by his men, the village was soon cleared of all but five of the native Floridians. These, apparently awed by the invulnerability of their opponents, gave in and surrendered. They were compelled to go along with the Spaniards as guides.

Passing through a country of well-tilled fields and gardens, where were picturesque clusters of native houses, the discoverers came to the waters of a great lake which was so wide that the woods were scarcely distinguishable upon the opposite shore. This was Lake Munroe, a broad expanse of the St. Johns River, which enters it at one end and flows from it at the other. De Leon here halted, sending the captured natives onward to find the chief of this country, telling them to assure him that the white men were peacefully inclined and were in search of the fabled and mystical Fountain of Perpetual Youth, which they had heard was in the territory over which he held dominion.

At nightfall, one of these native runners appeared at the camp, bearing the reply of the great chief Olatheta, which was that he was delighted to learn that the strangers did not wish to war with him and requested that their leader should meet him at the council house upon the following day.

Ponce de Leon was overjoyed. Now he was nearing his goal, for he believed that the Fountain of Perpetual Youth lay only a few leagues before him. Eagerly he awaited the morrow, and, at the time set for the advance, heralds came from Olatheta to conduct the Spaniards to their chieftain. The Castilians soon came upon a great collection of dwellings, many of which were quite large, and before the largest of all was the chieftain with his principal men. As they entered the town, the signal was given for the trumpeters to blow and the drums to beat. This caused great fear among the natives so that many ran away; but, seeing that there were no signs of hostility on the part of the strangers, they resumed their wonted attitude of stoical reserve.

"Pray, why have you come to this country?" asked Olatheta. "Are you peaceful, or are you warlike?"

Ponce de Leon bowed.

"I am the servant of a Great King beyond the water," said he, "and he has given me the Governorship of these islands. So I have brought with me a holy man to teach you the true religion, and, as I have heard that you have here the Fountain of Perpetual Youth, I would like to visit it and to drink of its wonderous waters."

Olatheta smiled, as he answered:

"There is a great fountain near at hand, which we all reverence and hold sacred. Yet, because my people have transgressed the proper laws of our tribe, the Great Spirit has taken much of its virtue from it. If, however, you wish to visit it, I will willingly accompany you. This holy man of yours may induce the great God to restore its power, which will be such a great blessing to my people that they will all rejoice at your coming, instead of being angry with you, as many are now, because of your attack upon Colooza."

"Let us journey to this spring immediately," said de Leon with enthusiasm. "Good chieftain, lead on!"

Olatheta arose, and, beckoning to the Spaniards to attend him, walked rapidly away. The Castilians followed, surrounded by a vast multitude of natives, who crowded around them in wonder and curiosity. As they wound through the thickets, Father Antonio's mule startled every one with a series of the most ear-piercing brays, which caused an instant panic among the Indians, coupled with loud laugher from the soldiers.

"By the Saint of San Sebastian," cried a Sergeant, called Bartola, "were that mule mine and were this indeed the fountain whereof we are in search, I should see to it that he drank not a drop of its waters."

"Why so?" asked a smiling comrade.

"Why? A pretty question truly. Because there would be no place for any sound on earth, if the waters would have such virtue to increase vigor as they are said to have. All would have to fly before the thunderous braying of yonder ass."

The cavalcade passed onward, and, nearing a grove of stately trees, the eager Spaniards saw a fountain such as they had never seen before in any other land. There was a brim as round as a huge cup, and inside were waters as clear as crystal, which boiled up from depths lost in inky shadows, and ran over the edge into a little water course, which gushed and bubbled towards the lake.

"Hurrah!" cried the eager de Leon. "It must indeed be the Fountain of Youth! Hurrah! Hurrah! Hurrah!"

The day was a beautiful one. Bright birds darted from the waving branches, the sun shone brilliantly upon the armor of the Spanish adventurers, as, with the horsemen in advance, clad with plumed helmets, silver shields, upon which were emblazoned red lions, and with sword and battle-axe clanking against their armored legs, the Spaniards neared the gushing waters of the fountain. In front of all was the good Father Antonio, who, holding with one hand the bridle-rein of his dun-brown mule, raised the other in blessing. The Indians crowded around him, awed by the sonorous Latin, and, as he finished his benediction, Olatheta stepped forward and filled an earthen cup, which he had brought, with water dipped from the fountain. Turning about he handed it to Ponce de Leon.

Smiling, and with a trembling hand, the good knight raised the cup to his lips. The cool liquid gurgled down his bronzed and weather-beaten throat. Yet—oh! Sad and distressing to relate! No part of his grizzled exterior changed to the freshness of youth.

As he was raising this goblet to his lips, his companions rushed tumultuously to the fountain and buried their heated faces in the clear and sparkling water. They drank deeply, and in silence awaited the beginning of miracles, each with eager eyes fixed upon his neighbor.

Again, alas! The miracles came not. Beards of grizzly gray remained the same. Wrinkles did not disappear, and stiffened joints still moved with the same lack of spring as of yore. Alack and aday!! The fountain had lost its charm and was not the fabled water of perpetual youth.

The silence was broken by the solemn voice of Father Antonio:

"God's will be done!" cried he. "Blessed be His holy name!"

In sorrow and with downcast faces, the Spaniards turned about, and wearily, dejectedly, mournfully, wended their way back to the camp of the friendly Olatheta.

The good Knight Ponce de Leon traveled through much of this beautiful land of Florida, fought many a stiff fight with the native inhabitants, and finally sailed back to the isle of Porto Rico, bearing marvelous tales of this land of promise, but no water which would restore the agèd to youth and beauty. He journeyed to Spain, was received right graciously by the King, and came back to his island home, expecting to remain there in peaceful pursuits, until his demise.

Figure 5. Juan Ponce de Leon at the Fountain of Youth.

Yet, still hoping to find that mystical and fabled fountain, he finally fitted out two caravels, and, with a larger force than had followed his banner in the first expedition, resolved to again explore the western coast of beautiful Florida.

This journey was to be his undoing. At every point naked savages fought desperately against his mailed warriors. In one of these encounters he was attempting to rescue one of his comrades, when he was hit by an arrow in the thigh. The barb penetrated the protecting armor to the bone. He was rescued by his faithful followers and was carried to his ship, weak and fainting from the loss of blood. It is said by some, that, although the arrow was withdrawn, a part of the arrow-head, which was of flint, did not come wholly away.

Suffering and delirious, the brave old navigator was borne to the harbor of Matanzas in Cuba, where was a settlement which he, himself, had founded. His adventurous companions lifted the pallet upon which he lay on the upper deck, where the cooling breezes might alleviate his fever, lowered it into a boat, and, when the shore was reached, carried him tenderly into an unfinished house, which he was having constructed. They brought his suit of mail, his banner, and his sword, placing them around him so that he might feel at home. Delirium now seized the care-worn explorer, and thus he lay for days, as, in fancy he saw himself a boy again, climbing the bold rocks of the Sierras after young eagles, contending in the courtyard with his brothers, or chasing the brown deer in the leafy forests.

Then the camp and battle scenes passed before his eager vision; voyages over vast seas among beauteous islands; expeditions through palms and moss-grown mimosas; journeying to the villages of brown-skinned natives.

One night, peace came to the old warrior, and there was weeping and sorrow among his staunch and battle-scarred companions.

They carried the body of the good knight to the Isle of Porto Rico, where they first gave him a sepulchre within the castle, but eventually his ashes were deposited beneath the high altar of the Dominican church in San Juan de Puerto Rico, where they rested for more than three hundred years.

When the American forces invaded the country in 1898, and took it away from the rule of Castile, his remains were placed beneath a monument, upon which was carved the trite but appropriate saying:

"This narrow grave contains the remains of a man who was a lion by name, and much more so by nature."

Chapter 5

VASCO NUÑEZ DE BALBOA

DISCOVERER OF THE PACIFIC OCEAN, (1475-1517)

A sob and a moan from the ocean; a voice from the swaying palm,
As a parroquet, brilliant with spangles, chatters and clatters alarm.
For a man stands gazing seaward, a man who is pale and worn,
With a lean hand shading his forehead, a doublet faded and torn.
"I take you, O brilliant waters, for the King and Queen of Castile
And I name you the Southern Ocean, Ye must know how joyous I feel.
For, from lands that are distant and foreign, I sailed to view and explore,
And what I have seen is o'erpowering; what I behold, I adore."
And the parroquet chattered and scolded, and the waters lay calm and gray,
As Balboa, who found the Pacific, gazed and dreamed through the day.

It is something to be a discoverer of anything. It must give the one who has that happy fate a great thrill of satisfaction. He should know that his name will go down to history as a man of particular eminence. Yet, do you think that any of these early Spanish voyagers held that thought? I doubt whether either de Soto, or Balboa, ever had any extraordinary feeling of elation when they had feasted their eyes upon the two great sheets of water, which, as far as we know, they were the first white men to set eyes upon; the first, the Mississippi; the second, the vast Pacific Ocean. Once I thought that I had discovered a wide plateau upon the summit of the Rockies. I knew that I was in an unexplored region which had never been mapped, and, as I scrambled to a high eminence to look down upon the headwater of a curving stream, I turned to my companion, exclaiming:

"This is magnificent! We are turning our eyes upon a scene of verdant beauty upon which no one but the wild Cheyenne, or roving Blackfoot warrior has ever gazed before! I feel thrilled! I feel awed! I feel in the same way that Columbus must have felt, when—"

"He saw that tomato can lying down there in that sage bush," interrupted my companion, dryly, and sure enough—some accursed white man had been there before me! It was a drop from the sublime to the ridiculous!

But Vasco Nuñez de Balboa, when he stood upon the shores of the Pacific, was aware that he was the first Spaniard to set eyes upon this particular sheet of water, because he had learned from the Indians that such an ocean existed, and, so far, no explorer had yet come to Spain who had brought word of it. The accounts of the scene say that he was thrilled and awed by the vision which came to him, and that, realizing, when approaching the water, that he was about to view an ocean which no other European had ever seen, he left his party behind him, so that no one else should share his honor. This shows a selfishness which is quite characteristic of these early Spanish adventurers and discoverers.

Balboa was not only selfish, but he was also daring. He was likewise a fellow of considerable humor, as the following incident will illustrate.

The adventurer and explorer was tall, red-headed and athletic. He had come from a good family in Spain, and, when a young man, had emigrated to the New World, where he had settled as a farmer in Hispaniola. Here he was soon overwhelmed with debt, as he was loose and prodigal in his habits. His creditors pressed him severely and it came to be quite a problem with him how to escape these persons who were hounding his trail. But he was clever, and eluded their watchfulness by having himself hauled in a cask from his farm to a vessel, which was about to set sail. As this barrel was supposed to contain provisions, he was soon safely out to sea. The contents of that cask were the most animated that the sailors had ever seen, and, when the stowaway gained the deck, shouting: "Good morning, Señors, I am going to be one of you henceforth," the Spanish stevedores nearly fainted from surprise.

In those days the Spaniards were continually making new settlements near the Isthmus of Panama, and the venturesome Balboa had fallen in with a body of adventurers who settled at Darien, a native village upon the east coast of the Isthmus and near a great bay. There were many natives at this town when the Castilians arrived, but, although they put up a sharp fight in order to protect their village and their possessions, they were routed by the navigators, who seized their village, with a large quantity of food and cotton, and also a great mass of gold ornaments, worth fifty thousand dollars. This place seemed to be healthy and fertile, so, from this time forth, it became the headquarters of the Spaniards in the New World.

As has seemed to be perpetually the case in Spanish America, when these settlers were not fighting Indians, they were fighting among themselves. There were two Governors in the country, at this period, who had the sweet-sounding names of Encisco and Nicuesa, and, as is customary with Spanish-American potentates, they were soon at daggers' points with one another.

Balboa carefully stirred up the resentment between them, hoping that there would come a revolution, after which he would step into the Governorship, himself. Encisco declared that he had control over the town and citizens of Darien, but Balboa contented that Darien was situated in the territory assigned to Nicuesa and that Encisco had no authority there, whatsoever. Stirred by the speeches of this cask-traveler, the Spanish adventurers refused obedience to the pompous Encisco.

Some one, at this moment, sent to Nombre de Dios, another settlement on the coast, and advised Nicuesa to come down to Darien in order to act as Governor. Balboa stirred up a revolution against him, while he was on his way, declaring that his reputation was that of a harsh administrator, that he ruled in a very high-handed fashion, and that he would be a worse ruler than Encisco.

The hot Spanish blood began to boil in the inhabitants of Darien, and had soon boiled to such a pitch that, when Nicuesa sailed into the harbor, he was greeted by an angry rabble who yelled at him derisively, refused to receive him as governor, and, when he attempted to march into the city, attacked him with swords and drove him into the woods.

To the credit of Balboa be it said that he now interceded for the poor fellow, so that no actual harm was done him, and, since he refused to return to Nombre de Dios, he was presented with the worst vessel in the harbor and the most unseaworthy, in which to return to Spain. This he did with a few faithful followers, and was never heard of again in the New World.

Now see how the crafty Vasco Nuñez de Balboa profited by this little revolution, for, having deposed one of the governors, and having sent away the other, the irascible inhabitants of the country chose Balboa and a man named Lamudio to rule them as magistrates.

Encisco was, of course, furious at this and shortly sailed to Spain in order to plead his own cause before the King; but Balboa was not to be caught napping. He dispatched his friend, Lamudio, along at the same time in order to offset the pleas of the angry Encisco, and, to further aid and abet his own cause, secretly loaded him with a sound sum of gold with which to ease the palm of the royal treasurer in old Madrid. He was crafty, as you can well appreciate.

What do you think of this fellow now? From being a mere stowaway, and an outcast who was hunted by his creditors and head over heels in debt, this adventurous Spaniard, at one bound had risen to be a governor and commander of troops. And in this new rôle he showed marked ability, for he not only led his men well against the native chiefs, but also managed to gain the confidence of these wild inhabitants of the Isthmus, so that, one after another, they became his friends and his allies.

Balboa kept up his expeditions into the unknown interior and more than once was told that a vast ocean lay beyond the mountains which jutted up from the table-land of the central portion of this strip of country between North and South America. Several natives spoke of a gray, glittering body of water, quite different from the Atlantic. The Indians said that "it was far away," so, as Balboa anticipated a long journey to see and make certain of the native tales, he determined to ask assistance from the King of Spain. In spite of the fact that he was really a rebel and was ruling over a colony of revolutionists, we find that he actually did send a letter to Ferdinand, asking for a thousand men to be dispatched to him, so that he might undertake the discovery of this fabled ocean. He was careful to send along some gold, for nothing spoke more loudly with the Spanish sovereign than this.

The ambitious Balboa waited patiently for a reply from far distant Spain; but, before it came, he received a very disquieting epistle from Lamudio, his faithful friend whom he had dispatched to court to plead his cause. Alas! Ferdinand had heard the complaint of the outraged Encisco and had given judgment in his favor against the upstart and revolutionist, Nuñez de Balboa. Worse yet! The adventurous Governor of Darien was to be summoned to Spain in order that he might answer to the King for his treatment of Nicuesa.

Balboa heard this with regret, also with some anger. He was clever enough to see that only one course could save him, and that was to act promptly, and at once; to find this ocean, and to travel to Spain with the news of this discovery, first hand. He knew King Ferdinand well enough to believe that, if successful in this venture, displeasure would be turned into favor. The royal order had not yet come—he was still free—so he determined to waste no moment in idleness.

This was to be no child's play, for dense tropical forests were in front of him; lofty mountain ranges; and deep rivers. There were also vindictive Indian tribes in the path, and warriors who had no love for those mail-clad white-skins. Balboa had less than two hundred soldiers and these were not properly armed, yet, should he stay where he was, ruin stared him in the face and disgrace confronted him. It was forward and success, or a future of oblivion in old Madrid.

The morning of the first day of September, 1513, dawned bright and sunny upon the harbor of Darien, as a small fleet of vessels sailed away, with Balboa in command. With them were several savage bloodhounds with which to chase and terrorize the Indians, and also a number of friendly natives who were to act as guides and interpreters. The journey up the coast was uneventful, and, having finally arrived at Coyba, the domain of a friendly chief, the soldiers were disembarked, the march was commenced, and all struck off cheerfully towards the high mountains which could be seen towering up in the interior. It was hot and the men suffered from the torrid blaze, because of their armor and steel caps.

Keeping on, and struggling through the tropic vegetation, the expedition made good progress, and reached a native village from which the inhabitants had fled as soon as they had learned of the approach of these adventurers. But it was quite necessary to obtain guides who knew the wilderness in front, so Balboa sent some of his Indians to find the chieftain, who had disappeared from this pleasantly situated little collection of huts. The chief was not far away and allowed the native pathfinders to approach without waylaying them. He was later persuaded to visit the camp of the Spaniards, and, after he had been feasted, consented to furnish the eager Castilians with trained men who could pilot them through the country.

"There," said he, pointing to a lofty ridge, "is a mountain from the top of which one may see the great waters upon the other side."

Balboa's eyes sparkled, for he was now within striking distance of his goal and he saw success written upon the banner, which, waving aloft, carried the blazoned arms of Castile. A number of the men were ill and exhausted, so they were sent back. The remainder were eager to get on, so, with renewed courage, the Spaniards again pressed through the tropic foliage and tangled undergrowth.

Advancing for about thirty miles, they came to the territory of a chieftain who was a deadly enemy of the native whose country they had just traversed. He attacked the small Spanish band with vindictive fury. The natives advanced with a great show of confidence,—yelling, screeching, and discharging a veritable shower of arrows. The first boom from the old-time guns made them cease their yelping and stop still. The Castilians now advanced for a little sword-work, but they were to find no brave foe who would engage in combat. The Indians fled. As they did so, the bloodhounds were let go and many of the redskins were overtaken and worried to death by these ferocious animals. In the native village was found a large quantity of both gold and jewels.

Some of the Castilians had been struck by arrows, so they were now left behind. The rest pressed on, for they had reached the foot of the large mountain from the top of which the friendly chief had declared that one could view the vast expanse of water beyond. All were cheerful and sang songs from old Madrid in order to make the journey a more joyous one.

That night they camped near a spring of crystal water and in the morning emerged from the forest at the foot of an eminence from which their friends, the natives, told them that they could see the ocean.

Now note how Balboa did the same thing which another explorer was criticized for doing many years later. He left his party behind, in order that no one might share the honor of discovery, and climbed alone to the mountain top. Up, up, he clambered, and at last stood upon the summit. Hurrah! He had found what he had suffered great hardship and privation to find. There before his eager gaze lay another ocean.

The adventurous explorer sank upon the soil and feasted his eyes upon the scene. Beyond a wide, intervening belt of rocks and forest, and seen through the swaying branches of green savannah trees, was that vast, mysterious ocean of which Columbus had heard, but which no European had yet beheld. It lay there gleaming, glistening, rising and falling, beckoning to the adventurous to sail upon its surface and find danger,— and treasure.

Balboa reclined there for a long time, dreaming, speculating, and thanking his lucky star that he had at last seen this once fabled sheet of water, for now he could go before King Ferdinand and be sure of a cordial reception. Then he arose and climbed down the side of the mountain to where his followers lay drowsing.

"Come, men!" he cried. "I have found it, the Mal de Sur (Southern Ocean)."

Figure 6. Balboa Taking Possession of the Pacific Ocean in the Name of the King of Spain.

The men scrambled to the summit in no time, and, when they, too, saw the gray, rolling billows, they set up a wild cheering. The Te Deum was chanted, a cross was erected, and, from this lofty eminence, Balboa cried out that he took possession of this sheet of water, with all of its islands and surrounding lands, in the name of his master, the King of Spain. Then again a hymn was sung and all clambered down to the lowland where they feasted right merrily. It had been an eventful hour for these hard-marching, hard-mannered swashbucklers from Darien.

This was the twenty-sixth day of September, 1513, a day to be long remembered by Balboa, for he felt a great weight lifted from his shoulders as he thought of that letter which Lamudio had sent all the way from Spain. His men had taken twenty days in crossing a strip of territory scarcely forty miles in width, so you can well imagine how tangled must have been this tropic underbrush. Yet, unmindful of their hardships, they now set forth to journey to the very sea-coast, and to there touch the water of this newly discovered Mal de Sur.

The Castilians descended the slope of the high mountains and sought for the rich kingdoms of which they had heard the natives speak. But they found nothing remarkable save some wild thickets and impenetrable bogs.

Finally they passed through the territory of a warlike chieftain who came out to stop their progress and forbade them to set foot within his dominions. He drew up his followers in close array, and seemed to be quite willing to fight; but a volley from the arquebusiers scattered his followers like chaff before the wind. The chieftain soon gave himself up, and, in order to gain the favor of the Spaniards, brought them a quantity of gold. This pleased Balboa greatly and he tarried in the native village for several days.

Then separate parties were dispatched to the sea in order to find the best route by which it could be approached. One of these bands, in which was a fellow named Alonzo Martin, reached the water before any one else, and at a place where were several canoes. Alonzo jumped into one of these, and, pushing it into the waves, cried out to his companions:

"See, my friends, I am the first European to ever sail upon the new ocean."

Balboa followed soon afterwards, and, taking a banner upon which was painted a picture of the Virgin and child, and under them the royal arms of Spain, drew his sword, waded to his knees in the water, and solemnly declared that this belonged to his sovereign, together with all the adjacent lands from pole to pole, as long as the world should endure and until the final day of judgment. Then he came back to the beach where his few followers cheered lustily.

The climate was hot and muggy, but the Spaniards were keen and enterprising and soon had explored a considerable area. The Indians were friendly and gave them gifts of gold and pearls, of which a quantity was set aside for shipment to Spain. Stories were told by the natives of a country far to the south where was more gold than could be ever seen in this particular land. The chattering brown-skinned Indians also spoke of animals, resembling a deer, which the southern people used for transporting their luggage. They showed the Spaniards a figure molded in clay which was said to be the baggage-bearer of these natives to the south. It seemed to be somewhat like a deer and somewhat like a camel in appearance, in fact, was the llama, which Pizarro later came upon in far-distant Peru. The tales of this country and these animals stirred up many thoughts in the active mind of Balboa, and he conceived the idea of sailing to that mysterious realm and taking possession of it, even as he had seized the Isthmus of Panama.

The Spaniards had now seen about all that was to be seen, and it was time to march across the mountains towards Darien. With their usual cheerfulness the adventurers started for their home port, carrying along a great quantity of gold and pearls, and also a stock of provisions, which was transported by friendly natives. But, as they tramped into the country, they secured more gold, and, because they loaded the Indians with this instead of with food, they came near dying of hunger. They met many hostile chiefs, among whom was a fellow who had eighty wives. He was called Tubanama, and, although he put up a stiff fight for his freedom, he was captured. His people ransomed him by means of many golden ornaments, and, thus appeased, the Castilians marched onward, naming this country Panama, after the wily chieftain.

Balboa was now prostrated by fever and had to be borne along in a hammock by the natives. The heat and humidity of the swampy country caused many of his followers to become ill and this delayed the march.

Still, the little caravan kept on, and, on the eighteenth day of January, reached Darien, after an absence of four and a half months in this journey of exploration. The entire population turned out to welcome the discoverer of the Pacific, who returned laden with pearls, golden ornaments and plates of embossed silver. There was also a long train of captive natives who followed in the rear. The trip had been a glorious success and all cheered lustily for Balboa: adventurer, explorer, and first European to view the Pacific Ocean.

The time was now opportune for a missive to the King of Spain, for the adventurous explorer knew that Ferdinand would not oust a man from office who had added such a vast domain to his possessions. So he dispatched a special envoy to Madrid, with a letter which gave a full account of this overland journey. He also added a gift of glittering pearls and one-fifth of the gold which he had secured, this being the regular tax which the Spanish government imposed upon all its subjects.

The vessel was delayed in sailing, and the delay was fatal, for the King of Spain had resolved to appoint another Governor of Panama in place of Balboa, as he had listened to the story of Encisco and had decided that he had been very unjustly treated by this upstart from Hispaniola, who had escaped from his debtors in a cask. A man named Pedrarias had been selected for the post and he was already on his way, accompanied by a host of adventurers who had heard that Darien was a country of enormous wealth. There were, in fact, fully two thousand men, who were eager for adventure in this new-found territory.

Pedrarias, with his many followers, had scarcely put to sea, before a ship sailed into the harbor of Seville bearing the envoy from Balboa. He delivered his letters to Ferdinand, told him of the discovery of this wonderful new ocean, and presented the King with the golden vessels and trinkets which his faithful subject had sent him.

The King opened his eyes in wonder and surprise. Why, he might have made an error after all! This fellow was a pretty good sort,—a discoverer of new territory, of a new ocean, indeed. He had also sent him considerable treasure. Well! Well! Well! The King decided that he had acted somewhat hastily. He would send another missive to far-off Darien, and would make the excellent Balboa a colleague of Pedrarias, and entitled to equal honor. That would be proper recognition for all that this man had done for the crown of Castile and should satisfy him, without a doubt. Meanwhile Pedrarias was sailing towards the Isthmus and eventually landed at Darien, where, at the head of two thousand men in gorgeous array, he made a triumphant entry into the town.

The cavaliers from Spain had expected to find a brilliant city, with food in abundance and treasure piled high on every side. Instead of this they found Balboa wearing a cotton suit and a Panama hat. His five hundred seasoned veterans were clad in loose cotton clothes, and were living in straw-thatched cabins on roots and cassava-bread. They also had no wine, but were drinking water.

The newcomers were grievously disappointed at what they found here in the colony. The climate was hot and sticky and fever soon carried off a score of victims. Others sickened and died of various complaints, so that, within a very short time, seven hundred of these dashing cavaliers had passed to the great beyond. A ship-load of the gay blades now sailed back to Spain, for they had seen all that they desired of this new country. Another ship-load soon followed them to Cuba. Several expeditions were sent into the interior after gold, but they suffered ill fortune. One of these parties was defeated by the warlike chieftain Tubanama. Another small army, sent out by Pedrarias, was overwhelmed and butchered to a man: only one small Indian boy escaping to tell the tale of the massacre. The friends of Balboa began to murmur against this newly-appointed Governor and to cry out, that, should their own leader be in control, there would be no such disasters.

Pedrarias realized that his own position was getting to be insecure, and decided that he had better form an alliance with Balboa by giving him one of his daughters in marriage. He suggested this to his rival and the other accepted the offer gladly. Thus a written agreement was drawn up and signed by both parties whereby the young lady was to be joined in wedlock to Balboa just as soon as she could be brought from Spain. All now looked favorable for a peaceful rule in the Isthmus.

Balboa's restless mind soon conceived the idea of another expedition,—or: a second journey to the Pacific coast. This he wished to explore, and, since there were no vessels upon the other side of the mountains, nor could he build any, should he attempt the feat, he decided to cut and shape the timbers on the Atlantic coast and to transport them across the Isthmus to the Pacific. A worthy undertaking and one which took great courage and perseverance! Let us see how it came out!

The Spaniards set diligently to work and soon had shaped the timbers for two brigantines, with all the necessary spars and rigging. It was a stupendous undertaking to transport these to the other shore, yet the feat was accomplished. The timbers were carried over the mountains by the miserable natives, who had been enslaved by the greedy Castilians, and they did good work. Although hundreds perished on the journey, the fact gave their master little concern.

Finally the caravan had arrived upon the Pacific coast, the ships were put together, and floated upon the waters of the new-found ocean. Hurray! The first European vessel had been launched upon the far away Pacific and the proud flag of Spain floated from her masthead.

Balboa and his compatriots boarded their ships and headed south, bound to sail to that far distant land of which the natives had told him. But stormy winds were met with, so the men put back, sailed to the point which they had started from, and determined to make two more vessels before they would again depart for the land of the llama and glittering gold. Alas! Busy tongues had been working against Balboa since he had left Darien and it was to go ill with this intrepid explorer.

The vessels were greatly in need of iron and of pitch, so it was decided to send across the mountains for these. Balboa, himself accompanied his men, and, as he advanced through the forest, was met by a messenger who presented a letter from Governor Pedrarias. It was couched in the friendliest of terms and bade him come at once to Darien in order to confer with him upon matters of the utmost importance. Balboa smiled, for matters were apparently going well with him. The weak old Governor, however, had been stirred up by the enemies of the discoverer of the Pacific, to such a point, that he was in a fit of jealous rage. Some had told him that Balboa had no intention of marrying his daughter, as he was about to take unto himself an Indian girl as wife. Others whispered that he and his men were about to start an independent government on the Pacific coast and throw off their allegiance to the Spanish crown. Pedrarias determined to arrest this successful adventurer as soon as he should arrive.

Balboa, meanwhile, was approaching the Atlantic sea-coast with a light heart, and a feeling that all would go well with him. What was his surprise when he was met by a cavalier called Pizarro, with an armed force, and was told that, by orders of the Governor, he was a prisoner. Yet he submitted quietly and was taken to Darien in irons. There he found that the irascible Governor had determined to try him for treason, and, if he could, to do away with him.

A trial was soon held, and the venturesome navigator was charged with treasonable intentions. There was no evidence against him that was not trumped-up for the occasion, yet he pleaded his innocence in vain.

"How preposterous is this charge of my determination to usurp the power here," said he. "I have four vessels and three hundred devoted followers upon the other coast. Should I have so wished, I could have sailed away far beyond the Governor's reach, and could have founded a colony of mine own in far-distant Peru. My coming here is good evidence that I had no desire to disobey the summons of the Governor. I am innocent of these so-called offenses."

In spite of all that he could say, the judges found him guilty, yet recommended mercy because of his wonderful discoveries and evident patriotism for Spain. The Governor, however, would entertain no suggestion of this nature.

"If he is guilty, let him die, and the sooner the better," said the irate Pedrarias, scowling. "To the block with him!"

So they took brave Balboa out and beheaded him in spite of all the renown which he had won. The discoverer of the Pacific met his end with calm indifference, and, as the news of this was borne to the people of Darien, many wept tears for the man who had founded their city and had brought much honor to the Spanish flag. Thus, in the very prime of his manhood, perished one of the greatest explorers which the world has produced, and, although he was foully and brutally murdered by his own people, his fame will last as long as men love those of courage, of daring, and of imagination.

Chapter 6

HERNANDO CORTÉS

CONQUEROR OF MEXICO, (1485-1547)

Lift high the golden goblets and quaff to our leader bold,
Who came from Cuba's heated sands to gather Aztec gold,
His heart was big with courage; with his hands he seized the helm,
And he gathered the power and gained the dower of Montezuma's realm.
The muffled war drums mocked him, from the top of the white stone wall,
And the maddened priests reviled him as they heard his trumpets call.
His Tlascalan allies trembled at the curse of the warriors red,
But the cry was ever "Onward!" to the city's fountain head.
To the top of the teocalli where the eagle banner floats,
Where the evil gods are smiling and Huitzilopochtli gloats;
Up! Up! our leader clambered. Up! Up! and won the prize,
Hurrah! Hurrah! for Cortés! Come victors, drink as we rise!

Song of the Spanish Cavaliers, 1519.

To the brave belong the spoils. To him, who ventures much, sometimes comes a great reward. Here is the story of a man who determined to conquer an empire with but a handful of followers,—and accomplished his purpose. Although it seems to be a romance, it is a series of facts. Strange, wonderful, almost unbelievable, yet true; for truth, they say, is sometimes stranger than fiction. Listen, then, to this tale of as valiant a soul as ever led fighting men on to victory!

Long, long ago, when fat King Henry the Eighth ruled over Merrie England, and Charles the Fifth was King of Spain, there lived a young Spanish cavalier called Hernando Cortés. He was a wild youth and did not care for books or study. In fact, although his parents wished him to be a lawyer and, when he was fourteen years of age, sent him to an excellent school, he would not learn his lessons and so was asked to leave the institution. Returning home, he greatly annoyed his good father and mother by cutting up and playing all kinds of pranks, so that they were glad to learn he had determined to join an expedition which was setting out for that New World so lately discovered by Columbus.

Shortly after this decision he fell from the top of a high wall, upon which he had been climbing after wild grapes, and hurt himself so grievously that he could not walk. It was therefore impossible for him to join the adventurers who were heading for the New World. The ship set sail without him. For two years longer, young Cortés remained at home, and then, finding that another expedition was about to set sail, he obtained permission to join this fleet, bound for the West Indies. He was now nineteen years of age and was extremely agile and sinewy. His face was pale, his eyes piercing, and his hair raven black. He was looking for adventure and was determined to bear himself right valiantly in whatever situation he should find himself.

The fleet set sail, and arrived without accident at Hispaniola. Cortés went immediately to see the Governor of the island, whom he had known in Spain.

"You must remain here and become a good citizen," said the Spanish dignitary to him. "I will therefore present you with a grant of land which I hope that you will cultivate."

"I came to get gold, not to till the ground like a peasant," said Cortés. "And I am anxious for adventure."

The Governor laughed.

"You had better become a farmer," said he. "There is more money in crops than there is in searching for gold."

Six years passed, six rather monotonous years for Cortés, although he occasionally joined some expeditions against the natives, where he learned how to endure toil and danger, and became familiar with the tactics of Indian warfare. At length, in 1511, when Diego Velasquez, the Governor's Lieutenant, undertook the conquest of Cuba, Cortés gladly became one of his followers, and, throughout the expedition, conducted himself right valiantly.

The Spaniards conquered the country; but when, later on, there was distribution of lands and of offices, great discontent arose. Those who believed that they had been ill-used, chose Cortés to journey back to Hispaniola and lay their grievances before the higher authorities. This reached the ears of Velasquez. He ordered that the youthful Cortés should be bound, loaded with fetters, and thrown into prison. The act was humiliating, but it was what those of Spanish blood were accustomed to do to one another. Note, however, how the young man conducted himself!

Cortés soon succeeded in escaping from the irons which encircled him, and, letting himself down from the window of the jail, took refuge in the nearest church, where he claimed that he could not be touched, as he was under the protection of the priests. Velasquez heard of this, was very angry, and stationed a guard near the sanctuary, with orders to seize the youthful Spaniard, should he endeavor to get off. Cortés was careless, wandered, one day, quite far from the church door, and was immediately captured.

Velasquez determined to get rid of the young adventurer, this time, so had him carried on board a ship which was to sail, next day, for Hispaniola. But Cortés was again too clever for him. By great exertion he managed to drag his feet through the rings which fettered him, and, dropping silently over the side of the ship into a little boat, made off in the darkness.

As he neared the shore, the water became so rough that the boat was useless, so he dove overboard and swam the rest of the way. He was tossed up upon the beach in a half-dazed condition; but finally arose, made his way to the church, and hid himself in the sanctuary. Velasquez had no idea where he had disappeared to.

Shortly after this the bold adventurer married a lady named Catalina Xuarez whose family was friendly with the hard-hearted Velasquez. Peace was therefore made with the Governor, and Cortés received a large estate near St. Iago, where he lived for some years and even amassed a considerable sum of money.

Here he was quietly residing when news came of an exploring expedition which had set out in 1518 to find out what lay farther to the west. It had been led by Grijalva, a nephew of Velasquez, and he had touched at various places on the coast of Mexico. This was a land inhabited by Indians called Aztecs who had named their country after "Mexitili": war god of their race.

These Aztecs, it seems, had originally come down from the north, and, after many wanderings, had halted on the western border of a great lake which lay in a long valley, situated at a height of about 7,500 feet above the sea, so that the air was cool even in the hottest weather. The valley, sixty odd miles in width, was surrounded by towering rocks which were a protection from invasion. The Aztecs were few in numbers when they first came to the shores of the lake, but they increased rapidly in population and in power. Nearby were other Indian tribes, and, as there was much warfare between them, the Aztecs united themselves with the King of the Tezcucans in order to aid him against a tribe called the Tepanics, who had invaded his territory. The allies won, and, as a result, an agreement was made between the states of Mexico, Tezcuco, and Tlacopan, that they should support one another in the wars and divide all the spoils between them. This alliance remained unbroken for over a hundred years.

Although fond of warfare and cruel in their tortures to prisoners, the Aztecs had many wise laws and institutions, and were, in some respects, highly civilized. They were governed by an Emperor, and, when he died, another one was chosen by four nobles from among his sons or nephews. The one preferred was obliged to have distinguished himself in war, and he was not crowned until he had waged a successful campaign, had captured large numbers of the enemy, and thus provided enough captives to grace his entry into the capital.

The Aztecs worshiped thirteen principal gods, and more than two hundred of less importance, whose temples were everywhere to be seen. At the head of all the gods was the great Huitzilopochtli, whose temples were in every city of the empire, and whose image was always loaded with costly ornaments.

They also had a legend that there had once dwelt upon the earth the great god, Quetzalcoatl, god of the air, under whose sway the Aztec people had flourished and there had been peace and prosperity among all men. He was said to have been tall in stature, with a white skin, long, dark hair, and a flowing beard. He had, in fact, quite resembled a Spaniard, and this led to the success which Cortés had with the Mexicans, as you will presently see.

Quetzalcoatl, it was said, had in some way incurred the wrath of the principal gods, so that he had been forced to leave the country. He had turned towards the Gulf of Mexico, had stopped at the city of Cholula, and had then departed in a magic boat, made of serpent's skins, to the fabled land of Tlapallan. Tradition had it that as he was leaving, he had turned to the faithful ones who had followed him saying: "Watch and wait for me, I shall come again." For this reason the Aztecs were ever on the lookout for the great and benevolent god of the white skin and flowing beard.

As horses were not known, communication was held by means of couriers, who, trained from childhood to run, traveled with amazing swiftness. There were relay stations, or post houses, for these couriers, and they would thus carry on their messages for a hundred to two hundred miles in a day. In this manner the Emperor of the Aztecs, as he sat in his palace in the City of Mexico, would feast upon fresh fish, which, twenty-four hours before, had been caught in the Gulf of Mexico, over two hundred miles away. Thus the news was transmitted when war was in progress, and, as the messengers came along the highways, the people knew whether the tidings were good or bad, by the dress which they wore. If bad news, the runners were in black. If good, in gay colors.

The one great object of all expeditions made by the Aztecs was to capture victims to be sacrificed upon their altars. They believed that the soldier who fell in battle was transported at once to the blissful regions of the sun, and consequently they fought with an utter disregard for danger. The dress of the warriors was magnificent. Their bodies were protected by a belt of quilted cotton, impervious to all darts or arrows, and over this the chiefs wore mantles of gorgeous feather-work. Their helmets were made of wood, fashioned so as to resemble the head of some wild animal, and embellished with bits of gold and of silver. Their banners were embroidered with gold and with feather-work.

After the prisoners had been brought from the battle field they were sacrificed to the gods in a most brutal and horrible manner. The poor victim was held by five priests upon a huge, round, sacrificial stone; while a sixth butcher, clothed in a scarlet mantle, plunged a long knife into the breast of the writhing captive, and, cutting out the heart, held it up first to the sun, which they worshiped, and then cast it at the feet of the stone god. The dagger used was as sharp as a razor and made of "itztli," a volcanic substance as hard as flint. This was not all. The body of the captive thus sacrificed was afterwards given to the warrior who had taken him in battle, who thereupon gave a great banquet and served him up among choice dishes and delicious beverages, for the entertainment of his friends.

The Aztecs called their temples, teocallis, which means, "Houses of God," and there were several hundred of them in each of the principal cities. They looked like Egyptian pyramids, and were divided into four or five stories, each one smaller than the one below it. The ascent was by a flight of steps. At the top was a broad space on which stood a tower, from forty to fifty feet high, which contained the images of the gods. Before such a tower was the stone of sacrifice and two lofty altars on which the sacred fires burned continually. The floor was dyed crimson from the blood of the helpless victims of the Aztec wars.

These people were unknown to the Spaniards, at this time, since of them Grijalva sent back to Cuba only a few vague reports. It was said, however, that the country was full of gold and of treasure.

When this news reached the ears of Cortés he was immediately fired with a resolve to penetrate into this unknown land and to gain great renown for himself. The Governor of Cuba, likewise, determined to send out ships in order to follow up the discoveries of Grijalva. Who should be put in command? Who was better, indeed, than Hernando Cortés!

The Spanish adventurer, with the utmost energy, at once began to purchase and to fit out ships. He used all the money that he had saved and as much as he could persuade his friends to lend him, so that it was not long before he was in possession of six vessels, while three hundred recruits had signified their intention of sailing with him.

But now the Spanish nature began to assert itself, for a jealousy and distrust of Cortés took possession of the mind of Velasquez and he determined to entrust the fleet to the hands of some one else. This would have put an end to the aspirations of the youthful leader, had it not been whispered to him that Velasquez was about to have him removed from his place. He took care to checkmate the plans of his former enemy. Summoning his officers secretly, he set sail that very night with what supplies he was able to put his hands on, although his ships were neither ready for a voyage, nor properly provisioned.

Morning dawned and Velasquez heard that the fleet was under weigh. He rose hastily, galloped to the ocean, and found Cortés in a small boat drifting near the shore. The commander of the expedition rowed back to within speaking distance.

"This is a courteous way of taking leave of me, truly," cried the angry Governor.

"Pardon me," answered the young mariner. "Time presses and there are some things which should be done even before they are thought of. Good-bye, my friend; may you live to see the day when I return a great man."

With that he paddled to the fleet and ordered all hands to sail away. This was November the 18th, 1518.

Shortly after this the vessels anchored off Trinidad, a town on the southern coast of Cuba. Here Cortés landed, set up his standard, and invited all, who wished to join the expedition, to come on with him. He told them that there was great wealth to be gained and attracted many volunteers to his banner. Finally, in February, he had sufficient reënforcements assembled, so he set sail. He had eleven vessels, one hundred and ten sailors, five hundred and fifty-three soldiers, and two hundred Indians. He likewise had sixteen horses, ten large guns, and four falconets, or light cannon.

The fleet set out, touched upon the coast in several places, and then reached the mouth of the Rio de Tabasco. The Spaniards landed and found that the Indians were hostile and were drawn up in great force against them. But Cortés had his cannon put ashore, ordered an attack, and soon had captured both the town of Tabasco and also many of the Indians, who saw the uselessness of further fighting, and consequently came humbly to the Spaniards, bringing presents and slaves. Among the latter was a beautiful Mexican girl called Malinche who had fallen into the hands of the cacique of Tabasco through some traders, to whom she had been sold by her mother. The Spaniards always called her Marina, and, as she quickly learned to speak their language, she was soon of inestimable assistance to them as an interpreter. Cortés made her his secretary and always kept her near him in the exciting days which followed.

By means of his interpreter, Cortés found that these Indians were the subjects of the emperor Montezuma, and were governed by Tenhtlile, one of the great nobles. He determined to send word to the potentate who ruled over this country and to let him know that he and his followers wished to see him.

Upon the day following, Tenhtlile arrived at the Spanish camp, accompanied by a numerous retinue. The Indian chieftain asked about the country of the strangers and the object of their visit. "We are subjects of a powerful monarch beyond the seas," replied the leader of the adventurers, "who has heard of the greatness of your Mexican Emperor and has sent me with a present to be delivered to him in person, as a token of his good will. I would be glad, therefore, to go immediately to his capital and trust that you can guide me there."

This seemed to annoy the Aztec noble, for he replied in a haughty manner:

"How is it that you have been here only two days, and yet demand to see my Emperor? I am surprised to learn that there lives another monarch as powerful as Montezuma, but, if it is true that you are his representative,

I will communicate with my Emperor and will forward to him the royal present sent by you. Meanwhile, pray receive the gifts which I have brought for you."

As he spoke, a number of slaves came forward and deposited ten loads of gorgeous feather- work, and a wicker basket filled with golden ornaments.

Cortés was greatly pleased with this show of friendliness, and ordered his own soldiers to bring forth the presents for Montezuma. These were an armchair richly carved and painted, a crimson cloth cap with a gold medal, and a quantity of collars, bracelets and other ornaments of cut glass, which much surprised the Aztecs, as this was a country where there was no glass, and hence these were more valuable than emeralds or sapphires.

"I see over there a soldier with a shining thing upon his head," now said Tenhtlile. "I should much like to send that to Montezuma, for it will remind him of the one worn by the god Quetzalcoatl. Can I not have it?"

"Certainly," replied Cortés, "and I trust that you will ask the Emperor to return it filled with the gold dust of the country, so that I may compare it with that which is in mine own. If you must know it, my kind friend, we Spaniards are troubled with a disease of the heart for which gold is the only sure remedy. I trust, therefore, that you will send us all that you can."

While he was speaking, Cortés observed that one of the Indians was busy with a pencil, and, on looking at his work, saw that he had made a sketch of the Spaniards, their costumes, and weapons. This was the celebrated picture writing, for which the Aztecs were famous.

"You see," said Tenhtlile, "the Emperor can thus get an excellent idea of you and your followers." "Bring out the cavalry," cried Cortés, at this. "We will show you our wonderful horses."

The appearance of the snorting steeds filled the natives with astonishment, and, when the General ordered a cannon to be fired off, the natives ran away in alarm. The painters, however, were very busy, and faithfully recorded everything which the Spaniards possessed, even putting in a picture of the ships as they swung at anchor.

At length the Aztecs departed, with much bowing and scraping. Their chief, Tenhtlile, seemed to be in a good humor and left orders with his people to supply the Spanish general with all that he might require until further instructions from the Emperor Montezuma.

Meanwhile great excitement was taking place in the Mexican capital, for many seemed to think that the great god, Quetzalcoatl, had returned to earth and was about to revisit the scenes of his former life. Montezuma, himself, seemed to be undecided how to act. When the picture writings, showing the Spanish invaders, reached him, he summoned the Kings of Tezcuco and Tlacopan in order to consult with them as to how the strangers should be received. The three differed in their ideas, but finally Montezuma resolved to send a rich present to Cortés which would impress him with a high idea of the Emperor's wealth and his grandeur. At the same time he determined to forbid him to approach the capital.

Eight days passed away—eight long days for Cortés and his men, as they were suffering greatly from the intense heat—and then the embassy, accompanied by the governor, Tenhtlile, arrived at the camp, and presented Cortés with the magnificent presents sent by Montezuma.

After the usual salute, the slaves unrolled some delicately woven mats and displayed the gifts which the Aztec Emperor had sent. There were shields, helmets, and cuirasses embossed with plates and ornaments of pure gold; with collars and bracelets of the same precious metal. There were also sandals, fans, plumes, and crests of variegated feathers, wrought with gold and silver thread, and sprinkled with pearls and with precious stones. There were golden birds and animals; curtain coverlets and robes of cotton. There were more than thirty loads of cotton cloth, and finally, the helmet which Cortés had sent, loaded to the brim with grains of pure gold.

This rich treasure fired the zeal and ardor of the Spaniards; yet they controlled themselves, and expressed admiration only for two circular plates of gold and of silver as large as carriage wheels. One, representing the sun, was richly carved with plants and with animals, and was worth a fabulous sum of money.

When the voyageurs had received the presents, the ambassadors courteously delivered their message, to the effect that Montezuma had great pleasure in holding communication with such a powerful monarch as the King of Spain; but could grant no personal interview to his soldiers.

That the way to the capital was too long and dangerous for the white men to attempt. Therefore the strangers must return to the land from which they had come.

Cortés received this message with coldness, and, turning to his officers, said:

"This is, indeed, a rich and powerful Monarch, and he does well to speak in this manner; but I am determined to visit him in his capital."

He then bade good-by to the Aztec ambassadors, who shortly withdrew. That night every neighboring hut was deserted by the natives, and the Spaniards were left quite alone in the wilderness. They prepared for an attack, but none came.

The soldiers now became mutinous, saying that it was about time they returned with what treasure they had already collected. Cortés had difficulty in keeping them out of the boats, but now an event occurred which aided him very materially in his design to march to the City of Mexico, a design which he had long ago determined upon.

Five Indians entered the camp who wore rings of gold and bright blue gems in their ears and nostrils. A gold leaf, delicately wrought, was attached to their under lip. These were not Aztecs and explained that they came from Cempoalla, the capital of a tribe called the Totonacs, who had been lately conquered by the Aztecs, and who greatly resented the oppressions of these bloodthirsty tribesmen. The fame of the Spaniards, said they, had reached their leader, who had sent them to request the strangers to visit him, and to aid him in throwing off the domination of the Aztecs.

It can be easily seen that Cortés was delighted to hear this. He saw that discontent in the provinces conquered by Montezuma could be turned to his own advantage, and that, by allying himself to these Totonacs, he might be able to conquer Montezuma himself. He therefore dismissed the tribesmen with many presents, promising that he would soon visit their city.

Not long afterwards, the army set out to march northward, to a place where it had been decided to build a town. The men crossed a river in rafts and broken canoes, which they found on the bank, and soon came to a very different kind of country than that which they had left behind them. There were wide plains covered with green grass and groves of palm trees, among which were deer and flocks of pheasants and wild turkeys. The trees were loaded with fruits and with beautiful clusters of bowers, while gayly plumaged birds fluttered in the branches. There were gardens and orchards on either side of the road. As the Spanish soldiers passed along, they were met by crowds of friendly natives, who mingled fearlessly with the soldiers, and hung garlands of flowers around the neck of the General's horse.

The cacique, or chief of the Totonacs, received Cortés with great courtesy, and assigned his soldiers to a neighboring temple, where they were well supplied with provisions. Cortés, himself, was presented with several vessels of gold and robes of fine cotton.

Upon the following day the General paid the cacique a visit, and, with the aid of Marina, held a long talk with him. He promised to aid the Totonacs against Montezuma. This pleased the chief greatly, and he promised to assist the Spaniards in every way that he could. Cortés returned to his troops, ordered an advance, and soon reached the town of Chiahuitztla, which stood upon a crag overlooking the valley.

As the Spaniards were halted in the center of the village, five men entered the market place where they were standing. Their dark, glossy hair was tied in a knot upon the top of their heads, and they carried bunches of sweet-smelling flowers in their hands. Their attendants bore wands, or fans, to sweep away the flies and insects from their lordly masters, who, by their disdainful looks, showed that they considered themselves to be superior to all around them. They brushed by the Spaniards, scarcely seeming to notice them, and were immediately joined by the Totonac chiefs, who seemed anxious to gain their favor. Cortés was much astonished, and, turning to Marina, asked what this meant.

"These are Aztec nobles," the girl replied, "and they are empowered to receive tribute for Montezuma."

"What are they saying?" asked he.

"They bring word that Montezuma is very angry with the Totonacs for entertaining you and your men without his permission," Marina replied.

"And, as a punishment, he has demanded twenty young men and maidens to be sacrificed to the gods."

Cortés was much irritated by this and told the Totonacs that they should not only refuse this demand but should seize the Aztec nobles and throw them into prison. This was done, but Cortés had the true Spanish character and now played a part of duplicity which was characteristic of the men from Seville. He had two of the captured Aztecs released, brought them before him, and very cunningly led them to believe that he was sorry to learn that they had been thrown into jail. He told them that he would help them to escape, and begged them to tell Montezuma that the great Emperor was held in high regard by the Spaniards. The two nobles were then hastily dispatched to the port where lay the Spanish vessels. They were taken on board, landed secretly upon the coast, and allowed to depart for the court of Montezuma. The Totonacs were very angry when they found that two of their prisoners had escaped, and determined to sacrifice the remainder; but Cortés interfered, had them taken to his vessels, and soon allowed them to join their companions. In this way he secured the friendship of Montezuma, while still appearing as the friend of the Totonacs.

Messengers were sent to all the other Totonac cities, telling the natives of the defiance that had been shown the Emperor, and bidding them, also, to refuse to pay tribute to Montezuma. The Indians soon came flocking into the town in order to confer with the powerful strangers, and thus Cortés managed to embroil them with the Emperor. At the same time he made them all swear allegiance to the Spanish King.

The Spaniards now busied themselves in building a town, for they had to have some place to store their belongings and also to retreat to in case of disaster. The Indians helped them willingly, so they soon had an excellent little village: the first one in New Spain.

When the Aztec nobles who had been set free reached the city of Mexico, and told Montezuma of the treatment which they had received, the Emperor of the Aztecs felt rather kindly disposed towards the Spaniards, and sent an embassy consisting of two young nephews and four of his chief nobles. They bore a princely gift of gold, richly embroidered cotton mantles, and robes of feather work. On coming before Cortés, the envoys presented Montezuma's thanks to him for the courtesy he had shown the captive nobles.

"We believe that you are the long-looked-for strangers who are to return with the god Quetzalcoatl," said the ambassadors, "and are therefore of the same lineage as ourselves. Therefore, out of deference to you, we will spare the Totonacs; but our day of vengeance against them will soon come."

Nothing was said about not being allowed to journey to the capital, so Cortés gave these Aztecs presents, as usual, and told them that he intended to soon visit Montezuma in the city of Mexico, when all misunderstanding between them would be adjusted. The Totonacs were amazed and awed by the influence which the Spaniards seemed to exert upon the Aztecs, and felt safe from further incursions by the terrible Emperor.

The bold and resolute Cortés was now determined to march to Mexico City, itself, to oust Montezuma, and to obtain possession of his country and his treasures. But he knew that the Governor of Cuba was his enemy, and also knew that, should he not send news of his discoveries to the King of Spain, he would be seriously interfered with by Velasquez. Consequently he prepared a letter setting forth the extent and magnitude of his discoveries, gave up all his own treasure which he had obtained from the natives, and persuaded his soldiers to do the same. This was placed in the hands of some of his followers who were given a ship, were bidden godspeed, and were told to sail to Spain. Cortés besought the King to make him Governor over all the new territory, so that he could add the great Indian Empire to the possessions of the Spanish crown.

Very soon after the departure of the treasure ship, Cortés discovered that there was a conspiracy among his followers, who had seized one of the ships, had stored provisions and water on board, and were just about to set sail for Cuba. One of the traitors repented of the part he had taken in the plot, betrayed it to Cortés, and thus made evident the extent of the conspiracy. In consequence, the ringleaders were hanged, and the Spanish commander determined to take the bold step of destroying the ships without the knowledge of his army. Accordingly he marched his entire force to Cempoalla, where he told his plan to a few of his devoted adherents, who approved of it. Nine of the ships were sunk; after the sails, masts, iron, and all movable fittings had been brought ashore.

When this act became known, it caused the greatest consternation among the Spaniards. They murmured loudly, and mutiny was threatened. Cortés, however, was equal to the emergency. He managed to reassure them, to persuade them that he had only done what was best for them, and so cleverly told them of the fame and treasure which they were on the eve of gaining, that not one of them accepted the chance of returning to Cuba in the remaining ship.

August the sixteenth, 1519, was a day ushered in by brilliant sunshine, as if the fates were friendly to the daring Spanish adventurer. Cortés was now ready to advance into the interior, for he had obtained from the cacique of Cempoalla, thirteen hundred warriors and a thousand porters to carry his baggage and drag onward the guns. His own force amounted to four hundred foot and fifteen horses, with seven pieces of artillery. Surely a small and insignificant army with which to attempt to conquer this vast and populous land!

The army set out upon its mission of conquest, and, at the close of the second day, reached Xalapa, a mountain town, and from which they looked back upon one of the grandest views which they had ever seen. Around were towering mountains; below lay the flat region, a gay confusion of meadows, streams, and flowering forests, with now and again a tiny Indian village dotting the brilliant landscape. Far, far away, to the eastward, was a faint line of light upon the horizon, which told them that there rolled the ocean which they had lately crossed, and beyond which slumbered their country, which many never expected to see again. To the south a mighty mountain, called "Orizaba," poked its head into the air, covered with a mantle of snow; while toward the southwest the Sierra Madre, with a dark belt of pine trees waving in the breeze, stretched with a long line of shadowy hills into the distance.

Onward and upward crawled the little army, pushing and jerking the guns over the rocks and crevices, and finally, on the fourth day, arrived at the town of Naulinco. The Indian inhabitants entertained the soldiers with great hospitality, for they were friendly with the Totonacs.

Cortés endeavored to persuade them to give up their savage idol worship, and, through a priest, Father Almedo, had them instructed in the teachings of Christianity and had a cross erected for future worship.

The troops pressed onward, entered a narrow, ragged valley, called "the Bishop's Pass," and, as they toiled around a bare, volcanic mountain, a snow-storm descended upon them with great violence. The Indians, who were natives of the flat region, suffered dreadfully, and several of them died by the way. The Spaniards, however, were protected by their thick coats of cotton, and thus bore up well beneath the change of climate.

For three days the little band pressed forward over the rugged mountain trail,—then emerged into an open country with a more genial climate. They had reached the great table-land which spreads out for hundreds of miles along the crests of the mountains, more than seven thousand feet above the level of the sea. Carefully cultivated fields of corn lay around them, and, as they trudged forward, they came upon a populous city made of substantial buildings of stone and of lime.

The army rested here for four or five days and then went on through a broad valley shaded by lofty trees and watered by a splendid river. An unbroken line of Indian dwellings extended for several leagues, and, on a knoll, stood a town of four to five thousand inhabitants, commanded by a fortress with walls and trenches. The army halted here and the troops were met with friendly treatment.

As the soldiers refreshed themselves, Cortés made inquiries concerning the route which he was to follow. The Indians, who were traveling with him, told him to go through Tlascala: a small republic which had always managed to maintain its independence against Mexican arms. The tribesmen had been friendly with the Totonac allies of the Spaniards, and had the reputation of being frank, fearless, and trustworthy.

Cortés decided to attempt to gain their good will, so he dispatched four or five of his principal Cempoallan allies to the Tlascalan capital with a cap of crimson cloth and a sword and cross-bow, as gifts. They were to ask permission to pass through the land and were to express admiration for the valor and the courage of the Tlascalans in resisting the Aztecs for such a long time. Three days after the departure of these envoys, the army resumed its march.

At last they reached the border of the Tlascalan territory, and were much surprised to find a strong fortification in their path. This was a stone wall nine feet high and twenty feet thick, with a parapet a foot and a half broad at the top, for the protection of those who defended the causeway. It had only one opening in the center, made by two semi-circular lines of wall which overlapped each other. As it extended for more than two miles and was built of natural blocks of stone, it could be easily seen, that, had the Tlascalans cared to dispute the passage of the Spanish invaders, not only would they have inflicted great damage upon them, but would undoubtedly have forced them to retire towards the sea-coast.

Fortune favored the Spanish command. No Tlascalans were there to hurl javelins and arrows into their ranks, so they pressed onward towards the capital.

"Tlascala" means the land of bread. The Tlascalans were an agricultural people and their country was very fertile. They had previously lived upon the western shore of Lake Tezcuco, a part of Mexico which was not very productive; but their neighbors had driven them from their original holdings and were now very jealous of their prosperity: so jealous, in fact, that the Tlascalans repeatedly had to defend themselves against their attacks. Montezuma, himself, had endeavored to conquer them, but they had defeated an army sent against them and commanded by the Emperor's favorite son. This had highly enraged the great ruler and he repeatedly harassed them with his troops, so that they were certainly glad to see some one journey to their land with whom they could ally themselves. They had heard about the Spaniards and their victorious advance, but they had not expected that they would venture their way. They were therefore much embarrassed when they saw the white-skinned strangers at their very gates, and demanding a passage through the fertile agricultural regions which they had so often defended with their lives.

While the Tlascalan chiefs were in the council chamber, trying to make up their minds what to do, Cortés and his men were advancing through their country. As they threaded their way through a steep gorge, they saw before them a small party of Indians armed with swords and bucklers. They fled as the Spaniards approached, but the men from Castile spurred their horses, and overtook them. As they were endeavoring to parley with them, the Indians turned and furiously assaulted those in armor. A stiff fight ensued and the native force would soon have been cut to pieces had not a body of several thousand Indians appeared, who rushed to their rescue. Cortés hastily dispatched a messenger to bring up his infantry and stood off the overwhelming masses of the enemy as best he could. The Indians fought like tigers, dragged to the ground one cavalier, who afterwards died of his wounds, and killed two horses by cutting through their necks with great broadswords. This was a serious loss to the Spaniards, as their steeds were very few, and they needed them, not only for battle, but also for hauling their possessions over the rough mountain trails.

Arrows were whizzing fast around the ears of the horsemen in the advance, when the infantry approached. Hastily falling into position, the soldiers delivered a volley from their crossbows, which not only astonished the enemy, but threw them into great confusion. The natives soon beat a hasty retreat, and the road towards the Tlascalan capital was left open to the adventurers.

This was not the only battle with the Tlascalans. Several other bands of natives were defeated as the Spanish pressed forward, so that, when the daring Cortés sent an embassy to the Tlascalan capital, his men received a most respectful hearing from the dejected natives. A free passage through the Tlascalan possessions was offered to these white gods and they were furnished with food.

Meanwhile, what of Montezuma?

As the terrible strangers advanced towards his capital, news of all of their doings had been faithfully reported to him by his runners, or messengers. He learned, with dismay, that these fair-skinned soldiers were defeating all of the natives that were sent against them. He saw that they were practically invincible, and that, before very long, they would be knocking at the very gates of his capital. With great satisfaction he had heard of their taking the road through the land of the Tlascalans, for he knew these Indians to be fiercely warlike, and he hoped that the white gods (so called) were only mortal men, and would prove to be no match for the natives who had defeated his own best troops. Alas! He now learned that even these gallant warriors had succumbed to the prowess of the strangers.

In his alarm and uncertainty, he dispatched five great nobles of his court, attended by two hundred slaves, to bear to Cortés a gift consisting of three thousand ounces of gold and several hundred robes of cotton and of feather-work.

The Spanish leader received the fawning natives with respectful attention. They laid the gifts at his feet and told him that they had come to offer him Montezuma's congratulations upon his many victories. They also stated that they wished to express their regret that the Emperor could not receive them at the capital, for his own population was so unruly, that, should they enter the city, he could not answer for their safety. He therefore respectfully requested Cortés to retire to the sea-coast.

"I wish to express my greatest respect for Montezuma," replied the artful Cortés, "and I wish that I could do as he desires. But I have received commands from my own sovereign to visit the City of Mexico, and it would go ill with me should I disobey the desires of the mighty Monarch of Spain. Tell the great and powerful Montezuma that I will some day repay him for his wonderful presents. And tell him, also, that I will be soon at the gates of Mexico City, where I hope to be received in a style befitting the Monarch whom I represent."

The Mexican ambassadors withdrew, but they were sadly displeased with the turn which matters were taking. They saw a firm friendship established between the Tlascalans—their mortal enemies—and the dreaded Spaniards. They also saw that nothing could deter the white men from coming forward. So, with gloomy faces and lowered eyes, they departed for the City of Mexico.

The Spanish troops were well treated by the Tlascalans, who feasted and entertained them in the four quarters of their city. But amid all these friendly demonstrations the General never relaxed, for a second, the discipline of the camp, and no soldier was allowed to leave his quarters without special permission.

Montezuma, meanwhile, had received the message from the doughty Spanish invader and was more frightened than even before. Had he exhibited a good fighting spirit, and had he been determined to expel the Spaniards, he could have raised a hundred thousand fighting men to overwhelm them as they advanced upon his capital. But he was lacking in resolution. Deep in his soul he had a suspicion that Cortés was really the god Quetzalcoatl, come back again to Mexico in order to bring peace and prosperity with him. In his heart he feared, that, should he kill the invader, he would be sacrificing one of the gods. And thus he vacillated, hesitated, and, at length, seeing that he could not buy off the invader with money, or frighten him by means of threats, determined to conciliate him. So he sent word that he invited the Spaniards to visit him in his capital, and requested them to take a route through the friendly city of Cholula, where arrangements were being made, by his orders, for their reception. He also besought Cortés to make no alliance with the Tlascalans; whom he called base, treacherous, and barbarous.

But now came startling events, yet events which pleased the daring Cortés greatly, for the conqueror was never so happy as when in the thick of fighting.

After a short consultation among the officers, the Spanish army moved forward on the road to Cholula. It was an ancient and populous place, six leagues to the south of Tlascala. Its inhabitants excelled in the art of working in metals, and in manufacturing cotton cloth and delicate pottery. They were not as bloodthirsty as the surrounding tribes, but were distinguished more for the skill in the arts than for their warlike attainments. Here it is supposed that the god Quetzalcoatl had paused on his way to the coast, many years before, and to his honor a great pyramid had been erected, upon which was a gorgeous temple and a statue of the fair-skinned god, bedecked with gold and with jewels.

Six thousand Tlascalan warriors allied themselves with Cortés in his march towards the capital. As the troops drew near the town of Cholula they were met by swarms of men, women, and children, all eager to catch a glimpse of these wonderful strangers. An immense number of priests, swinging censers, mingled with the crowd, and, as the Spaniards moved onward, they were decorated with garlands of flowers; while musicians filled the air with strange, melodious symphonies. The strangers were given lodgings in the court of one of the many teocallis and were well supplied with provisions.

All seemed to be going well, and the Spaniards were highly pleased with their reception, but soon the scene changed. Messengers arrived from Montezuma, who told Cortés that his approach occasioned much disquietude to their royal master. They hinted that he would not be well received, and then had a separate conference with the Cholulans. When they departed they took one of them off with them. The Cholulans now kept away from the Spanish camp, and, when pressed for an explanation, made many excuses, saying that they were ill. The supply of provisions ran short, and, when asked to bring more corn, the Indians answered that they were unable to do so, as it was very scarce.

The doughty General of the Spanish forces became alarmed at this sudden change. His allies, the Cempoallans, now told him, that, in wandering about the city, they had seen several streets barricaded, and, in some places, they saw where holes had been dug and a sharp stake planted upright in each. Branches had been strewn over these pits in order to conceal them. They also announced that the flat roofs of the houses were being stored with stones and with other missiles. Cortés prepared for an attack, particularly as his Tlascalan allies announced, that, in a far distant quarter of the town, a number of children had been sacrificed to the war god: the mighty Huitzilopochtli. They reported, too, that numbers of the people had taken their wives and children out of the city, as if to get away from the battle which was imminent.

Shortly after this, Marina made a discovery which proved that the Spaniards were in a most precarious position. The wife of one of the Cholulan caciques had taken a great fancy to the Mexican girl, and had continually urged her to visit her house; hinting, rather carefully and very mysteriously, that she would, in this way, escape a great danger which threatened the Spaniards. Marina appeared to be delighted with this proposal, and pretended to be glad to have a chance of escaping from the white men. She, at length, won the confidence of the Cholulan lady, who revealed the entire plot to her, a plot which had originated with Montezuma, and by which he hoped to get rid of these terrible strangers.

A force of twenty thousand Mexicans, said the wife of the cacique, were already near the city, and were to fall upon the Spaniards and their allies as they left. They were to be assisted by the Cholulans, who had stored great quantities of rocks and arrows to hurl upon the unsuspecting white men as they defiled along the roadway leading to the City of Mexico. After the fair-faced strangers had been captured, some were to be left with the Cholulans for sacrificial victims to their gods; the rest were to be sent in chains to Montezuma.

Marina rushed to the gallant Cortés with the news of this impending disaster to his army. The General at once ordered the cacique's wife to be seized, and she repeated to him the same story that she had told to Marina. The Spanish leader was not slow to act. Two native priests were immediately summoned into his presence, one of whom was a person of much prominence. By courteous treatment and many presents, he secured from them a complete confirmation of the story which Marina had told him. There was no time to be lost and Cortés was a man of action. Sending for the more prominent Cholulans, Cortés asked them to supply him with two thousand porters, next morning, as he had determined to move his army away from the town, and would need this many additional men, in order to transport his luggage and the many presents which had been given to him. After some consultation, the chiefs decided to give him this number of men, as it would assist them in their own plan of annihilating the invaders of their country. But Cortés had made up his mind how to act, and intended to annihilate the Cholulans when once he had them in his power. Night fell upon the city and every Spanish soldier lay down fully armed. The sentinels were doubled, but all remained quiet.

When the first streak of dawn reddened the east, next morning, Cortés was ahorse, and was directing the movements of his little band of heroic Spaniards. He placed the greater portion of his small force in the large oblong court in the center of the town. These were lined up in a hollow square, facing the center, all fully armed, with pouches filled with bullets, and quite ready for anything that might occur. A strong guard was placed at each of the three gates leading from the town, and a number of the best soldiers were stationed in charge of the cannon, which were pointed so as to command all the more prominent roads leading to the center of the native stronghold.

Hardly had this disposition of the troops been made than the Cholulan caciques arrived, bringing a much larger body of porters than Cortés had demanded. They were placed within the hollow square formed by the Castilian infantry.

The Spanish leader now took the caciques aside and said in a stern tone:

"Know, O Chiefs, that I have learned of your conspiracy to destroy me and my followers. I am fully aware that you intend to fall upon me and my men when we leave town, and I am determined to deal a just and summary vengeance upon you."

The Cholulans were thunderstruck, and gazed with awe upon these strangers, who seemed to have the power of reading their inmost thoughts. They made no attempt to deny the accusation, but tried to excuse themselves by throwing the blame upon Montezuma.

"The great Emperor made us do it," said they.

"I do not care whether he made you do it or not," answered the irritated leader of these Spanish conquerors. "For daring to think that you could capture and defeat me and my men, I will put you all to death, so that it will teach any others who may have designs upon my person, in the future, to leave me alone. 'Fire!'"

As he spoke a cannon growled out an ominous roar. It was the signal for which the Spanish soldiers had been anxiously awaiting.

In an instant the muskets and crossbows were leveled at the startled Cholulans, as they stood crowded together in the center of the market place. A crash of firearms,—and many of them lay groaning upon the pavement. Then, with a fierce and vindictive yell, the Spanish soldiers rushed at the natives with their swords, and mowed them down as they stood. The Indians had heard nothing of what was going on, and offered but slight resistance to the armored men of Castile.

Wild shrieks and yells arose above the din of firearms, as the massacre took place, and, attracted by the noise, the Cholulans from outside began a furious assault upon the Spanish soldiers. The heavy cannon opened fire upon them as they approached, and, when they advanced in close formation, many were swept off their feet. The cavalrymen now charged into their midst and hewed a passageway of blood in the lane of human beings. The Tlascalan allies of the Spaniards fell upon the rear of the battling Cholulans. Thus, harassed upon every side, the Cholulan townsfolk could no longer maintain their ground. They fled, some to the buildings nearby, others to the temples of the gods.

Headed by several priests, one strong body of fugitives ran to the largest of all the temples, the great teocalli. As the Spaniards came storming up the steps, these rained down stones, javelins, and burning arrows upon them. In spite of this shower of missiles, the soldiers pressed hard upon the heels of the fugitives, set fire to the wooden tower, and cheered wildly when they saw the natives throw themselves headlong from the parapet.

All was confusion and slaughter in the city of Cholula. The Spaniards and Tlascalans plundered and burned wherever they went, and, as the Tlascalans seemed only to want clothes and provisions, the adventurers under Cortés secured all the gold and jewels that they cared to have. Thus fire, plunder, and murder went on for many hours, until the General yielded to the entreaties of the Cholulan chiefs, who had been saved from the massacre, and, calling off his men, put an end to further violence. By degrees the tumult was appeased. The terrible vengeance of the invaders made a great impression upon the natives, but no one trembled more than did Montezuma on his throne within the mountains.

The Mexican Emperor, in fact, felt his empire melting away from him. His former vassals, on every hand, were sending envoys to the Spanish camp to tender their allegiance to the crown of Castile, and to attempt to secure the favor of the conqueror by rich gifts of gold and of slaves. Montezuma made up his mind to send another embassy to Cortés, the members of which were to impress upon him the fact that the Emperor had nothing to do with the conspiracy at Cholula. The envoys carried splendid presents of golden vessels and ornaments, including artificial birds made in imitation of turkeys with their plumage worked in gold, and also fifteen hundred robes of delicate cotton cloth. When they spoke to Cortés they told him that Montezuma had no knowledge of the plot to attack the Spaniards after they had left the town of Cholula and that the Aztec force had been sent there, not to assist in annihilating the Spaniards, but to quell a disturbance in the neighborhood.

Cortés, who was not fooled by this series of lies by Montezuma, remained quietly in the confines of Cholula. He restored the city again to order, seized upon the great temple, or teocalli, of which all the woodwork had been burned, and built a church out of the stones which remained. He also opened the cages in which hundreds of captives were kept until the day should come when they were to be sacrificed. After this had been done, he called up the chiefs of his Tlascalan allies, told them that the armies would now march toward the City of Mexico, and, upon the day following, set his own troops in motion.

He moved slowly, and soon was met by another embassy from the Emperor, consisting of several Aztec noblemen who brought a rich gift, indeed, and also a message from the trembling Montezuma to the effect that he would give four loads of gold to the General, each year, and one load to each of his Captains, if he would turn back from the city and would leave him alone. Cortés was surprised at this show of weakness and also pleased that the Aztec sovereign did not attack him. He replied that he could not return to the King of Spain without first visiting the Emperor at his capital.

"We Spaniards," said he, "are advancing in a spirit of peace, and wish to be courteously received. If, after a short stay, you find our visit burdensome, it is very easy for you to notify us that our presence in your beautiful city is no longer desired."

The ambassador reported this answer to Montezuma, who called a council of his chief advisors to determine what was now to be done. A great difference of opinion arose. Cacama, the Emperor's nephew, counseled him to receive the Spaniards courteously, as the ambassadors of a foreign prince; while his brother, Cuilahua, urged him to muster all his fighting men and to drive back the invaders, or die in the defense of his capital.

Torn with doubt and distress, the Emperor did not know which way to turn. It would not have been impossible to strike the invaders with his warriors, but Montezuma feared these white-skinned travelers as he had never before feared any enemy.

"Of what avail is resistance," said he, "when the gods have declared themselves against us? I must face the storm as best I may. I see my empire crumbling to dust before these invaders, and I am prepared to fight only when I see that I cannot rid myself of them by peaceful means."

Thus, trusting that he would eventually free himself from this menacing band, Montezuma awaited the entry of the Spaniards into the city.

The followers of Cortés, with their Tlascalan allies, now marched along the southern shores of Lake Chalco, through forests of strange-looking trees, such as they had never seen before, and orchards growing with unknown fruits. At length they came to a great dike, or causeway, four or five miles in length, which divided Lake Chalco, from Xochicalco, on the west. It was sufficiently wide, in some parts, for eight horsemen to ride abreast; and was solidly built of stone and of lime. At its narrowest part it was only a lance's length in breadth.

From the causeway the army descended upon a narrow point which lay between the two lakes, and, quickly crossing over this, reached the royal residence at Iztapalapan, a place governed by Montezuma's brother. Here Cortés was presented with gifts of gold and costly stuffs, and then the Spaniards were led into the gorgeous halls of the palace, the roof of which was of odorous cedar wood, while the stone walls were hung with brilliant tapestries. Here, also, the army rested for an entire night, ready and prepared for the advance upon the following morning into the sacred precincts ruled over by Montezuma.

Day dawned. As the sharp tones of the bugle woke the echoes in the quaint Aztec village, the Spanish adventurers bestirred themselves, formed in line of march, and followed by the dark horde of Tlascalan warriors, advanced upon the capital. Cortés' force was not more than seven thousand in all, and of this number less than four hundred were Spaniards. The adventure seemed foolhardy indeed. How could four hundred Spaniards hope to conquer an entire country?

At the distance of half a mile from the capital the invaders encountered a solid fortification, like a great curtain of stone, which was built across the dike. It was twelve feet high, and had a tower on each end; in the center was a battlement-gateway through which the troops passed. This was the fort of Xoloc, and here the Spaniards were met by several hundred Aztec chiefs. After the usual salutations, the march was resumed, and the army reached a wooden drawbridge which crossed an opening in the dike. As the soldiers left it, they realized that they were in the power of Montezuma, for, had he so wished, he could cut them off from communication with the country, and hold them prisoners in his capital.

But now the Emperor Montezuma, himself, approached. A crowd of Indian nobles surrounded him, and he was preceded by his officers of state, bearing golden wands. Reclining upon the royal palanquin, blazing with burnished gold, he was borne aloft by four attendants, who were barefooted, and who walked with a slow, measured pace, their eyes bent upon the ground. Montezuma wore a square cloak of the finest cotton, on his feet were sandals with soles of gold, and both cloak and sandals were sprinkled with pearls and with precious stones. On his head was a plume of royal green feathers, the badge of his military rank. He was at this time about forty years of age, was tall and thin, and lighter in color than most of his countrymen.

The Emperor received Cortés with princely courtesy, and appointed his brother to conduct the Spaniards to their quarters. The adventurers followed their guide, and, with colors flying and with music playing, entered the southern portion of the Aztec capital. As they proceeded, they crossed many bridges which spanned the canals, and at length halted in a wide, open space, near the center of the city and close to the temple of the war god. Here were a number of low, stone buildings, once a palace belonging to the Emperor's father, but now to become the lodging of the Spaniards.

After a rapid survey the General assigned the troops to their respective quarters. He planted his cannon so as to command the approaches to the palace, stationed sentinels along the walls, and ordered that no soldier should leave his quarters under pain of death. When all these precautions had been taken, he allowed his men to enjoy the banquet prepared for them.

Not long after this, Montezuma came to visit the fair-skinned strangers, and was received with great courtesy by Cortés, who had the faithful Marina to interpret for him. The Emperor made many inquiries concerning the country of the Spaniards, and particularly asked why Cortés and his men had visited Mexico.

"We have desired to see you," answered the General, "and to declare to you the true faith which we, as Christians, believe. We think that your own worship is most pernicious, and we do not approve of the many human sacrifices which you are continually making to your gods. We therefore pray that you give up the worship of idols, adopt the faith of Jesus Christ, and cease to tear out the hearts of poor human beings as a sacrifice in your temples."

The Emperor smiled at the reference to the ancient customs of the Aztecs, and made many inquiries concerning the rank of the cavaliers in their own country and their positions in the army. He then commanded a gift of cotton robes to be distributed among the Spaniards and their Tlascalan allies, and returned to his own palace. When he had departed, Cortés ordered a general discharge of his artillery, so as to impress the natives with his power. The noise of the guns and the smoke filled the Aztecs with alarm and dismay, and put them in great fear of these strangers from another country.

Cortés had several other audiences with the Aztec ruler, who seemed to wish to treat these adventurers with kindness and consideration; but the Spanish general was harassed by many doubts. He was in the heart of a great capital, with dikes and drawbridges on every side, which might be converted into serious obstacles against him and his men, should the

Aztecs determine to crush the small Spanish army. At a nod from the mighty Montezuma all communication with the rest of the country would be cut off, and the whole population would be immediately hurled upon him and his handful of followers. Against such odds, of what avail would be his armor, his muskets, and his cannon? Montezuma had a thousand warriors to his one. His best policy, therefore, seemed to be to keep up the superstitious reverence in which he seemed to be held by both the Emperor and his people, and to find out all that he could about the city and its inhabitants. Then, should the opportunity occur, he would seize the chief power for himself.

Next day the General asked the Emperor's permission to visit the principal public buildings and received a willing assent. Putting himself at the head of his cavalry, and, followed by nearly all of his foot soldiers, he set out, under the guidance of several caciques, to view more closely what he had only seen at a distance. He was led to the great teocalli of the god of war, Huitzilopochtli, which stood in an open court surrounded by a wall of stone and lime, about eight feet high, and ornamented by raised figures of serpents, so that it was called the "wall of serpents." It was pierced by huge gateways, opening upon the four principal streets of the city, and over each gate was an arsenal filled with arms and other warlike gear.

The Spanish visitors climbed up the flights of steps and reached the great paved space at the summit, where was a huge, round stone upon which the victims were stretched before their hearts were cut out to propitiate the feelings of the great god. At the other end of the platform stood two towers, each three stories in height, in which were the images of the gods.

Montezuma came forward to receive Cortés and conducted him into the first tower, at the end of which, in a huge recess, stood a colossal stone image of Huitzilopochtli, the god of war. In his right hand he held a bow: in his left a bunch of golden arrows. The second sanctuary was dedicated to Tezcatlepoco, who was believed to have created the earth and to watch over it. He was represented as a young man, although his image was made of polished, black stone, garnished with gold plates and with ornaments. A shield, burnished like a mirror, was upon one arm; and in this was supposed to be reflected the doings of the world.

On descending again to the courtyard, the cavaliers took a careful look at the other buildings in the inclosure, and saw, to their horror, a great mound with a timber framework upon its summit, along which were strung hundreds of thousands of skulls: those of the many victims which had been sacrificed. The rest of the space was filled with schools, granaries and gardens. Several fountains, spouting crystal streams of water, played gracefully in the clear air. It was a combination of barbarism and civilization which was quite characteristic of the Mexican people.

Upon the day following, the Spaniards asked permission to convert one of the halls in their palace into a chapel where they could hold the services of their church, and Montezuma readily granted their request. While the work was in progress, a young cavalier discovered what seemed to be a door which had only recently been plastered over. There was a rumor that Montezuma kept the treasures of his father in this place, so, to satisfy their eager curiosity, the plaster was knocked away. Sure enough, a doorway was beyond the plaster, and, pushing this aside, a great hall was disclosed, filled with all manner of rich and beautiful stuffs. There were also much gold and silver in bars, and many jewels of inestimable value. Some thought that all the riches in the world were in that room. Afraid to touch it, then, by command of the General, the wall was again built up, and strict orders were given that the discovery must be kept a profound secret.

Time was passing and Cortés grew somewhat worried over his position. Some of his officers were for an immediate retreat. Some, and these were in the majority, were well satisfied with the plan which their General now disclosed to them, which was: to march to the royal palace, and by persuasion, or force, to induce Montezuma to take up his abode in the Spanish quarters. When they had taken possession of his person, it would be easy to rule in his name, until they had made their position secure. Then, too, reënforcements might reach them at any time.

An excuse soon offered itself, for two of the Spaniards were treacherously murdered by the Aztecs, when upon a journey to Vera Cruz, and this was sufficient pretext to seize the person of the Emperor. Having asked for an audience with Montezuma, which was granted, the Spanish adventurer immediately made the necessary arrangements for this hazardous enterprise. The principal part of his force was drawn up in the courtyard, next day, but one detachment was stationed in the avenue leading to the palace, so that no rescue could be attempted by the citizens. Twenty-five or thirty soldiers were ordered to drop into the palace by twos and by threes, as if accidentally, and Cortés was accompanied by five cavaliers upon whose courage and coolness he could perfectly rely. All were in full mail and were armed to the teeth.

Montezuma seemed to be in great good spirits when the Spaniards arrived, and paid Cortés the compliment of offering him one of his daughters in marriage; an honor which the general most respectfully declined, because of the fact that he already had one wife. Not long after this he saw that all of his soldiers were ready, and, turning to Montezuma, asked him why the Aztecs had murdered his two soldiers at Vera Cruz. The Emperor listened to him with great surprise, and said that such an act had never been by his direction.

"I care not whether you ordered this massacre or not," replied Cortés, "this native chief, Quanhpopoca, whose men killed my soldiers, must be sent for at once, so that I may deal with him as he deserves."

Montezuma agreed to this, and, taking his royal signet ring from his finger, gave it to one of his nobles, with orders to show it to the Aztec governor and require his immediate presence in the capital. In case he resisted, the bearer was to call in the aid of the neighboring towns and their fighting men.

The messenger had soon disappeared, and Cortés assured the smiling Montezuma that he was now perfectly convinced of his innocence in the matter, but that it was quite necessary that his own sovereign should be assured of it. Nothing could therefore be better than that Montezuma should transfer his residence to the palace occupied by the Spaniards, as this would show a personal regard for the Spanish monarch which would free him from all suspicion.

To this proposal Montezuma listened with the greatest amazement, and then exclaimed, with resentment and offended dignity:

"When was it that a great prince like myself willingly left his own palace to become a prisoner in the hands of strangers?"

"You will not go as a prisoner," replied the artful Cortés, "but will simply be changing your residence."

"If I should consent to such a degradation," cried Montezuma, wrathfully, "my subjects never would."

But Cortés was obdurate and insisted that the Aztec should go, in spite of the fact that the Emperor offered him one of his sons and two of his daughters as hostages, so that he might be spared this disgrace. Thus two hours passed by in a fruitless discussion.

Finally Velasquez de Leon, one of the cavaliers, who was impatient at the long delay, cried out in loud tones:

"Why do we waste words on this barbarian? Let us seize him, and, if he resists, let us plunge our swords into his body!"

The fierce tones of the man in armor, coupled with his menacing gesture, alarmed Montezuma, who asked Marina what the angry Spaniard had remarked. The Mexican girl explained, as gently as she could, what had been said, then besought him to accompany the white men, who would surely treat him with respect and kindness.

"If you refuse," she whispered, "you will, perhaps, be killed."

As she said this, the Emperor shuddered, and, looking around for some sympathetic glance, saw only the stern faces and mail-clad forms of the Spaniards. He felt that, should he refuse, he would be immediately dispatched.

"I will go with you, Malinche," said he, in a scarcely audible voice. "Bring forward the royal litter!"

As the Aztec retinue marched dejectedly down the avenue to the Spanish quarters, the people crowded together, crying out that Montezuma had been carried off by force.

"Disperse, subjects!" cried the Emperor. "I am visiting my friends of my own accord."

The crowd remained quiet, and, on reaching the Spanish quarters, Montezuma sent out his nobles to the mob with similar assurances, and bade them all return to their homes.

The Spaniards received him with great respect and allowed him to choose his own apartments, which were speedily furnished with tapestry, feather-work, and all other Indian luxuries. Yet it was only too clear to the Aztecs themselves that their honored Emperor was a prisoner, as by day and night the palace was guarded by sixty sentinels, both in the front and in the rear, while yet another body was stationed in the royal antechamber.

In a day or two, the native chief, Quanhpopoca, arrived from the coast. He was asked by Cortés why he had made an attack upon his soldiers, and, as he could make no satisfactory reply, was immediately condemned to be burned to death. Montezuma made no objection to this, so a funeral pile was erected in the courtyard before the palace, and upon this the chief and his attendants were burned. Just before the execution took place, Cortés entered the Emperor's apartment, followed by a soldier bearing fetters in his hands. The Spanish general accused Montezuma of having been the instigator of this treacherous deed, and said that a crime which merited death in a subject, must be likewise atoned for by a king. With this, he ordered the soldier to fasten the fetters upon Montezuma's ankles, and, after coolly waiting until this was done, turned his back upon the outraged Aztec Emperor, and quitted the room.

After the execution was over Cortés came in and unclasped the irons with his own hands. Montezuma thanked him as if he had received some great and unmerited favor.

Not long after this the Spanish commander told Montezuma that he could return to his own quarters. But the Emperor declined to go back, for, realizing how his conduct must be viewed by the great nobles of his Empire, he decided that his life was safer with the Spaniards than with them. Although he had thus resigned himself, without a fight, to a life of captivity, some of his kinsmen were determined to rescue their Emperor from the clutches of these fair-skinned invaders. His nephew, Cacama, lord of the Tezcuco, was especially incensed at the method by which Montezuma had been stolen, and tried to stir up the Aztecs to make an attack upon the Spanish robbers. Actuated by jealousy, the other nobles refused to join Cacama, declaring themselves unwilling to do anything without the Emperor's sanction.

Cortés heard of this, and wished to march at once upon Tezcuco, in order to stamp out the spark of rebellion, but Montezuma persuaded him to get hold of Cacama personally, and to make away with him. Cacama was enticed into a villa overhanging the lake, where he was overpowered, forced into a boat, and speedily brought to Mexico City. Here he was fettered and imprisoned. His kingdom was given to his brother,—a mere boy,—to reign in his stead.

Now Cortés felt himself powerful enough to demand that Montezuma and all his nobles should formally swear allegiance to the King and Queen of Spain. He accordingly requested the Emperor to call together his principal caciques, and, when they were gathered together, Montezuma addressed them as follows:

"You all know, O caciques, our ancient tradition, how the Great Being who once ruled over the land, declared that he would one day return and reign again. That time has now arrived. The white men have come from the land beyond the sea, sent by their master to reclaim the obedience of his ancient subjects. I am ready, for my part, to acknowledge his authority. You have been faithful vassals of mine all through the years that I have sat upon the throne of my father; I now expect that you will show me a last act of obedience, by acknowledging the great King beyond the waters to be your lord also, and that you will pay him tribute as you have hitherto done to me."

As he spoke, the tears fell fast down his cheeks, and his nobles were deeply affected by the sight of his distress. Many of these fierce fighting-men had come from a great distance, and had no idea of what was going on in the capital. Hence they were filled with astonishment at seeing the voluntary submission of their master to this mere handful of Spanish soldiers. They had always reverenced him as their all powerful lord, and, therefore, were willing to obey him and to swear allegiance to the white men's sovereign. Accordingly the oaths were administered, with due solemnity, and a full record of these proceedings was drawn up by the royal notary to be sent to Spain.

The Spanish explorer had now gained the greatest object of the expedition, but in the conversion of the natives to Christianity he seemed to have made little progress, and the horrible sacrifices, where human hearts were torn from the breasts of captives, were occurring every day. What could be done? With the blatant disregard for the sentiments of the natives that had always characterized his actions, Cortés determined to hold the services of the church in the temple of the great god, Huitzilopochtli, and notified Montezuma to this effect. The Emperor listened in great consternation.

"Malinche," said he, "why will you push matters to an extremity that will surely bring down the vengeance of our gods and stir up an insurrection amongst my people? They will never endure this profanation of their temple. Do not attempt to destroy their gods, for, if you do so, you will be driven from the land by the enfuriated populace."

In spite of what the weak-minded ruler had said, Cortés decided to hold the services of the church in one of the sanctuaries of the famous temple, which was dedicated to the fearful god of war. Consequently, the whole army moved, one day, in a solemn procession up the winding ascent to the pyramid, and mass was celebrated by Father Almedo. The Aztecs crowded around in order to view this ceremony, and looked on with repugnance plainly showing in their dark faces.

As Montezuma had prophesied, the Mexican people were greatly outraged by this profanation of their temple, and many conferences now took place between the Emperor and the nobles. After several weeks, Cortés received a summons to appear before the Aztec chief, who said, in rather apologetic tones:

"What I told you in connection with the insult to our gods has come to pass. The gods are offended and they threaten to forsake our city if you and your men are not driven from it. If you regard your safety, you will leave the country without delay. I have only to lift my finger and every Aztec in the land will rise against you."

"I shall greatly regret to say good-bye to your capital," Cortés answered. "I cannot leave your country, for I have no ships in which to sail. Besides, if I am driven out, I shall have to take you with me."

Montezuma, although troubled with this last suggestion, offered to send workmen to the coast to assist the Spaniards in building ships. In the interim he assured the populace that the white men would leave in a very few weeks. Cortés, meanwhile, sent word to delay the construction of ships as long as possible, for he hoped, in the meantime, to receive reënforcements from Spain, so that he could hold his ground. The Spaniards were now thoroughly frightened, for they were surrounded by hundreds of thousands of the enemy, and, should these break loose upon them, they knew that they should have to fight for their lives.

This was the state of affairs, in May, 1520, after the Spaniards had been six months in the country of Mexico. Then came an unexpected thunderclap, for Cortés received word from the coast that the jealous Governor of Cuba, hearing of his great success, was forwarding an expedition to attack him. Think of it! To attack the one who had accomplished that which he had been sent to accomplish!

The commander of this second expedition, Narváez, sent several of his most trusted adherents to Villa Rica, where Cortés had left a body of men under one Sandoval, to demand his capitulation. But, Sandoval would hear nothing of this, and, binding the emissaries to the backs of several sturdy porters, like bales of cotton, he sent them, under guard, to Mexico City, where Cortés received them courteously. He learned that the principal object of Narváez was the finding of gold, and that the soldiers of this interloper had no particular regard for their leader, as he was arrogant and by no means liberal.

The General decided that the only thing to do was to march against this man, to defeat him, and to unite the new forces with his own. This he did. The newcomer was captured, his troops willingly joined with the followers of Cortés, and the bold Spaniard returned to Mexico City, where he had left his Lieutenant Alvarado in command. But he found that matters had gone very ill since his departure, and that insurrection and bloodshed were rampant in the once quiet capital.

The General eagerly inquired what had transpired during his absence, and found that Alvarado had acted in a manner that was not only undiplomatic but also bloodthirsty. A few days after Cortés had marched towards the coast, the Aztec festival of "The Incensing of Huitzilopochtli" was celebrated, and, having asked permission to use the teocalli, the Aztecs assembled to the number of at least six hundred. The natives wore their magnificent gala attire, with mantles of feather-work sprinkled with precious stones, and collars, bracelets, and ornaments of gold. Alvarado and his men, fully armed, attended as spectators, and, as the natives were engaged in one of their ceremonial dances, fell upon them suddenly,— sword in hand. A great and dreadful slaughter now followed, the Aztecs being hewn down without resistance. Those who attempted to escape by climbing the wall of serpents, were cut down to a man, until not a single one remained alive. The tidings of this awful massacre flew instantly through the capital, and the city rose in arms against these terrible invaders, who would do such a dastardly deed.

The Spaniards made themselves secure in their citadel, but they were attacked with the greatest fury. The works were undermined, and some of the more courageous assailants set fire to the walls. Montezuma was entreated to interfere, and, mounting the battlement, requested the howling mob of Aztecs to desist from storming the fortress, out of regard for his own safety. This they did, although a regular blockade was begun, and high walls were thrown up around the citadel in order to prevent the egress of the Spaniards. The Aztec warriors chanted defiance at Alvarado and his men, while sullenly awaiting the time when the Spaniards would be starved into submission.

Cortés was angered and ashamed at the action which his Lieutenant had taken, and, calling him to him, roundly upbraided him for attacking the natives in this brutal fashion. As an explanation for his atrocious act, Alvarado declared that he had struck this blow in order to intimidate the natives and crush an uprising which he had learned was about to occur.

"You have done badly!" cried Cortés. "You have been false to your trust and your conduct has been that of a madman!"

The Spanish commander lost his self-control for the first time, and allowed his disgust and irritation to be plainly seen. He bitterly regretted that he had entrusted so important a command to one who had such a rash and cruel nature. But the deed was done. The Aztecs were now in open revolt, and the Spaniards had to battle for their very lives. The whole city was in arms, the drawbridges were raised, and the enemy was collecting from every quarter.

As Cortés directed the troops within the citadel, to which he had had to fight his way after the destruction of Narváez, he heard a long, hoarse, sullen roar from the streets of the city. It became louder and louder, until, as he stood upon the parapet and looked into the distance, he could see dark masses of warriors rolling towards the citadel in a confused tide, while the flat roofs of the houses nearby were covered with swarms of menacing figures, who brandished their weapons, and cried out with shrill voices: "Death to the invaders! Death to the enemies of our gods! Death to the dogs from Spain!" The great war drum upon the teocalli rolled out a mournful and doleful sound of battle, while gay banners fluttered from the serried ranks of the approaching army.

On, on, came the wild Aztecs, their shrill yells sounding high above the rolling of their rude drums, and, as they came within sight of the Spanish quarters, they let loose a perfect tempest of stones, darts, and arrows. At the same time those upon the roofs let drive a blinding volley. The men under Cortés waited until the enemy were within a hundred yards of the ancient palace, in which they had barricaded themselves, and then thundered a return volley from their cannon and guns. The first few ranks of the Aztec warriors were swept to the ground, but, leaping over the prostrate bodies of the slain, the great horde of fighting men came on. Soon some of the bolder warriors succeeded in getting close enough to the wall to be sheltered by it from the fire of the Spaniards, so they made a gallant yet futile effort to scale the parapet. As soon as their heads appeared above the ramparts, they were shot down, one after another, and fell to the street below. Great piles of the slain lay heaped before the ancient palace of the Montezumas.

Burning arrows were now shot upon the buildings in the courtyard, and several of them took fire. So severe was the conflagration that a part of the wall had to be thrown down, thus laying open a formidable breach, which the Aztecs endeavored to storm. But cannon were pointed at the spot, and a file of arquebusiers kept up an incessant volley-fire through the opening, so that those who attempted to get through were killed as fast as they reached the portal. All day long the fight raged with fury, and, when night came, the Spaniards could get no sleep, for they were in hourly expectation of a new attack.

Next morning the mournful war-drum again groaned out its call to the battle, and again the serried ranks of the enfuriated Aztec warriors came on to the attack. Showers of burning arrows, darts, and heavy stones fell against the Spanish battlement, and the mass of warriors struggled with renewed fury to gain possession of the breach. Cortés ordered a sortie, hoping to drive this body of invaders away, but, when the gates were thrown open and he dashed forward with the cavalry, assisted by a large force of Tlascalans, the natives retreated behind a barricade. Heavy guns were ordered up, and the barriers were demolished; but, as he pressed the Aztecs backwards, so many came in upon the flanks that he was forced to retreat. As the Spaniards reëntered their fortress, pursued by a shower of darts and arrows, the Indians once more closed around it, with menacing cries and insults.

"The gods have delivered you into our hands at last!" they called. "Huitzilopochtli has long been crying for his victims, and the stone of sacrifice is ever ready. Our knives are sharpened. The wild beasts in the palace are roaring for their feast."

Yet they cried piteously for Montezuma and entreated the Spaniards to deliver him up to them. "Oh, give us back our Emperor!" said they. "You have willfully and falsely detained and imprisoned him!"

At this, Cortés determined to induce Montezuma to exert his authority, in order to allay the tumult. So he requested the captive Emperor to speak to the howling mob. Montezuma had soon arrayed himself in his finest robes, and with a guard of Spaniards around him, and preceded by an Aztec carrying a golden wand (the symbol of sovereignty) the Indian monarch ascended the central turret of the palace.

A marvelous and magical change now came over the scene. The fierce and vindictive war cries of the Aztec warriors ceased. Great rows of Indians prostrated themselves on the ground, while all eyes were turned upon the monarch whom they had been taught to venerate with slavish awe. The Spaniards were startled at the homage which was given to the cowardly Emperor, and Montezuma, himself, saw his advantage. He felt himself once again a king, and addressed the multitude with all of his former authority and confidence.

"Why do I see my people here in arms against the palace of my father?" said he. "Is it that you think your sovereign a prisoner and wish to release him? If so, you have done well; but you are mistaken. I am no prisoner. These strangers are my guests. I remain with them only by choice and I can leave them when I will. Have you come to drive them from the city? That is unnecessary; they will depart of their own accord, if you will open a way for them. Return to your homes! Lay down your arms! Show your obedience to me, whose right it is. The white men shall go back to their land, and all shall be well again within the walls of Mexico."

A murmur of contempt ran through the multitude. Rage and desire for revenge made the Aztec warriors forget their reverence for their former beloved Emperor, and they now turned against the very man whose word had once been their law.

"Base Aztec!" they cried out in loud tones. "You are a woman and a coward! The white men have made you a female, fit only to weave and to spin! Begone! Back to your needlework and to your Spanish brothers!"

Immediately the Emperor was assailed by a cloud of rocks and arrows. A stone struck the miserable man in the head, with a sickening thud, and knocked him to the ground. A chief of high rank hurled his javelin at him, but it just missed him as he fell. The Mexicans were shocked at their own act of sacrilege and set up a dismal cry. They dispersed, panic-stricken, and not one remained in the great square before the palace.

With care and gentleness the Spaniards carried the body of Montezuma to his own apartments. As soon as he recovered from his insensibility, the full misery of his situation broke upon him. He, the once great and powerful Montezuma, had been reviled and rejected by his own people. Utterly crushed in spirit, he refused all food or assistance, even tearing off the bandages which the Spaniards applied to his wounds. He sat motionless, with eyes cast upon the ground, perpetually brooding over his humiliation, and gradually grew so weak that he could scarcely sit upright.

A body of Mexicans now took possession of the famous temple to the war god, Huitzilopochtli, which was opposite the Spanish palace, and rose to a height of nearly a hundred and fifty feet. From this vantage point the Aztecs discharged such a volley of arrows upon the garrison, that it was impossible for any soldier to show himself for an instant outside the wall of the palace, without being immediately struck. The Mexicans, meanwhile, were completely sheltered. As it was absolutely necessary that they be driven from this point of vantage, Cortés intrusted the task to his chamberlain, Escobar, giving him a hundred men for the purpose. Three desperate attempts were made, but being repulsed with considerable loss, this officer returned, and Cortés determined to lead the storming party himself. A wound in his left hand had almost disabled it, but he strapped his shield to the injured member and thus sallied forth.

Several thousand of the Tlascalan allies were with him, and, at the head of three hundred chosen cavaliers, he now dashed from the palace. In the courtyard of the temple, a body of Mexicans was drawn up to dispute his passage, but he charged them briskly, and, although the horses could not stand up and had to be returned to the Spanish quarters, the Aztecs were dispersed. The cavaliers and their Indian allies now pressed up to the flight of stone steps which led into the teocalli. The warriors were drawn up on every terrace, as well as on the topmost platform, and showered down heavy stones, beams, and burning rafters. The Spaniards kept on, in spite of the fact that many of them were badly wounded by the falling beams and arrows, and, aided by a brisk fire from the muskateers below, soon drove the Aztecs to the broad summit of the teocalli. Here a desperate hand-to-hand fight took place.

As the edge of the platform was unprotected by either battlement or parapet, many of the combatants, as they struggled together, rolled off, locked in a deadly deathgrip. Two powerful Aztecs seized upon Cortés, at one stage of the battle, and were dragging him violently toward the side of the pyramid, when, by sheer strength, he tore himself from their grasp and hurled one of them over the edge.

At the beginning of the fight for the possession of this temple, the priests ran to and fro among the contestants, with their long hair streaming out behind them. With wild gestures they encouraged and urged on the Indians, until they were all either killed or captured by the onrushing Spanish cavaliers.

One by one the Indian warriors fell dead upon the blood-drenched pavement, or were hurled from the dizzy height to the pavement below, until, at last, none were left to oppose the white men. The Spaniards, with yells of victory, now rushed into the sanctuaries. In one was the hideous image of Huitzilopochtli with an offering of human hearts before him. Possibly these were those of their own countrymen! With loud shouts of triumph the Spaniards tore the hideous idol from its niche, and, as the Aztecs watched, hurled it down the long steps of the teocalli. Then the sanctuaries were set on fire, and, descending joyfully to the courtyard, the soldiers set up a great song of thanksgiving for their victory.

Cortés now hoped that the natives were sufficiently subdued to be willing to come to terms with him, so he invited them to a parley, and addressed the principal chiefs. He talked to them from the turret previously occupied by Montezuma, and, as usual, had Marina to interpret for him.

"You have brought all this slaughter upon yourselves by your rebellion," he said. "Yet, for the sake of the affection felt for you by the sovereign whom you have treated so unworthily, I would willingly stay my hand if you will lay down your arms and return once more to obedience to me. If you do not do this, I will make your city a heap of ruins, and will leave not a single soul alive to mourn over it."

The Aztecs replied in a manner which was quite unexpected.

"It is quite true that you have destroyed our gods, massacred our countrymen, and broken our temple to pieces. But look out upon our streets and terraces. You see them thronged with warriors as far as your eyes can reach," said the Indian who had been chosen spokesman. "Our numbers are scarcely diminished by our losses. Yours, on the contrary, are lessened every hour. Your provisions and your water are failing; you are perishing from hunger and from sickness; you must soon fall into our hands. The bridges are broken down and you cannot escape! There will be few of you left to glut the vengeance of our gods."

With this tart reply, they discharged a volley of arrows, which compelled the Spaniards to beat a speedy retreat.

To retreat was hazardous, indeed, and it was mortifying to abandon the city; but, with his men daily diminishing in strength and in numbers, and with his stock of provisions so nearly exhausted that one small daily ration of bread was all that the soldiers had, there was nothing else for Cortés to do. Montezuma had lingered feebly along, after the day in which he had been struck by a stone, and now passed to another world. "The tidings of this," says an old historian, "were received with real grief by every cavalier and soldier in the army who had access to his person, for we all loved him as a father." The Emperor's death was a misfortune for the Spaniards, because, while he lived, there was a slight possibility of using his influence with the natives. Now that hope had disappeared.

A council was called to decide as speedily as possible the all-important question of the retreat. It was agreed that they should leave at once, and at night, so that darkness would cloak their movements. The safe conveyance of the treasure was quite a problem, but the soldiers had converted their share into gold chains, or collars, which could be easily carried about their persons. The royal fifth, however, was in bars and wedges of solid gold. It could be carried only by horse, and a special guard had to be provided for it. But much treasure had to be abandoned, and it lay in shining heaps upon the floor of the palace.

The soldiers who had come with Cortés, being old campaigners, did not load themselves down with more than they could safely transport. The soldiers of Narváez, however, being keen for the accumulation of treasure, loaded themselves down with all that they could possibly carry off with them.

As the retreat was to be over the causeway and dykes, a portable bridge was constructed which could be laid across the open canals. This was entrusted to the care of an officer named Magarino and forty men. Cortés arranged the order of march. First was to go two hundred Spanish foot soldiers, commanded by a Captain Sandoval, with twenty other cavaliers. The rear guard was formed of infantry under Alvarado and de Leon, while the center was in charge of Cortés, himself, with some heavy guns, the baggage and the treasure. There were also the prisoners, among whom were a son and two daughters of Montezuma, Cacama, and several nobles. The Indian allies, the Tlascalans, were divided up among the three divisions. There were several thousand of these.

Midnight came and all was ready for the journey. A solemn mass was celebrated by Father Almedo, and, keeping as quiet as they possibly could, the Spaniards sallied forth from the ancient palace of the Aztecs, which had been the scene of so much suffering and fighting. The night was a dark one, and a fine, misty rain fell steadily upon the serried columns of Spanish cavaliers and brown-skinned natives.

The vast square before the palace was deserted. Through some superstitious dread, the natives had not frequented the plaza since the death of their Emperor, Montezuma, and the Spaniards crossed it as noiselessly as possible, entering the great street of Tlacopan. They peered anxiously into the gloom, expecting to be attacked at any moment by a swarm of Aztecs, but all went well with them until the first files of soldiers drew near the spot where the street opened upon the causeway, which led by the side of the lake. Here there were Mexican sentinels at their posts, and, as the bridge was being adjusted across the uncovered breach, the Aztecs fled, crying out in loud tones that the hated white men were leaving the city.

Immediately there was a commotion. The priests heard the shouting from the summits of their teocalli and beat upon the peculiar shells which were used for rousing the people. The huge drum upon the temple of the god of war was struck and gave forth a hollow, moaning roar which vibrated through every corner of the capital. The Spaniards were alarmed and worked with desperate fury to place their bridge across the causeway so that the army could escape. But, as the soldiers labored valorously, a sound was heard like a stormy wind as it rises in a forest. Nearer and nearer it came, and, from the dark waters of the lake came the splashing of many paddles. A few stones and arrows fell among the hurrying troops. More and more followed in rapid succession until they became a veritable blinding storm. Yells and shrill war-cries rent the air, and, before the Spaniards well realized their position, they found themselves surrounded by myriads of the enemy, who were swarming over land and lake.

The Aztecs ran their canoes along the sides of the causeway, climbed up, and charged the ranks of the Spaniards, with their Tlascalan allies. The soldiers shook them off as best they could, rode over them with their horses, and, with their pikes and their swords, drove them headlong down the sides of the dike. They halted and waited for the bridge to be brought up; but a terrible calamity had occurred, for the bridge had been so borne down by the weight of the artillery passing over it, that it had jammed firmly into the sides of the dike and was immovable.

The tidings spread rapidly from man to man and a cry of despair arose, for all means of advance were cut off, and the Spaniards were caught in a trap. Those behind pressed forward, trampling the weak and the wounded under foot, and forcing those in front over the gulf. Some of the cavaliers succeeded in swimming their horses across, but many rolled back into the lake when attempting to ascend the opposite bank. The infantry followed in a panic, and many of the men were pierced by the Aztec arrows, or struck down by war clubs. Some were dragged into the canoes to be later sacrificed to the great and awful stone god. Fierce battle cries rose above the tumult of war, and these were mingled with the cries of despair of the drowning Spaniards.

By degrees the opening in the causeway was filled up by the wreck of the wagons, guns, rich bales of stuffs, chests of solid ingots, and bodies of men and horses. Walking on top of this dismal ruin, those in the rear were able to reach the other side.

As the attention of the Aztec warriors now fell upon the rich spoil that strewed the ground, the pursuit of the Spaniards ceased. The troops pressed forward through the village of Popotla, where Cortés dismounted from his weary war-horse, and, sitting down upon the steps of an Indian temple, looked mournfully at his broken army, as the thin and disordered ranks filed past. It was a heartrending spectacle. He knew, however, that this was no time to give away to vain regrets, so he speedily mounted, and led his men through Tlacopan.

The broken army, disorganized and half starved, moved slowly toward the sea coast. On the seventh day it reached the mountain range which overlooks the plains of Otumba, and the scouts, climbing the steep hillside, reported that a mighty host of warriors was in the valley, ready to dispute their passage. Every chief of importance had taken the field, and, as far as the eye could reach, extended a moving mass of glittering shields and spears, mingled with the banners and the bright feather-mail of the caciques.

Cortés disposed his army to the best advantage, and prepared to cut his way through the enemy. He gave his force as broad a front as possible, protecting it on either flank by his cavalry, now reduced to but twenty horsemen. His directions to his infantrymen was that they were to thrust, not strike, with their swords, and were to make for the leaders of the enemy, whom they were to dispatch as soon as met with. After a few brave words of encouragement, the little band began to descend the hill. The enemy set up fierce war cries, as they approached, and met the Spaniards with a storm of stones and arrows.

Now occurred a bitter fight. The Spaniards, at first, beat through the crowd of natives, but, as the battle progressed, they were surrounded on every side by a swarm of warriors. Cortés received a wound in the head and his horse was killed beneath him, so that he was obliged to mount one taken from the baggage train. His men became exhausted beneath the fiery rays of the sun and began to give way. The enemy, on the other hand, was constantly being reënforced from the rear, and pressed on with redoubled fury.

Matters were critical for the Spaniards, when Cortés did a deed of daring which was quite worthy of the Chevalier Bayard, or Murat, the famous Napoleonic leader of horse. With his keen eye he discovered in the distance a chief, who, from his dress and surroundings, he knew to be the leader of the Aztec forces. Turning to his favorite henchmen, the brave Spaniard cried out, while pointing his finger at the chief:

"There is our mark! Follow and support me!"

Then, shouting his war cry, he plunged into the thickest of the press and bore towards the noble Aztec.

The enemy was taken completely by surprise and fell back. Many could not dodge aside and were trampled down by the war-horse, or pierced by the long lance which Cortés wielded with all the skill of a trained fencer. The cavalier companions of the gallant Spaniard followed him closely, and, in a few moments, they had come within striking distance of the Aztec chieftain. Cortés rode speedily at him, and, thrusting with his lance, brought him to earth, where he was stabbed to death by a young Spaniard called Juan de Salamanca. Tearing his banner from his clinched fist, the Castilian presented it to Cortés, who waved it triumphantly above his head. The caciques' guard, surprised by this sudden onset, fled precipitously, while the panic spread to the other Indians. The Spaniards pursued them for several miles, then returned to secure the rich booty which they had left behind them. Truly the battle had been won by the daring and personal initiative of the brave Spanish leader.

The adventurers were now safely out of their grave peril. They reached Tlascala in a few days, and, with the assistance of their native allies, at once prepared to revenge themselves upon the Aztecs. Several Spaniards were at Vera Cruz and these joined them. But there was much need of gunpowder, and there was no way of getting sulphur for its manufacture, unless it was obtained from one of the many volcanoes in the neighborhood. How was this to be done?

A cavalier, named Francio Montaño, was equal to the emergency and suggested that he be allowed to descend into the terrible volcano of Popocatepetl, where sulphur, in a crude form, hung to the side of the crater. Cortés was only too willing to allow him to make the attempt, so accompanied by several others, he set out. After great hardship, and, after passing through a region of perpetual snow, the explorers reached the mouth of the fierce volcano, and, crawling cautiously to the very edge, they peered down into its gloomy depths. At the bottom of the dark abyss a lurid flame was burning, and, every now and again, arose a sulphurous stream, which, cooling as it came upward, fell again in showers upon the side of the cavity. It was necessary to descend into this crater, with the boiling lava below, in order to scrape some of the sulphur from the sides.

Montaño himself drew the longest stem of grass, when the Spaniards had prepared lots to see who should descend, and, clinging to a basket and rope, was soon four hundred feet within the horrible chasm. As he hung there, he scraped the sulphur from the sides of the crater, descending again and again, until he had procured enough for the wants of the army. Then, with great elation, the adventurous sulphur hunters returned to Tlascala, where their arrival was greeted with shouts of joy.

Cortés was fully prepared to march again to the Mexican capital and to wreak vengeance upon the Aztecs, who were now governed by Guatemozin, a young prince who had married one of Montezuma's daughters.

The Spanish army consisted of about six hundred men, of which forty were cavalry, and eighty were arquebusiers and cross-bowmen. There were nine cannon. The men were armed with swords and with long copper-headed pikes, which had been specially constructed under the direction of the General. There were, also, the Tlascalan allies, who were still anxious and willing to fight their hated enemies, the Aztecs. Numerous other bands of Indians also flocked to the Spanish standard.

Cortés determined to march to Tezcuco, establish his headquarters upon the side of the great lake which was near the Mexican capital, and to begin a blockade of the city of the Aztecs, until some ships, which he was having constructed, could be brought to him. Then he could transport his troops to the edge of the city and begin a direct assault.

Everything went well with both ships and men. The vessels reached the lake in good order, were launched, and were filled with soldiers. The plan of action against the city was to send the cavalier, Sandoval, with one division, to take possession of Iztapalapan at the southern end of the lake, while Alvarado and Olid were to secure Tlacopan and Chapultepec upon the western shore, destroy the aqueduct, and thus cut off the city's supply of fresh water. This was successfully done and soon the Spaniards had penetrated into the city as far as the great teocalli. The natives were driven before them, while the Tlascalans in the rear filled up the gaps and brought up the cannon. As you remember, it was at the great teocalli that the most serious fighting occurred when the Spaniards were previously driven from the city. Now still fiercer battling took place and the Spaniards again captured this temple of the war-god. Some of them rushed to the top and there found a fresh image to Huitzilopochtli. Tearing off the gold and jewels with which it was bedecked, they hurled it, with its attendant priests, over the side, with a mighty yell of defiance. Then they hastened below to the assistance of their comrades, who were being furiously assailed by the Aztecs.

Things were going ill with the Spaniards and they were being driven down the great street of the city in hopeless confusion and panic. Luck was with them, however, for a small force of cavalry now arrived, charged into the mass of yelping Indians, and drove them back again to the teocalli. Here Cortés attacked by the flank and the natives retired in confusion and dismay. Evening was now coming on, so the Spanish troops retreated in good order, their Tlascalan allies pulling down many of the houses as they departed. The palace of Montezuma was set afire, and this sight so maddened the Aztecs, that they redoubled their efforts to head off the disappearing white men. It was of no avail. The attacking Spaniards soon reached Xoloc, where they learned that many of the native tribes, seeing the Mexicans unable to hold the city, would join with the men from Castile. After months of siege the Aztecs still defied the conquerors and fiercely rejected all overtures of peace, although the banner of Castile floated undisturbed from the smoldering remains of the sanctuary on the teocalli of the war-god. Hundreds of famishing wretches died every day and lay where they fell, with no one to bury them. In the midst of all this brutality and misery, Guatemozin remained calm and courageous, and was as firmly resolved as ever not to capitulate.

An assault was ordered, and, although the Mexicans fought valiantly, they were weakened by starvation and could not struggle as before. After a bloody battle, the Spanish commander withdrew to his quarters, leaving behind him forty thousand corpses and a smoldering ruin. This blow seemed to utterly stun the Aztecs.

Cortés now determined to secure the person of Guatemozin, so, upon the following day, August 13th, 1521, the Spaniards again advanced into the town and were soon battling fiercely with the Aztecs. While this was going on several canoes pushed off across the lake. The Spanish ships gave chase and sunk most of them, but a few succeeded in getting into open water. Two or three large canoes, close together, attracted the attention of a soldier, named Garci Holguin, who instantly gave chase, and, with a favorable wind, soon overtook the fugitives, although they rowed with great energy. The Spaniards leveled their guns at the Indians, when one rose, saying:

"I am Guatemozin. Lead me to Malinche. I am his prisoner. But let no harm come to my wife and to my followers."

Figure 7. Capture by Cortés of the City of Mexico.

The Emperor was taken on board one of the ships and was ordered to call upon his people to surrender.

"There is no need of this," he answered sadly, "for they will fight no longer when they see that their Emperor has been captured."

He had spoken correctly, for, when the news of his capture reached the shore, the Mexicans at once ceased to defend themselves. They had put up a hard battle in order to give their Sovereign an opportunity to escape.

Cortés had been watching the affair from the flat roof of one of the houses and now sent word that Guatemozin should be brought before him. He came, escorted by Sandoval and Holguin, both of whom claimed the honor of having captured him. The Spanish conqueror came forward with dignified courtesy to receive the noble prisoner.

"I have done all that I could to defend myself and my people," said Guatemozin. "I am now reduced to this awful state. Deal with me, Malinche, as you will." Then, laying his hand upon a dagger which hung from the belt of the Spanish invader, he added: "Better dispatch me at once with this, and rid me of life."

Cortés smiled.

"Fear not," said he. "You will be treated with honor. You have defended your capital like a brave warrior, and a Spaniard knows how to respect valor, even in an enemy."

In spite of these remarks he treated him with great cruelty, for, when the city was entered and less treasure was found there than had been expected, Cortés caused poor Guatemozin to be tortured. Fire and cord could not, however, wring the secret of the treasure from this illustrious Prince. Later on he was hanged, upon the pretense that he had conspired against the Spaniards.

The Aztec dead were now collected and burned in huge bonfires. Those who were still alive were allowed to leave the city, and for three days a mournful train of men, women, and children straggled feebly across the causeways, sick and wounded, wasted with famine and with misery. Again and again they turned to take one more look at the spot which had once been their home. When they were gone, the Spanish conquerors took possession of the place and purified it as speedily as possible, burying those who were not burned in the bonfires.

The treasures of gold and of jewels which were found fell far short of the expectations of the conquerors, for the Aztecs, no doubt, had buried their hoards, or sunk them in the lake on purpose to disappoint the avarice of their enemies.

Thus, after three months of continued fighting, the renowned capital of the Aztecs fell before Cortés and his men. The Mexicans had put up a courageous fight and had suffered much, but they had been no match for the soldiers from Cuba and from Spain.

The Aztecs would not have thus gone down to ruin, had they not ruthlessly made war upon the neighboring states, which caused them to be hated. Their human sacrifices had angered their weaker neighbors, and thus Cortés had secured the aid of the Tlascalans, without whose assistance he could never have won the fight.

Cortés and his Spaniards were now masters of Mexico. A brave man with equally brave followers had conquered an entire empire!

And what of the future days of this bold-hearted explorer? Alas! These were similar to those which came to Columbus, the Navigator. Poor, forsaken by the King of Spain, surrounded by persons who were jealous of his position and his fame, the once rich and prosperous adventurer died miserably at Castilleja, Spain, on December second, 1547, at the age of sixty-two. With him was his devoted son, Martin, a youth of fifteen.

Cortés was entombed in the land of his birth, but this was not to be his last resting place, for his remains were taken across the sea to the country which he had conquered. He was buried for the second time in the Franciscan monastery at Tezcuco; then, for a third time, in the church of St. Francis in the City of Mexico. On this occasion, which was sixty-seven years after the first entombment, all the dignitaries of Mexico marched in procession through the streets of the city. Still again, in 1794, there was another removal of the General's moldering dust to the hospital of Jesus, where a monument of bronze was erected to his fame and glory.

In 1823 there was yet another disturbance of what remained of our hero. The previous removals of his ashes had been inspired by regard, but now a revolutionary mob of frenzied Mexicans, in order to show its hatred and detestation of the Spanish conquerors, endeavored to desecrate the tomb. To prevent this, the casket, in the dead of night, was secretly carried away by the Duke of Monteleone, a descendant of Cortés on the female line, and for more than seventy years remained in a place of safety. Monteleone, himself, was killed in one of the many Mexican revolutions, and all knowledge was lost of the spot where he had hidden the ashes of the conqueror. Yet, within a few years, the remains have been discovered and a movement has been started to have them placed in the national pantheon, a temple in the City of Mexico, erected to all those who have made great names in the history of this turbulent republic.

So at last, perhaps, the valiant Cortés will receive the honor that is due him.

Chapter 7

FERDINAND MAGELLAN

EXPERT MARINER, WHOSE FOLLOWERS WERE THE FIRST TO CIRCUMNAVIGATE THE GLOBE, (1480-1521)

"Come hither, page, I want you."

A little boy ran through the corridors of the palace of King John of Portugal as this cry rang out, and, kneeling at the feet of the Queen, kissed her hand.

"That is a good boy," said Queen Leonora, smiling. "Ferdinand, I wish to say that you need not accompany me this afternoon, but can go out hawking."

"Thank you, Your Majesty," said the little boy, and, scampering off, he was soon outside the palace, where some of the men-at-arms took him hunting. This was much more to his liking than staying near the Queen and carrying messages for her, which he was expected to do nearly every day in the week.

Little Ferdinand had been born about the year 1470 at the Villa de Sabroza, which is situated about the center of that part of Portugal which lies north of the River Douro. His family was a noble one and consequently it had been easy for the youth to obtain a position of page at Court, a position which in those days, was equivalent to going to boarding-school at the present time.

In 1470 a page was taught something of the history of his own country, and a little about the history of others. He was instructed in Latin,—enough to enable him to understand the church service,—and was also taught how to read and to write. He was shown how to use the rapier, the lance, and the arquebus; how to ride a horse; how to swim and to dance. This was supposed to constitute the education of a Portuguese gentleman, and, as there was some rivalry among the nobles in regard to their respective households, the retinues of a Count or a Baron quite resembled a modern boarding-school.

These were days when all eyes were turned upon the New World and the recent discoveries in America. Every Portuguese youth was anxious to follow the sea, perhaps to become a great explorer or navigator. The discovery of a route to the Indies by a mariner in the service of Spain had awakened a jealousy in the hearts of the Portuguese, and all patriotic sailors were anxious to coast down the African shore, and, if possible, to find a way to the Indies by the Cape of Good Hope. Young Ferdinand grew up in this atmosphere, so you can readily see that he eagerly looked for a chance when he could leave the court and could become a mariner upon the wide and surging ocean.

The ambitious Ferdinand did not have to look far, or long, before he had an opportunity to follow the sea. We find that he served an apprenticeship under a famous navigator called Albuquerque, who, although he maintained a strict military discipline over his followers, was wise, humane, and just in his dealings with them. Young Ferdinand spent much time in the Indies, where he had an excellent opportunity to study and learn by experience how to govern men, so, when Albuquerque was recalled to Portugal, he went with him, only to find that the King would give him but slight recognition for his services. This angered the high-spirited young fellow.

"I will leave the service of such a monarch," said he, "and will go to Spain. There, I hear, they know how to treat a valiant man."

So, accompanied by one Roy Falero, who had earned quite a reputation as a geographer and astronomer, he sought out Charles the Fifth at Seville, proposing that the King allow him men and money for a journey of exploration.

"I wish to sail westward," said he, "and will discover a new route to the Indies. If your gracious Majesty will but help me, I will find new lands which will become the possessions of the Crown of Castile."

Charles the Fifth, the grandson of Ferdinand and Isabella, was King of Spain, and also Monarch of Austria; one crown being his by right of his mother, the other by inheritance from his father. He was a man of large ideas, so, when this project was presented to him, he heartily approved, saying:

"Of course you shall go, and I will give you the money, the men, and the ships. But all that you discover must belong to the King of Spain.— Understand this!"

"We do."

"Then you may sail, and God be with you!"

Five ships were soon fitted out for the expedition. Their crews numbered two hundred and thirty- seven men and Ferdinand was commissioned Admiral of the squadron, a position which pleased him mightily. The caravels turned southward, and, leaving Seville on August 10th, 1519, lazed along until they reached the Gulf of Guinea on the west coast of Africa, where the ships cast anchor. By and by a trade-wind came along, and aided by this and by the South Equatorial current, the vessels made a safe and easy passage across the Atlantic, to the shore of Brazil.

The Spaniards were delighted with what they saw, for they found a large, fresh-water river, seventeen miles across, and at its mouth were seven islands. Going ashore the sailors saw many brown-skinned natives, who ran away whenever they approached, yelling like demons. One of them "had the stature of a giant and the voice of a bull," but even he skipped headlong into the brush as the men from Castile made after him. When the Spaniards reached the village of these Brazilians they found the remains of human beings roasting on their fires. They stood aghast, for these fellows were cannibals!

The ships were headed southward and languidly cruised along the coast to Patagonia where the explorers lingered for two full months, eagerly looking for precious stones and for human beings. But they found none of the former and only one of the latter, this fellow being a giant who came down to the shore dancing, singing, and throwing dust over his head.

He was so tall, says an old chronicler of this voyage, that the head of a middling-sized man reached only to his waist; he was well-proportioned; his visage was large and painted with different colors, principally with yellow. There were red circles about his eyes and something like a beard was pictured on either cheek. His hair was colored white and his apparel was the skin of some beast, laced together, the head of which appeared to have been very large. It had ears like a mule, the body of a camel, and the tail of a horse: the skin of it was wrapped about his feet in the manner of shoes. In his hand was a short, thick bow and a bundle of arrows, made of reeds and pointed with sharp stones.

Magellan invited the giant Patagonian on board his flagship, and, when the old fellow had mounted the rope-ladder leading over the side, presented him with hawk's bells, a comb, some blue beads, and a looking glass, into which the dusky-hued savage took a glance.

"Hu—rruu!!" No sooner had he seen his own horrid appearance than he started backwards, with such violence, that he knocked down two sailors who were standing behind him. He slipped, fell down on the deck, and, when he arose, stood there shivering. His own face, never seen before, had terrorized him. After awhile he was rowed ashore, still quaking and rolling his eyes with unpleasant recollections of what he had seen.

The Spaniards laughed heartily at what had occurred, but the next day a man of still greater stature came to visit them. He sang some native songs, danced on the deck, and brought out some skins which he traded for glass beads and other trinkets. Then he disappeared and did not return, which led the voyagers to the belief that his countrymen had made away with him because of the friendship which they had shown towards him.

This did not deter other natives from paddling out to the ships, and four soon came on board. These were presented with beads, with bells, and similar trifles. But the Spaniards determined to trick them, so fastened iron shackles around the ankles of two of them, as if for ornaments. The ignorant Indians professed great delight with the shining bands of metal, but, when they were ready to leave the vessel, the fraud was discovered. It was certainly a cruel way to treat the poor South Americans.

As for the other two, they dove over the side of the vessel and swam to land, as soon as they perceived what had happened to their companions, who began to roar "as loud as bulls," and implored the assistance of their God, the great devil Setebos. It was of no avail. The Spaniards would not let them go and took them with them when they sailed further south. They called them Patagonians, for their feet were covered with skins, and the Portuguese word pata means a hoof or paw.

Now trouble beset Magellan, the same kind of trouble which Columbus had with his men. His followers grew rebellious, and threatened to break into open mutiny. Winter was at hand, and the ships were laid up for the cold weather, but this forced inactivity made the sailors begin to think about home, and they grew restless and discontented. They requested their commander to set sail for Spain, but this he refused to do. The sailors talked the matter over, and their sense of oppression grew stronger and stronger. So they decided to take possession of the ships, put the Admiral to death, imprison or kill such of the superior officers as refused to acknowledge the authority of the mutineers, and to return to Spain with a story that their commander had been swept overboard in a storm.

The leader of this conspiracy was one Luis de Mendoza, who was assisted by a Roman Catholic priest, Juan de Carthagena, who had accompanied the expedition so that the Spaniards might not be without spiritual assistance during their roving trips into unknown seas. Fortunately for the Admiral this plot was disclosed to him in time to prevent its execution. He had a trial and found the mutineers guilty. Many were sentenced to be hanged, drawn, and quartered.

But the priest was allowed to have his life, for the Spaniards were too good Catholics to harm any one who had devoted his days to the Church. Carthagena was not injured; but was simply put under arrest, guarded by one of the captains. The man of God was forced into the stocks: an instrument made of two pieces of wood placed one upon the other and pierced by two holes in which were inserted the legs of the person who was to be punished.

There were many others who were less guilty than Mendoza, but who were deserving of punishment. To have retained these on board, after a short period of imprisonment, was to invite another mutiny, so Magellan determined to put the remaining mutineers on shore and leave them to the mercy of the native Patagonians. They were seated in the boats, were landed, and the ships sailed southward, never to return.

The men had now been away from Spain for about a year; the long and cold winter was drawing to a close; they were plowing towards the south with the land ever in view upon the starboard. Would they reach a point where the ships could enter the South Sea from the Atlantic?

Magellan was determined either to die or to bring the expedition to a successful conclusion, so one day he addressed his sailors as follows:

"My men," said he, "the Emperor has assigned me to the course which I am to take, and I cannot and will not depart from it under any pretext whatsoever. If our provisions grow scarce, you can add to your rations by fishing and hunting on the land. I will not put back, under any consideration, and if any of you speak to me again of this, I will throw you overboard where the sharks can have a full meal."

Seeing the determination of their leader the sailors said nothing more.

The vessels kept onward, and, having reached a point about fifty-two degrees south of the equator, were obliged to lay to in a harbor near the shore. The men secured an ample supply of fish, of fuel, and of fresh water, and, thus well provided, the prows were again turned in a southerly direction. Suddenly the coast seemed to turn westward. The sailors saw land on either side of them: sometimes there was scarcely a mile between coast and islands.

This began to look interesting, as if, at last, they were nearing that unknown sea for which they searched. The prows of the caravels were now turned due west, and, with sails well filled by tempestuous winds, the Spanish ships plowed onward, ever onward, until they emerged from among the rocky islands, which surrounded them, into a broad and peaceful ocean. Hurrah! Magellan had entered the gray waters of that sea which Balboa had seen from the palm-clad hills of the Isthmus of Panama.

It was a warm, still day when the caravels forged ahead through the straits which were ever afterwards to bear the name of this Spanish adventurer, and, remembering the dreary winter upon the coast of Patagonia, Magellan named the ocean the Pacific, for all seemed beauty and peace after the troublous times which had passed. His men scrambled ashore, erected a huge cross, and called the place Cape Desire, a name well suited to their hopes of finding a route to India with its treasures of gems and of spices.

There was trouble in store for them, in spite of the pacific greeting which the vast ocean had given them. Turning westward and northward, for three long months the caravels tossed upon the oily swells with no sight of land. All the provisions were finally consumed and the water casks were almost empty. Food was obtained by soaking old leather in sea-water to soften it, and so weak were many of the sailors that they could not perform their duties. Nineteen died, including the two Patagonians.

But the ocean was truly pacific, it was like glass. No storms threatened, no tempests alarmed them, and, after sailing four thousand miles, the adventurers suddenly were cheered by the sight of land. Eagerly they drew near and went ashore, only to find two small, treeless, and uninhabited islands which they called the Unfortunate Isles. Certainly these sea rovers were having a rough time of it!

The Spaniards were upon the outskirts of Polynesia, and, as they sailed onward, soon came upon a number of islands where they obtained plenty of food from the dusky-hued natives who eagerly swarmed around them in skin boats. The islanders also stole everything which they could get their hands on, including one of the long boats, which they paddled ashore and hid near their village. This angered the men from Castile exceedingly, so they determined to punish the Polynesians, and that right quickly.

Arming themselves, and putting on their steel helmets and breastplates, the Spaniards now went ashore, shot at the natives with their guns, drove them from their village, smashed their canoes, and burned their huts. After killing seven of the yelping brown-skins, they seized their lost boat, rowed it back to the ship, hoisted sail, and left for other scenes. Magellan revenged himself further by calling these islands the Insular Latronum, or "Islands of Thieves." They are now called the Ladrones.

It was the month of March, 1521. The air was balmy and the navigators much enjoyed the sight of many beauteous islands in the South Sea. They landed upon one of them, pitched a tent for the accommodation of the sick, and killed a stout porker which they had obtained from the thieving natives. After their diet of leather, soaked in sea water, this fresh meat was appreciated. In fact they had a good, old-fashioned banquet, such as one is accustomed to on Thanksgiving Day. After this they chanted the Te Deum and had a siesta beneath the shadows of the trees.

They had remained here about a week when nine men came paddling up in a canoe, and brought presents of cocoa-wine and some golden trinkets. These were eagerly accepted, and the visitors rowed away, promising by signs to return in four days with flesh, fowls, and rice. This promise they kept, and, when they arrived, offered to exchange various kinds of spices and articles made of gold, for the beads and trinkets which the Spaniards showed them. Magellan wished to impress the natives with his reserve power, so he ordered one of the cannon to be discharged, while the visitors were on board his vessel. This so frightened them that they ran to the gunwale in order to jump into the sea. The sailors interfered, and, assuring them of the friendliness of the Admiral, soon had them quieted.

Leaving this island behind them, the Spaniards now steered west and southwest, and, after a run of three days, anchored near a large body of land which was inhabited by a tribe of brown-skinned natives, who seemed to be well-disposed towards these strange foreigners. Magellan presented the King with a red and yellow garment made long and flowing, and gave his principal courtiers knives and glass beads.

The Spaniards were well received by these people, so well received, in fact, that the King of the island offered to furnish them with pilots when they wished to sail away. This offer was accepted, and, steering westward, they soon reached another island, called Zubut, where they learned that a vessel manned by a Portuguese crew, and having a cargo of gold and of slaves, had anchored opposite the capital only the day before Magellan's arrival, and had offered tribute to the King. Rendered bold by this deference, the native proceeded to exact tribute from Magellan, informing him that all who came to his dominions were obliged to pay it.

"I cannot pursue the same course that these Portuguese have done," answered Magellan. "For the King of Portugal is a far less powerful monarch than he whom I serve, for my Emperor has such power that his subjects pay tribute to no one. If, therefore, you persist in your claim, you may find yourself involved in a war with one who will crush you at the first conflict."

These words made the bold native reflect, and, as a Moorish trader, who was present, informed him that what he told him was the truth, the monarch asked for a day in which to consider his answer to Magellan's refusal. In the meantime he entertained the sailors right royally.

While deliberating how to gracefully withdraw from the arrogant position which he had assumed, the savage ruler was visited by the native monarch who had accompanied Magellan on board his ship from the island which he had recently visited. This fellow spoke so well of the Admiral that his words had great weight with the proud islander. The demand for tribute was withdrawn, and the people of the island entered eagerly into traffic with the newcomers, who became missionaries and preached the Christian faith with so much earnestness, that, within a very short time, the whole territory was converted to the religion of Jesus Christ. The native idols were destroyed and crosses were erected in many places.

After a lengthy stay at this island, the Spaniards again went on board their ships, and, sailing away, reached the Philippine Islands, which were called Mathan by the natives. Here were two native rulers, Tual and Cilapulapu, whom Magellan summoned to pay tribute to the King of Spain. The first acceded to his demand, the second refused indignantly to do so.

This roused the hot blood of the Castilian adventurer, and he determined to enforce his claim with cold steel. He, therefore, chose sixty of his bravest men, armed them with coats of mail and steel helmets, and, taking to the boats, soon landed. They marched inland in order to chastise this independent ruler.

Cilapulapu had hastily collected all of his fighting men, arranged them in three divisions, and awaited the oncoming Spaniards. His soldiers were many—there were two thousand in each division, or six thousand in all—armed with spears, lances, darts, javelins, and arrows dipped in poison. The Spaniards little knew what they were marching against, yet, like Custer at the Little Big Horn, they kept on moving. And, like Custer, there was soon to be an equally severe defeat. The mail-clad Castilians advanced boldly through the jungle to where the enemy was lying concealed, and there a shower of arrows beat down upon them, rattling like hail upon their steel coats. Many of the barbs were turned aside, but some penetrated the joints of the armor, and, entering the skin of the Spaniards, sent the deadly poison coursing through their veins.

Magellan urged on his followers by voice and waving sword, but, as he led the advance, a sharp barb penetrated a joint of his armor, and forced the deadly poison into his blood. The enemy now rushed in on every side, in overwhelming numbers, and showered their javelins upon the sixty brave soldiers of Castile. The wounded leader bravely endeavored to direct his men, in spite of his injury, but, as he shouted his battle-cry, a cane-lance struck him full in the face. The blow was fatal and he sank dead upon the ground.

His soldiers were now almost surrounded. Eight of them were killed, the rest retreated (as best they might) to the beach, leaving the body of their dead leader in the hands of the exultant savages, who made the air hideous with their exultant battle-cries.

So died the brave Portuguese navigator, on an island which was to belong to the Spanish Crown for many, many years. He had fallen as he had always wished to do, in the front of battle, and, although his followers endeavored to secure his body from the wild Filipinos, they were unable to do so. Their emissary to the barbarous Cilapulapu was murdered by this wily monarch, and, seeing that it was impossible to remain longer in this region, the navigators sailed away, bitterly cursing their misfortune in losing such a brave and courageous leader.

Reduced to forty-six in number, the survivors of this expedition of adventure and discovery continued their journey among the various islands of Polynesia until February, 1522, when they passed the extremity of Molucca, and, keeping outside of Sumatra, sailed due west toward the eastern coast of Africa. Twenty-one of the forty-six died of hunger before they reached the Cape Verde Islands, where, sending deputies ashore to represent their pitiable condition to the Portuguese authorities, they were allowed some rice, which was quickly disposed of. Thirteen of the sailors went on shore again to secure a further supply of provisions, but the Portuguese considered that they had done quite enough for them, so seized them and threw them into prison. The others, panic-stricken, hoisted sail, and, without endeavoring to release their companions, set out for their beloved Spain.

Figure 8. The Death of Magellan.

On September the seventh, 1522, twelve miserable-looking Spanish sailors landed at the port of St. Lucar, near Seville. They were ragged, bare-foot, and gaunt from hunger. Proceeding to the Cathedral, they sank to their knees and thanked God for their preservation, for, out of the two hundred and thirty-seven who had sailed gayly away from Seville more than three years before, these were all that remained to tell the tale.

And it was a pretty good tale they had to tell, for they had been the first white men to circumnavigate the globe. But the bones of their gallant leader lay among the wild and bloodthirsty natives of the Philippine Islands, with not even a stone to mark the last resting place of the brave and energetic Portuguese mariner.

Chapter 8

GIOVANNI VERRAZANO

FIRST NAVIGATOR TO EXPLORE THE COAST OF NEW JERSEY AND NEW YORK, (1480-1527)

It was a calm, still day off the coast of Spain. A light, southerly breeze rippled the surface of the water, and, if you had been standing on the Cape St. Vincent, you would have seen the sails of six vessels which were headed for the shore. If you had been nearer, you would have seen that here were three Spanish galleons of war and three treasure ships from far distant Hispaniola, on the Isthmus of Panama. They were loaded with gold, with silver, and with spices, which had been sent to the King of Spain by Hernando Cortés, conqueror of Montezuma and the Mexican people.

But, ah! What is this!

As the treasure ships and their convoys approached the shore, suddenly a fleet of six vessels could be seen boiling along under full canvas, and rushing to meet them. They were armed corsairs under Juan Florin, fitted out at New Rochelle, in France, and having on board a man who was to have some prominence in later years, as he was to be the first European to view the broad salt marshes of New Jersey. This was Giovanni Verrazano, a Florentine navigator, who, like all the mariners in those days, was a sea robber, a pirate, and an explorer.

The Spanish ships were about thirty-five miles from the shore, and rollicked along right merrily, under a full spread of canvas. Their steermen thought, no doubt, that these were friendly vessels coming to greet them and to convoy them home. But in an hour they found out their mistake. The flag of France flew defiantly at the mast-heads of the oncoming galleons, and, as they drew near, cannon were trained upon the Spaniards and balls began to fly dangerously close. One of the treasure ships turned around and took flight, but the others had to fight it out.

Now was a sharp little battle. Around and around went the boats, banging away at a good rate; but the French corsairs were accurate marksmen and were keen to win, for they longed for all that Mexican gold. At the end of two hours' time the French were alongside, had boarded, and the yellow flag of Spain came fluttering to the decks of the galleons from the coast of Mexico. The treasure of Cortés was to find a safe home on the shores of Merrie France.

The King of Spain was deeply grieved to hear of this loss and thereupon ordered all homeward- bound vessels to rendezvous at Hispaniola, in order to be safely convoyed to Spain. He also offered one-half of the treasure captured to any Spaniard who would chase the French and get back that which had been stolen. Hernando Cortés, too, was greatly disappointed when he heard of this loss, but he took measure to avoid such mishaps in the future. As for Verrazano: he reaped such a large share of this treasure, that he soon owned some vessels of his own.

For several years this Florentine corsair, now sailing under the flag of France, made it a business to lie in wait for treasure ships coming from Mexico, and the West Indies, to the shores of Spain. He did well, captured many a prize, and on one occasion took a Portuguese ship bringing from the Indies a freight valued at 180,000 ducats. He grew rich and prosperous, and, as he was of an adventurous disposition, determined to, himself, sail to the New World, and make an attempt to find that passage to Cathay, for which all European navigators were then searching. The Spaniards, at this time, had just about given up all hope of finding Asia connected with the continent of North America.

In the year 1522, with four ships, Verrazano turned his face towards America and started across the Atlantic. But fierce storms beset his path; he was driven back to the coast of Brittany, where his vessels, badly damaged by wind and waves, were refitted. After this he gathered a fleet of armed caravels, cruised southward into Spanish waters, took several prizes, and then returned. This was in the spring of 1524. He then determined to sail for the land of America, in one ship, the Dauphine. He took fifty men, with ammunition, arms, and stores sufficient to last them for eight months, and turned the prow of the trim little vessel towards the west.

Heading straight across the broad Atlantic, Verrazano and his Frenchmen passed north of the Bermuda Islands, and, drifting northward in the Gulf Stream, sighted land about the sixth day of March. Many fires were seen on the beach, made by the Indians, who flocked to the shore at this season to feast on shell fish and to manufacture wampum, or shell money. The explorers were off the coast of New Jersey, probably near Cape May.

Verrazano was much pleased to see that he had reached the shores of America and ordered a boat to land. As the sailors scrambled up on the sandy beach, a number of natives came down to the shore; but fled as the white men approached, sometimes stopping, and turning about, gazing with much curiosity at the white-skinned navigators. Being reassured by signs that they would not be injured, some of them came near, and, looking with wonder at the dress and complexions of the foreigners, offered them food. This was accepted, and then the sailors returned to their vessel.

The explorers sailed northward, again landed, and, going inland, found this to be a country full of very great forests. They marveled at the many trees and shrubs which stretched away in unbroken splendor. Verrazano was undoubtedly in the harbor of New York, at this time, and saw Shrewsbury River, the Kills, and the Narrows. He says: "The land has many lakes and ponds of fresh water, with numerous kinds of birds adapted to all the pleasures of the chase. The winds do not blow fiercely in these regions and those which prevail are northwest and west."

Leaving New York harbor, the explorers followed the coastline, and sailed along the shores of Long Island, where they saw many great fires made by the native inhabitants. Approaching the beach in order to get water, the Captain ordered the boat to land, with twenty-five men, but there was such high surf that it was impossible to do so. Many Indians came down to the sand, making friendly signs, and pointing to where the white men might gain a footing.

Figure 9. Giovanni Verrazano.

Rockaway Bay was a great resort of the Indians for the purpose of manufacturing wampum or seawan, the money of the Native Americans. Numerous shell beds now line the shore where the manufacture was carried on. The navigators must have therefore landed on Rockaway

Beach, where the shore-line meets the narrow and barren outer-bar, which for over seventy miles separates the ocean from the bay, or lagoons, behind it.

Still coasting along, the keen Verrazano went ashore again near Quogue or Bridgehampton, where he found the place full of forests of various kinds of woods, but not as odoriferous as those on the Jersey shore; the country being more northerly and colder. Here the Indians again fled into the thickets, as the white men approached, but the Frenchmen saw many of their boats, made of a single log twenty feet long and four feet wide, hollowed out with sharp knives and axes.

After remaining here three days, the navigators departed, running along the coast in a northerly direction, sailing by day and dropping anchor at night. At the end of a journey of a hundred miles they found a very pleasant place, indeed, where a large river, deep at its mouth, ran into the sea between high cliffs upon either side. The explorers proceeded up the curving stream in a boat and soon found themselves surrounded by the redskins in canoes, these natives being dressed with bird feathers of gay colors. They came towards the Frenchmen, joyfully, and emitted great shouts of admiration.

The sailors ascended the river for about half a mile, "where," says Verrazano, "we saw a fine lake about three miles in circumference through which were passing many canoes of the red men." But a violent wind sprang up, so that the explorers had to return to their ships, "leaving the land," continues Verrazano, "with much regret, as the hills there showed minerals." The navigators had entered the river Thames, the vessel being anchored well within Fisher's Island, where many a steam-yacht would afterwards cast its anchor, while the sailors would watch the rival crews of Yale and Harvard, as they battled for supremacy on the waters of the shimmering stream.

But the navigators would not remain to make friends with the Indians, and, weighing anchor, sailed eastward, where they saw an island, triangular in form, distant about ten miles from the mainland, full of hills and covered with trees. Judging from the fires which they viewed along the shore, the Frenchmen considered it to be thickly inhabited. This was Block Island, but the sunburned explorers called it Louisa Island, after the mother of King Francis the First, of far distant France.

Fourteen miles from Block Island is Narragansett Bay, and hither the Dauphine was headed, anchoring first at its mouth, then between Goat Island and the present town of Newport. Immediately the vessel was surrounded by canoes, filled with wondering savages, who at first did not venture to approach the ships, but, stopping about fifty paces away, gazed in silent admiration at the strange object which had risen, as if by magic, before them. Then, all of a sudden, they broke into a loud shout of joy.

The Frenchmen crowded to the rail, reassuring the natives and imitating their gestures. The Indians therefore, came nearer, and, as they approached, the navigators threw them bells, mirrors, and other trinkets, which they picked up, laughing, and then paddled up to the sides of the great hulk. Catching hold of the gunwales with their hands, they crawled up on the deck, saying: "Ugh! Ugh!"

Among the visitors were two kings, one of whom seemed to be about forty, the other twenty-four years of age. The elder was arrayed in a robe of deer skins, skillfully wrought with rich embroidery; his head was bare and his hair was carefully tied behind him; his neck was adorned by a large chain, set off with various colored stones. The dress of the younger monarch was nearly like that of his elder companion.

The followers of these kings crowded around them, "and," says Verrazano, "they were the most beautiful and genteel-mannered people I had met in all the voyage." Their complexions were remarkably clear; their features regular, their hair long, and dressed with no ordinary degree of care; their eyes black and lively. Their whole aspect was pleasing, and their profiles reminded the Frenchmen of the busts of the ancients. The wives and daughters of the native Narragansetts were not allowed to come on board, and had to wait for their husbands in the canoes. These, too, were richly dressed in deer and beaver skins. The early inhabitants of Newport, it seems, were as gaudily arrayed as were their white-skinned descendants to be many centuries later.

The Frenchmen lingered here for more than two weeks, while Verrazano made numerous trips into the many estuaries of Narragansett

Bay, finding a pleasant country with all kinds of cultivation going on. Corn was being grown; wine and oil were being manufactured by the native inhabitants. The corsair was particularly struck with the total ignorance shown by the natives of the value of gold, and the preference which they gave for beads and for toys, over more costly objects. So, in trade, he was able to get many valuable furs and skins for a few, shining, glass beads.

But, in spite of the charms of the scenery and the pleasant reception given him by the friendly Narragansett Indians, the Frenchmen decided to continue their journey northward. So, leaving Newport behind them, the Dauphine was steered along the coast. The vessel passed around south of Martha's Vineyard and Nantucket, and, steering well clear of Cape Cod, lazed along the rocky shore of Massachusetts near Cape Ann.

Occasionally the explorers landed in their boat, finding dense woods of pines and hemlocks. The natives seemed to be quite different, also, from those farther south, for, while the southerners had been gentle in their behavior, these were more barbarous and rough. They were dressed in the skins of bears, wolves, and foxes, and, although the Frenchmen endeavored to hold conversation with them, this was found to be impossible, as they would run into the forest whenever the white men approached.

Finally, somewhere between Cape Ann and Nahant—probably where the Myopia Hunt Club now rests in peaceful seclusion—twenty-five of the explorers went inland for two or three miles, seeing many natives, who would not be friendly, and, when they returned to the shore, the primitive sons of Massachusetts shot at the interlopers with their bows and arrows, shouting loudly as they did so. Many of the redskins had copper rings in their ears. The forests were very dense hereabouts, and the savages hid themselves whenever the white men turned to fight.

Not pleased with their reception, the navigators coasted northward, passed the rocky promontory of Cape Ann, the wind-ripped Isles of Shoals, and finally reached Portland Harbor. They were charmed with the magnificent scenery, and, coasting along the hemlock-clad shores, passed thirty-two islands, all lying near the rocky beach, which impressed the voyagers greatly with their beauty. But alas! Provisions now began to fail, and it was time to hark back to France.

All the crew were well and happy, for they had had a wonderful trip along the coastline of America, then unspoiled by the erection of houses, towns, and villages.

On board was an Indian boy, whom they had kidnapped, and he, too, seemed to be well and contented. When off the Jersey coast, Verrazano had landed and had journeyed about two miles into the interior, with about twenty of the crew. The natives had fled to the forest; but two,—a young girl and an old woman, less fortunate than the rest,—had been overtaken by the Europeans. The Frenchmen seized the girl, and also a boy of about eight years of age, who had been hanging on the back of the old woman. Then, they began to retrace their steps to the sea.

As they proceeded, the girl made a vigorous resistance, and set up violent cries of rage and terror. She clawed with her nails, struck with her hands, and struggled to free herself. At last, wearied with the attempt to transport this virago, the Frenchmen let her go, keeping the boy as a less troublesome, though less valued prize. The girl bounded away into the forest like a deer, and was soon lost in the shadows of the trees.

The Dauphine was now somewhere near the mouth of the beautiful Penobscot River, in Maine. It was the end of June and the breath from the hemlock forests along the shore was filled with the scent of the balsam bough. Verrazano would have lingered longer in this lovely country, but the object of the voyage had now been accomplished; over seven hundred leagues of the new world had been explored, and the French corsair had held sufficient communication with the native redskins to form some idea of their state and character.

The bow of the Dauphine was therefore turned towards France; she made a safe passage, propelled by favorable winds, and, in the month of July, 1524, about five and a half months after her departure, Verrazano, the corsair, landed at Dieppe. The Indian boy was well, and he was taken ashore: but what happened to him afterwards is not known.

The adventurous explorer now wrote a letter to the King of France telling of the land which he had discovered and of the Indians and wild beasts which he had seen. To Francis the First, the French Monarch, he offered a vast province in the temperate latitude, on which France might well have expended her enterprise, and which would have repaid her efforts a thousand fold. But, alas! France was then in dreadful straits, for she was near annihilation from her recent struggles with Germany. The King was a prisoner in the hands of the Emperor; his army had been dispersed; his treasury was exhausted.

Thus the vast and fruitful land of America was left to the English and the Dutch to explore, to colonize, and to subdue. Could the rough, old corsair have seen in dreams the beach of Atlantic City, four centuries later, with its board walk, its towering hotels, its thousands of bathers, and its wheeled chairs, he would have, indeed, been surprised, for the old fellow was the first European who had seen the surf on the shelving sands of New Jersey.

Chapter 9

FRANCISCO PIZARRO

CONQUEROR OF PERU, (1475-1538)

An eagle soared o'er the heights of Quito,
Its talons were hard, and it screamed as it flew;
For, far down below, in gleaming chain mail,
Was a Spanish corsair with his murderous crew.
The Spaniard looked upward. "Ah, brother," said he,
"Are there doves here below? If it's so, I am here
To plunder such weaklings, despoil them of home,
To pillage and burn without shedding a tear."
The eagle said, "Yes; you, I see, are my mate,
For I am a harpy; bring ruin in my path.
Let's form an alliance, and kill all we can,
What matter to us if we stir up fierce wrath!"
So the Spaniard and eagle swept o'er poor Peru;
Each sought out the doves, e'en at the church portal.
'Midst fire and pillage, 'midst carnage and death,
Both carved a career,—the Spaniard's immortal.

There was a Spaniard once, who lived in Panama and who had the high sounding name of Vasco Nuñez de Balboa.

Like all of the adventurers in the early days, he was ever on the lookout for gold. Do you wonder, therefore, that his brown eyes glittered and gleamed when an Indian chief came to him and said:

"If this yellow gold is what you prize so greatly that you are willing to leave your home and risk even life itself, for it, then I can tell you of a land where they eat and drink out of golden vessels, and gold is as common with the natives as iron is with you."

It is unnecessary to add that the keen Balboa eagerly inquired where this place was to be found. And the Indian, sweeping his hand toward the South, said: "It is there,—Peru, the land of the Incas!"

The Spaniard did not forget what the native had said, and he told it to some of his friends, among whom was a young adventurer by the name of Francisco Pizarro, who had been sent to Panama to traffic with the natives for pearls. This fellow, who was a distant kinsman of Hernando Cortés, conqueror of Mexico, was a true adventurer; but he was the least educated of all the Spaniards who have made names for themselves in the New World. He had, indeed, been employed as a swine-herd near the city of Truxillo, in Spain, where he had been born. He could neither read nor write with any fluency. From childhood he had been neglected and had been left to make a living as best he might.

We know that he sailed away from Seville, in Spain, when quite a young man, and that he embarked, with other adventurers, to find his fortune in the New World. We hear of him in Hispaniola, and, later on, know that he was employed by Balboa in several enterprises. He seems to have been ever on the lookout for adventure and anxious to mend his fortunes, which were so low, indeed, that, when he heard of this land of gold, he had not the means to fit out a ship in order to sail thither and find out whether or not what the native had said was true. Still, the matter rankled in his mind, so that he, at length, found a way to go where was wealth, fame, and fortune. There were two people in eastern Panama who knew young Pizarro, and who decided that, perhaps, there was some truth in what the Indian had said about the land of the Incas.

"I wish to go there," said the Spaniard. "If you will assist and aid me, we may be all wealthy together."

"That sounds well," answered Hernando de Luque, one of these friends, "and I believe that I will give you the necessary funds, so that you may fit out a ship."

The other friend, named Diego Almagro, was also a badly educated individual, but he was one who eagerly listened to tales of adventure. A compact was thus made between these three, most of the money being supplied by de Luque, Almagro undertaking the equipment of the ship, and Pizarro taking command of the expedition. It was difficult to get men to join in such a venture, but eventually about a hundred were obtained, mostly idlers in the colony who eagerly grasped at anything that would mend their broken fortunes. They were a rough lot.

Everything was finally ready for the journey to that fabled land of Peru, so Pizarro set sail with his following of ne'er-do-wells in a large ship, some time during the month of November, 1524. Almagro followed in a second vessel, with the rest of the Panama ruffians, and thus began a movement which was to bring a rich and populous region beneath the banner of Castile.

Pizarro and his friends embarked at a most unfavorable time of the year, for it was the rainy season, and the coast was swept by violent tempests. They had no knowledge of this fact and consequently kept on until they reached the Puerto de Piñas, or Port of Pines, a headland upon the other side of which was a little river. The ship was brought to anchor and the crew landed in order to explore the country, but the Spanish adventurers found only thick, impenetrable forests, and deep swamplands which were filled with quagmire and with fever. So they returned to the ship, exhausted; hoisted sail, and proceeded again upon their voyage to the southland. They met with a succession of fearful storms which buffeted their vessel so severely that she began to leak. Their stock of food and water became nearly spent, and the members of the expedition had to subsist upon two ears of Indian corn a day. In this dreadful condition they were only too glad to turn back, and anchor, again, a few leagues from the place where they had first hauled down their sails.

The Spaniards were now in a desperate state of mind, for the food supply was about gone, and, upon the shore, all that they could discover were a few unwholesome berries. So the ship was sent back to Panama in order to lay in a fresh stock of provisions, while Pizarro, himself, with about half of his company, made a further attempt to explore the country. The climate was hot and enervating, so that more than twenty men died of fever, but the energetic Pizarro kept on, and at last succeeded in reaching a clearing where stood a small Indian village.

To the half-starved Spaniards this was a godsend, indeed, and, rushing forward, they broke into the rude huts and seized what food was there to be found; which they devoured ravenously. The natives dispersed into the woods, but, seeing that the white-skins offered them no violence, they came back and, by means of signs, began to converse with these haggard adventurers. There was a rich country lying far to the south, said they, where the people had much gold. They, themselves, wore large ornaments of the shining metal, and this the Spaniards eagerly gazed upon, for it was substantial evidence that the precious material could be found at no far distant place.

Cheered, but miserable, the adventurers camped here for six weary weeks, when the ship returned with provisions. Those on board were horrified at the gaunt and haggard faces of their comrades, who looked like wild men, and who fell upon the provisions as if they had never before seen food. They soon revived, and, embarking once more, sailed southward along the coast, and away from that dismal and cheerless spot, which they named the Port of Famine.

The vessel crept along near the shore, and the Spaniards again landed, when they saw an Indian village among the trees. The inhabitants fled into the forest as the white-skinned men approached, leaving behind them a goodly store of corn and other food, and also a number of gold ornaments of considerable value. The adventurers found that these were a race of cannibals, for human flesh was roasting before a fire near one of the huts. So they hastened back to their ship, with no cheerful feelings, and again set sail, touching here and there upon the shore, where they found bold and warlike natives, who showed no disposition to be friendly.

Almagro, meanwhile, had succeeded in equipping a small caravel, and had followed in Pizarro's wake with about seventy men. At different places he touched the shore, even as Pizarro had done, and had several severe fights with the natives, in one of which he was struck in the forehead by a javelin, which deprived him of the sight of one eye. Nothing daunted by this mishap, he kept on down the coast, collected considerable gold, and finally gained tidings of his friend Pizarro, whom he came upon at a seaport called Chicama. The two adventurous commanders embraced with much fervor, and each told the other of his many exciting encounters with the natives. They both were sure that they had not yet gone far enough to the southward, and, after a long consultation, Pizarro decided to join with Almagro, and return to Panama for more men, more arms, and better supplies.

Alas! When the adventurous sea rovers reached Panama, the Governor lent an unwilling ear to all of their schemes.

"You have wasted men and money enough already," said he. "Away with you!"

But here the friendly de Luque interposed, and, by the payment of a large sum, was able to buy off this official interference with future explorations. A contract was now drawn up and signed between de Luque, Pizarro and Almagro, whereby the two latter agreed to pursue the undertaking until the treasures of Peru were discovered, and were to divide all the lands, gold, jewels, or treasures equally between the three, in consideration for further sums which de Luque was to furnish for more ships and provisions. Should the expedition fail utterly, de Luque was to be repaid with every bit of property which the two sea-captains might possess. Two large and strong vessels were now engaged, and, procuring a few horses and one hundred and sixty men, the second expedition was started for the fabled land of promise.

There was to be no easy or garland-strewn road to success. One of their ships, under an experienced pilot called Ruiz, sailed on ahead, leaving Pizarro with a number of his men at a place on the sea-coast, which seemed to be healthful, and in an excellent position for defense. A good deal of treasure had been gathered as the adventurers coasted along, and this was sent back to Panama, under the care of Almagro, who was instructed to bring reënforcements. By the exhibition of the gold, which had been discovered, it was hoped to tempt other Spaniards to this hazardous adventure.

Ruiz had a successful voyage. He sailed across the equinoctial line and entered a great bay, called the Bay of St. Matthew, where he found the natives hospitable, and somewhat afraid of these white-skinned strangers, in their curious house, which floated upon the blue water. The people wore robes of a woolen cloth of fine texture, dyed in brilliant colors, and embroidered with figures of birds and of flowers. They had a pair of balances for weighing gold and silver, a utensil never seen before among the natives of South America, and told him that they possessed large flocks of llamas, or Peruvian sheep, from which their wool was obtained, and also, that, in the palaces of their rulers, gold and silver was as common as wood. Ruiz took several of the most intelligent natives on board, in order to teach them Spanish, so that they could act as interpreters, and then sailed back to the place where he had left Pizarro and his men.

He arrived in the very nick of time, because the Spaniards had met with nothing but disaster. They had journeyed into the interior, hoping to find treasure and populous cities, only to become lost in dense forests of gigantic tropical vegetation. Many were waylaid and killed by lurking natives; some died of fever; and all suffered great privation and distress. Hideous snakes and alligators infested the many swamps which they came across; so, discouraged and depressed, they had retreated to the sea-coast, only to be so tormented by swarms of mosquitoes, that they had to bury themselves in the sand, in order to rid themselves of the pests. Harried by fear of starvation, and worn out by suffering, they wished to go no farther; but to sail immediately for Panama. Luckily, at this juncture, Almagro returned with a goodly supply of provisions, and with eighty new adventurers, whose enthusiasm speedily revived the drooping spirits of Pizarro's men. Sailing southward, under the pilotage of Ruiz, they again reached the Bay of St. Matthew, and cast anchor opposite the Peruvian town of Tacamez, which was swarming with natives who wore many ornaments of gold and of silver. Nearby flowed a river, called the River of Emeralds, because of the quantities of the gems which were dug from its banks, and, when the Spaniards heard of the vast stores of these gems which the natives had gathered, they were eager to come into possession of them.

With this thought in view, they landed, but were immediately surrounded by nearly ten thousand natives, who were well-armed, and seemed to be hostile. The adventurers were helpless; but, just as they expected to be assaulted, one of their number was thrown from his horse, and this caused a great commotion among the Peruvians.

"See," they cried, "what was all in one part has divided, so that it is now two portions. Make way for the sorcerers!"

A lane was immediately opened for the Castilians, and down this, with thankful hearts, they retreated to their boats.

Shortly after this, Almagro returned in one of the ships to Panama, for it was plain that they could never gain any treasure from these natives by force, unless they had a greater number of soldiers. Pizarro chose a small island as his headquarters until the return of his comrade; but this decision caused great discontent among his men, and many of them wrote to friends in Panama bewailing their condition, and begging them to use their influence with the Governor to send speedy relief. As Almagro did his best to seize all letters directed to Panama, one of these was hidden in a ball of cotton, and sent as a present to the wife of the Governor. It was signed by several soldiers, who begged that a ship be sent to rescue them from the dismal isle before they should all die of starvation and exposure. This epistle reached its proper destination, and, when the Governor viewed the haggard faces of Almagro's men, he determined, in his own mind, that the few ill-fated survivors of the expedition were being detained by Pizarro, against their will, and upon a desolate island. He was also angered by the number of lives which had already been lost, and the money which had been spent upon the unsuccessful expedition to the land of the Peruvians. Consequently he refused to help Almagro further, and, instead of this, sent off two ships to bring back every Spanish adventurer who was then with Pizarro. The vessels were commanded by a certain Captain Tafur.

The followers of Pizarro were overjoyed to see two well-provisioned ships come to their assistance, and were quite ready to return to Panama; but Pizarro received letters from both Almagro and the priest, de Luque, begging him to hold fast to his purpose. They furthermore advised him that they would come to his assistance in a very short time.

Now occurred a famous incident in the career of this noted explorer, an incident as famous as the passage of the Rubicon by Julius Cæsar, and of the Alps by the redoubtable Napoleon Bonaparte. Pizarro, indeed, was determined to press on, for he had in him an adventurous soul and the wealth which he had seen at the Bay of St. Matthew had fired his zeal and cupidity.

"Comrades," said he to his men, "I understand that many of you would put back from this hazardous enterprise. As for me, I intend to go onward."

Then, seizing his sword, he drew a line upon the sand from east to west, for all were collected upon the beach.

"On this side," he continued, pointing to the south, "are toil, hunger, the drenching storm, desertion, and death; on that side, ease and pleasure. Here lies Peru with its riches; there is Panama and its poverty! Choose each man what best becomes a brave Castilian! For my part I go to the south!"

So saying, he stepped across the line and was quickly followed by Ruiz, Pedro de Candia, and eleven other adventurous souls. The remainder made no movement, so Tafur sailed away with them, next day, leaving a goodly portion of his provisions to help out those who determined to cast their fortunes with the danger-loving Pizarro.

Now, constructing a raft, the adventurous Castilian transported his men to an island which lay farther north. There were pheasants and rabbits here, and also swarms of gnats, flies and mosquitoes. The rain fell incessantly, and, although the Spaniards built rude huts in order to keep out the water, they had hard work to be comfortable. For seven months they thus lived, until Almagro arrived from Panama, with only just enough men on board to work the vessel, and with commands from the Governor for Pizarro to report immediately at the Isthmus.

In spite of this mandate, the adventurous Spaniards headed the vessel for the southern coast, soon came in view of a great gulf, the Gulf of Guayaquil, and saw, far above them, the snowy crests of the towering mountains: the Cordilleras. Between these and the sea-coast, lay a narrow strip of land, which was highly cultivated by the natives. Some of these Pizarro persuaded to accompany him, and he left one of his own company, who was fair of complexion and wore a long beard, to learn the language of the Indians, so that he could act as an interpreter upon his return. He also took several of the native sheep, or llamas—"the little camels"—to exhibit to those who would doubt his story at Panama, or in Spain, for he had decided if necessary to seek assistance from the King.

The natives received these fair-skinned navigators with kindness and much curiosity, for the armor, guns, and horses of these so-called "Children of the Sun" greatly interested the gentle Peruvians. Several of the Spaniards penetrated into the interior, and came back with wondrous tales of temples filled with gold and silver ornaments. So Pizarro was determined, upon his return to Panama, to gather a force sufficient to conquer the entire country, for his desire for wealth and the power which this brings, was quite similar to that of those who penetrate the arid wastes of Nevada, at the present day, or search for the precious metal amidst the hemlock-forests of Alaska.

Now, satisfied that a rich and populous kingdom lay before him, Pizarro turned about and sailed northward, and, after an absence of a year and a half, once more talked with the irate Governor of Panama. As he was supposed to have perished with all his men, the representative of the Spanish King was quite considerate in his treatment of him; but, when Pizarro asked for further assistance in his scheme for the conquest of Peru, the Governor seemed to have other use for his money and his soldiers.

"What do I care?" cried the adventurer, in some heat. "I can visit the King of Spain and he will help me, I know. I am determined to succeed."

This man, you see, had the power of will. Although he had suffered hardship, mental anguish, famine; he was certain that he could become master of the gentle Peruvians, and so was determined to crush any obstacles which came in his path and obstructed this ambition. So far, his conduct had been noble, his treatment of his friends and companions had been just, his own cheerfulness and self control had been commendable. Let us see how he conducted himself, when he had secured that for which he sought?

Taking passage for Spain, he appeared at the Spanish Court with two or three llamas, several natives, and specimens of the woolen cloth and gold and silver ornaments of the Peruvians, to bear witness to his tales of this wonderful country. The King lent a ready ear to his request for assistance; he was empowered to conquer and take possession of Peru in the name of Spain; and was requested to transport many priests along with him, in order to convert the Indians to the Roman Catholic religion. The ignorant swine-herd, in fact, had become a man of some merit and mark, which so greatly pleased his four half-brothers—who possessed the high-sounding names of Hernando, Gonzalo, Juan, and Francisco de Alcantara—that they all desired to follow him to this land of the llama and the snow-capped mountains.

"Hurray for Brother Francisco," said they. "He will make us all rich! Hurray and God be with him!" Finally, two hundred and fifty men were gathered for the conquest of Peru. The Pizarros set sail for Panama—it was a family party now—and soon all were again upon the shores of the New World. Three ships were speedily loaded with equipment and provisions, and, with one hundred and eighty followers and twenty-seven horses, the Spanish free-booters and adventurers sailed for the Bay of St. Matthew. They landed, and immediately started operations in the usual high-handed and brutal manner of the Spanish conqueror.

The little band of cut-throats went ashore and advanced along the coast, while the three ships drifted along in a parallel line, keeping as close inshore as discretion would permit. When the Castilians reached a town of some importance, they would rush in upon the inhabitants, sword in hand, and would cut down all who opposed them. The poor, frightened natives would run away tumultuously, while the Pizarro brothers, and other Castilian robbers, would collect all the gold and silver ornaments that they could find. Many emeralds were also secured, which were sent to the ships, and back to Panama, in order to impress those who were left behind with the fact that the army was really accomplishing something. It was also done for the effect that it would produce upon the irate and unaccommodating Governor.

The Spaniards suffered greatly from the heat, for the sun beat upon their iron breastplates and quilted cotton doublets with most uncomfortable fury. In spite of this, they kept on, and, as they advanced, the natives fled before them.

They spent the rainy season upon an island; but, when the weather grew clear again, being reënforced by a hundred volunteers from Panama and more horses, they again crossed to the mainland and resumed their former operations.

They advanced to the town of Tumbez, expecting to find a rich and populous city; but, greatly to their surprise, they saw that this Peruvian stronghold had been burned and abandoned, owing to a recent disagreement between the inhabitants and the followers of the Inca. This ruler, Atahuallpa Capac, had fallen out with his brother, Huascar, and had advanced into his country in order to humiliate him and to become master of all Peru. Pizarro immediately made up his mind to march and capture the Inca Atahuallpa, himself, and to seize all of Peru for the Crown of Spain.

Some years before, the country had been conquered by a native soldier and statesman, named Huayna Capac, who left three sons: Huascar, the heir, and son of the Queen; Manco Capac, a half-brother; and Atahuallpa, a son of the Princess Quito. At the death of Huayna Capac, the kingdom was divided into two parts; Huascar succeeding to the empire of Peru, Atahuallpa to the empire of Quito. The latter was of a warlike disposition; the former was gentle and retiring. They thus did not long remain at peace with one another, for, Atahuallpa coveted the land of his brother, advanced to take it, and, after a great battle, in which he was victorious, overran, with his adherents, all the territory of his rival. This had all happened only a short time before Pizarro had landed, and the ruins of Tumbez bore full witness to the ruthlessness of the Inca's wrath.

The conqueror, it was said, was but twelve days' journey inland, so the Castilians struck boldly into the country, where they were everywhere received with hospitality by the natives. The invaders were now careful to give no offense, for they were very few and were surrounded by many thousands, who could quickly annihilate them, should they so wish.

An Indian gave Pizarro a scroll, as they advanced, upon which had been written: "Know, whoever you may be, that may chance to set foot in this country, that it contains more silver and gold than there is iron in Biscay." This was shown to the soldiers, but they laughed good-humoredly at it, believing that it was only a device of their leader to give them confidence and hope.

Pizarro halted his men, after five days of marching, and told them that the expedition was to be a hazardous one and that those who wished to retire could do so. Nine of the soldiers availed themselves of this opportunity to turn away from what lay in front, and, thus rid of what would undoubtedly be a dangerous element, the daring explorer pressed onward. He reached the foot of the great mountains which tower above the plains of Peru, and, sending forward a cavalier to speak with Atahuallpa, received word from this native ruler that he would be delighted to entertain the Spaniards at his camp in the mountains.

The little army now toiled up the steep slopes of the Cordilleras and came to many fortresses of stone which overhung their path, and where a mere handful of men, with little difficulty, could have barred their way. All was quiet and deserted, for luck was with this adventurer, and finally his band of treasure-seekers reached the summit of the mountains. An Indian messenger appeared from the Inca, who requested that he be informed when the Spaniards would reach Caxamalca, where they were to be entertained by the proud and imperious Atahuallpa. The messenger spoke glowingly of the might of his master; but Pizarro assured him that the King of Spain was the mightiest monarch under the sun, and that his servants would convince the Inca that they bore nothing but messages of good will from their master in far distant Castile.

The Spaniards marched onward for two days, then began to descend the eastern side of the Cordilleras, where they met a second envoy from the Inca. Seven days later the valley of Caxamalca lay before them, and, to the startled eyes of these adventurers, came the vision of several miles of white tents: those of the Inca's followers. Pizarro put on a bold front, marched towards the encampment, and, sending forward a cavalier with thirty-five horsemen to the Inca's pavilion, entered the outskirts of the town of

Caxamalca. The Peruvian nobility was in the courtyard, so, tramping onward, the Spanish adventurers passed through a long line of nobles to where Atahuallpa himself sat upon a low stool, distinguished by a crimson ribbon bound around his forehead, which he had placed there after the defeat of his brother, Huascar.

Pizarro rode up to the monarch of the Peruvian wilds, and, bowing in a lowly and respectful manner, informed him that he was the subject of the mighty Prince across the ocean, and that, attracted by the report of the warlike prowess of the Inca, he had come to offer him his services and those of his men, and to impart to him the doctrines of true faith, which they professed. He also invited Atahuallpa to visit him in his own encampment.

The Inca seemed to be dazed, and listened with his eyes fixed upon the ground. One of his nobles then said: "It is well."

"Can you not speak for yourself," asked Pizarro, turning to the Inca, "and tell me what is your desire?"

At this the proud native smiled faintly, and replied, through an interpreter:

"I am keeping a fast which will end to-morrow morning. I will then visit you. In the meantime, pray occupy the public buildings on the square and no other, until I order what shall be done."

Pizarro bowed. At that moment one of his soldiers, who was mounted upon a fiery steed, touched it with his spurs and galloped away. Whirling around, he dashed back through the crowd of natives and drew rein before the immobile Atahuallpa, who never, for an instant, lost his composure. Several of his soldiers, however, shrank back in manifest terror as this strange creature passed by, for such a wonderful animal had never been seen before in this country. The Spaniards now left, and, after they had departed, all of those who had shown fear of the galloping horse in the presence of the strangers, were put to death by order of the Inca.

That night Pizarro perfected his plan for the capture of Atahuallpa. He saw that, should he give battle to the Inca in the open field, it would doubtless end in disastrous defeat for the Spaniards, as the natives far outnumbered this handful of Castilians. His only chance for victory seemed to be to capture the Inca, to hold him prisoner, and to intimidate the vast horde of natives, by threat of death to their ruler, if they attacked the Spanish invaders. He therefore determined to entice the native to the building in which he and his men were lodged, which was built upon a square courtyard. His soldiers were to remain hidden around the central court, and, when Atahuallpa and his retainers should be in the very middle of the square, the Spaniards were to rush in upon him, and, putting the Peruvians to the sword, were to seize the unfortunate native ruler and hold him fast. This was the bold conception of this heartless adventurer, a veritable dare-devil, whose conscience was free from the lofty and proper conceptions of brotherly love.

The night was a quiet one. The Spaniards made a careful inspection of their arms and equipment, loaded all their guns, and stationed themselves at the places designated by their artful leader. At dawn they were ready, but it was late in the day before the Inca approached. He was preceded by a native courier, who informed Pizarro that his master was coming armed, even as the Spaniards had come to him.

"Tell your master," said the Castilian, "that come as he may, I will receive him as a friend and a brother."

Shortly afterwards the procession approached. First came a large number of natives, who had brooms in their hands and who swept all rubbish from the roadway. Then came a crowd of Peruvian soldiers. In their center the Inca was carried aloft upon a litter, surrounded by his nobles, who wore quantities of golden ornaments which glittered and gleamed in the sunshine. The Peruvian army followed, and, when they had all arrived within half a mile of the gate to the city, Pizarro was startled to see them halt. They seemed to be preparing to encamp, and a runner came to the courtyard, stating that the Inca had decided to delay his entrance into the city until the following morning.

"Tell your master," said Pizarro, "that I have provided a feast for his entertainment, and that my followers will be grievously disappointed if he does not come to visit us this day."

The runner went away, and Pizarro beat his foot upon the floor in anxious solicitude, for, should the Inca not come at this time, he feared that he would not be able to control his own followers, who had been under arms since daylight.

To the delight of the Spanish, a second runner now approached, who announced that the Inca would meet the white men; but would bring into the town with him only a few unarmed warriors. Pizarro breathed easier, and then inspected his followers, finding that all were in their places and eager for the attack.

The day was wearing to a close. Deep shadows from the gabled ends of the ancient buildings fell upon the courtyard, as the Peruvians, chanting their songs of triumph, entered the city gate and unsuspectingly marched onward to their destruction. Atahuallpa was in an open litter, lined with the brilliantly colored plumes of tropical birds and studded with burnished plates of gold and of silver. Around his neck hung a collar of large and brilliant emeralds. His dress was of the richest silk. At this time he was about thirty years of age and had a fine frame, a large and handsome head; but bloodshot eyes, which gave him a fierce and vindictive appearance. His bearing was calm, yet dignified, and he gazed upon the natives about him as one accustomed to command. He was surrounded by nobles, who were clad in blue uniforms studded with gold.

The procession entered the great square of the house which had been assigned to the Spaniard, but not a Castilian soldier was there. Only a priest, Father Valverde, Pizarro's Chaplain, was to be seen. He came forward, bible in hand, and, walking to the Inca's litter, began to explain to him the doctrines of the Christian religion.

"The Pope at Rome has commissioned the Emperor of Spain to conquer and to convert the inhabitants of this western world," said he to the Inca, "and I beseech you, therefore, to embrace the Christian faith and acknowledge yourself a tributary to the Emperor Charles of Spain, who will aid and protect you as a loyal vassal."

As he spoke, fire flashed from the eyes of Atahuallpa, and he answered: "I will be no man's tributary. I am far greater than any Prince on earth. Your own Emperor may be a great prince, I do not doubt it when I see that he has sent his subjects so far across the waters, and I am willing to hold him as a brother. As for the Pope of whom you speak, he must certainly be insane to give away countries which do not belong to him. As for my faith, I will not change it. Your own God, you say, was put to death by the very men whom he trusted, but mine"—here he stretched out his hand towards the setting sun—"my God still lives in the heavens and looks down upon his children. By what authority, man of Spain, do you say these things?"

The friar pointed to the well-worn bible which he held in his hand.

The Inca took it, looked at it for an instant, and then threw it violently down, exclaiming: "Tell your comrades that they shall give an account of their doings in my land. I will not go from here until they have given me full satisfaction for all the wrongs which they have committed."

This startled Valverde, and, rushing to Pizarro, he cried out:

"Do you not see that, while we stand here wasting our breath in talking with this dog—full of pride as he is—the fields behind him are filling up with his Indian allies? Set upon him at once, I absolve you."

Pizarro smiled, for he saw that the moment to strike had arrived. So he waved a white scarf, a gun was fired as a signal for the attack, and from every opening, the Spaniards poured into the great square, sword in hand, shouting their old battle-cry: "St. Iago and at them!"

A few cannons, which they had dragged up the mountain slopes with much stress and difficulty, were turned upon the startled Peruvians, and were discharged. The Indians were unarmed and were taken totally by surprise. Stunned by the noise of the artillery and blinded with smoke, they rushed hither and thither in confusion, as the Spanish free-booters pressed in upon every side. Fierce and agonizing cries went up from the courtyard, as nobles and Peruvian soldiers were ruthlessly cut down and trampled under the feet of the Spanish horsemen. So great, indeed, was the impact of these writhing Indians when they were pressed back against the wall of clay and stone, which surrounded the courtyard, that they broke through it, and, clambering over the débris, rushed headlong into the open country, hotly pursued in every direction by the Castilian cavalrymen, who cut them down with their sharp broadswords.

Meanwhile, what of the Inca, for the possession of whose body the invaders were making such a desperate effort?

Atahuallpa sat as if stunned. His litter was forced this way and that by the swaying throng, while his native attendants faithfully endeavored to defend him. As fast as one was cut down, another took his place, and, with their dying grasp, they clung to the bridles of the cavaliers in a vain endeavor to keep them away from the body of their sacred master. Fearing that the Inca might escape in the darkness, a few cavaliers now dashed in, in an attempt to end the battle by taking the life of the Peruvian chieftain; but Pizarro saw this action, and cried out: "Let no man who values his life strike at the Inca!"

As he spoke, he stretched out his arm in order to shield him, and received a wound in the hand from one of his own men. This, strange to relate, is said to be the only wound received by any Spaniard during the entire action.

The litter was now overturned, and Atahuallpa would have fallen violently to the ground, had not Pizarro and two of his soldiers caught the now humiliated chieftain in their arms. A soldier immediately snatched the crimson ribbon from his forehead. The helpless Peruvian monarch was taken to the nearest building and was carefully guarded, while his followers ceased their fruitless struggle and ran away as fast as they were able. The Castilian horsemen pursued them, until night fell, and the sound of the trumpet recalled them to the square at Caxamalca. It is recorded that many thousand of the Indians lay dead about the city, while not a single Spaniard had forfeited his life in this sharp but important engagement.

The Spaniards now had the Inca in their possession; but they were very few, in a great country, and surrounded by enemies. Atahuallpa seemed to be resigned to his unfortunate position; but he was determined to gain his freedom, if possible. He saw that gold was what his captors chiefly desired, and decided to try to buy his freedom, for he feared that Huascar might wrest the kingdom from him when he discovered that his brother was in captivity. He therefore promised Pizarro that he would fill the room in which they stood with gold, if he would but set him free.

"I will stuff with gold this chamber in which we stand," said he. "Not only will I cover the floor with it, but I will pile it up to a line drawn around the walls as high as you can reach."

Pizarro was dumb-founded, for the room was seventeen feet broad by twenty-two feet long, and the line upon the wall was nine feet high. He was still more affected when the Inca agreed to fill a smaller room, adjoining this one, with silver twice over, if he were given two months' time.

The Spaniard decided to accept, for, should Atahuallpa really do this, he could even then make way with him and still have possession of the gold.

"Go ahead," he remarked. "When you have fulfilled your contract, you shall have your freedom." Alas for the Inca! He did not know that treachery was the chief trait of all these Spanish adventurers.

The collection of the treasure went rapidly on, while Atahuallpa remained in the Spanish quarters, treated with great consideration, but strictly guarded. He even learned to play chess, and, although closely watched, was allowed to see his subjects freely. His dress was sometimes of vicuña wool, sometimes of bats' skins which were velvety sleek. He changed this often, but nothing which he had worn could be used by another, and, when he laid a robe aside, it was burned.

Huascar, meanwhile, had heard of Atahuallpa's capture and this roused in him a hope that he could regain his own kingdom, of which he had been recently despoiled. He sent word, therefore, to Pizarro, that, should the Spaniards wish it, he could pay a far greater ransom than his brother. He would expect to be reinstated to the chief command after this had been done.

News of this came to Atahuallpa, who also learned that Pizarro had said that Huascar should be brought to Caxamalca, so that he, himself, might determine which of the two brothers had a better right to the scepter of the Incas. This aroused in him a furious jealousy, and, fearing that the claims of his brother might be respected, he ordered secretly that Huascar should be put to death by his guards as he approached. He was accordingly drowned in the river Andamapa, as he neared Caxamalca.

"The white men will avenge my murder," said he, with his dying breath, "and my brother will find that he will not long survive my assassination!"

He was quite correct in this surmise, for the Spaniards grew suspicious of the Inca, and pretended to believe that he was arranging a general uprising among the Peruvians against the white men. When the treasure had nearly all been collected, they demanded that Pizarro should disburse it among them, which was done, after the golden vases and ornaments had been melted down into solid bars. What do you think? It was worth nearly three and a half million pounds sterling, or seventeen million five hundred thousand dollars ($17,500,000.00).

This distribution practically ruined the soldiers. They squandered it recklessly, or lost it over dice and cards. Very few were wise enough to return to Spain in order to enjoy their ill-gotten spoils in their native country, and one, indeed, lost a portion of one of the great golden images of the Sun, taken from the chief temple, in a single night of gaming; whence came the famous Spanish proverb: "He plays away the sun before sunrise!"

The wild and reckless Castilians, drunk with gold and sudden power, clamored for the life of the unhappy Inca, for rumors reached them that an immense army was mustering at Quito to attack them. Atahuallpa denied any knowledge of this, but his protestations of innocence did him little good. Pizarro, taking advantage of the absence of some of the cavaliers who would have defended the poor, helpless Indian, ordered him to be brought to instant trial. Several brown-skinned witnesses were produced, who gave testimony which sealed his doom; and, in spite of the fact that a few of the Spaniards staunchly stood up for him, he was found guilty of having assassinated his brother Huascar, of raising an insurrection against the invaders, and was sentenced to be burned alive.

The miserable Inca, when informed of his impending fate, lost, for a moment, his courage, which had heretofore never deserted him.

"What have I or my children done," said he to Pizarro, "that I should meet such a doom? And, from your hands, too! You who have met with nothing but friendship and kindness from my people, and who have received nothing but benefits from my hands."

In piteous wails he begged for his life.

"I promise to pay double the ransom already given you, if you will but spare me," said he.

It was all of no avail. After he had consented to give up his own religion and be baptized, he was executed, as the Spaniards were accustomed to put all their prisoners to death,—by strangulation.

Figure 10. Execution of the Inca of Peru.

Pizarro had no easy time after this. Although Almagro had arrived with reënforcements, there was serious trouble with all the Indians in the country. Freed of the power which governed them, they broke into fierce excesses, the remote provinces threw off their allegiance to the Incas, the great captains of distant armies set up for themselves, gold and silver acquired a new importance in their eyes; it was eagerly seized and hidden in caves and in forests. All Peru was in an uproar. Thus it remained for many years until, at last, the Spaniards successfully defeated all the native forces and secured the country to their own dominion. But now they began to fight among themselves for the possession of the fruitful land. Almagro lived to be seventy years of age, after a life of continual battle and adventure. Finally he was put to death by Hernando Pizarro, the brother of Francisco, who had followed him here from Spain. The murderer also dispatched his son, but he himself was imprisoned in Madrid for these acts. He lived for many years after his release, some say to be a hundred. Francisco's other brother, Gonzalo, was beheaded in Peru for rebelling against the Spanish emperor.

As for Francisco, that swine-herd who had conquered the fair land of Peru and had let no obstacle stand in the way of his chosen purpose, he, himself, came to no peaceful end. Brutal, remorseless, ambitious, greedy, it was only natural, that, when he had acquired power, he should stir up enemies even among his own people. In the lovely month of June, 1541, he was murdered in his own house at Lima by the desperate followers of the young Almagro, or the "Men of Chili," as they called themselves. Secretly and hastily he was buried by a few faithful servants in an obscure corner of the cathedral, and thus miserably ended the life of this man of adventurous spirit and desperate courage.

One cannot but admire the will-power of this Castilian, his serene calmness in time of danger, and his indifference to physical suffering. But his ruthlessness and cruelty to the Inca, his vindictive lust for riches, his lack of feeling for the inoffensive natives, can give him no such position in the Hall of Fame as is held by a Lincoln, a Gordon, or a George Washington.

Peace to your restless and ambitious soul, Francisco Pizarro!

Chapter 10

HERNANDO DE SOTO

DISCOVERER OF THE MISSISSIPPI RIVER, (1496-1542)

"Through the muddied lagoon we clambered, through the mire, the slime, and the muck;
O'er hills and valleys we hastened, through the creeks where our cannon stuck.
We were stung by the fierce mosquitoes, and were mocked by the chattering jay;
But we hewed and hacked a passage through the grass where the moccasin lay.
Fever, and heat, and ague were friends of our ceaseless toil,
And many a brave Castilian was interred 'neath the friendless soil.
We searched for the El Dorado, yet no gilded man found we,
Instead, a bed for our numberless dead, near the sob of the sun-gilded sea."

Song of de Soto's Men —1541.

In the old Spanish town of Seville, at the time when Pizarro and his numerous brothers were conquering the gentle Peruvians, the streets were often filled with the adventurers who had returned from Mexico, Panama, and South America, laden with the treasures of plundered cities. Among these successful cavaliers, no one had a more gallant bearing, or a more captivating presence, than Hernando de Soto, who had been with the Castilian troops in their battles upon the lofty Peruvian plains.

When the rapacious Spaniards had divided the ransom of the helpless Atahuallpa, which amounted to such a fabulous sum, the ambitious de Soto's share, it is said, was fully a million dollars of our own money. You see, therefore, that, when he returned to Spain, he could set up a princely establishment and was one of the most important citizens of the country. But, dissatisfied with the humdrum life of the civilized community in which he had hoped to end his days, he longed to go once more to this New World and discover other cities and other mines of treasure. He therefore asked the King to allow him to undertake an expedition at his own expense, for he was so rich in worldly goods that he had no need of financial assistance from the throne, which all the other discoverers and explorers has been seriously in need of. None, in fact, could have succeeded in their hazardous enterprises without the aid of the Castilian gold.

Romance is a vast assistance to exploration. Men look towards the unknown, wonder what is there, and, in order to verify their conjectures, go and explore. They bring back many stories. This element was of great aid to the daring Cavalier, for a fanciful legend was then current in Spain to the effect, that, in that far-distant America, was a country so rich in gold, that its King was completely gilded. He was known as El Dorado, the gilded man, and it became generally believed that this Kingdom of the Gilded Man lay somewhere in that vast, unexplored region, then called Florida.

The King of Spain appointed de Soto Governor of this fabled country, and decreed that he should have the power to subdue and to rule it. When it became known that the famous cavalier was about to start for the New World, recruits flocked to his standard, and both high and low-born vied with each other to gain a place in his company of explorers. Men of noble birth even sold their estates in order to properly equip themselves for this expedition, as they expected to duplicate the experiences of the cavaliers in

Peru and in Mexico. Many a tradesman, also, parted with his little shop in order to purchase armor, guns, and supplies for the great undertaking. The conquest of Florida was the talk of the hour and was upon every lip. It was a popular enterprise.

One beautifully clear morning in spring a fleet of white-winged galleons swept from the harbor of Seville. Crowds lined the quays, and, although a faint cheer or two was heard, there were many gloomy faces, for there was a multitude of disappointed aspirants who could not find a vacant place upon the overcrowded ships. Bugles blared a parting salute, the yellow flag of Spain was dipped into the blue Atlantic, and with cries of "Adios! We will find El Dorado!" the cheering followers of this swashbuckling hero of that day, gazed eagerly towards the now well-known passage to the Spanish Main. It was more like a monster picnic party than a serious expedition. The Spaniards landed at Cuba, where they delayed for nearly a year, and passed their time in a round of balls, tilting-matches and bullfights. After having enjoyed themselves to the full, they again embarked and headed for Florida, landing upon the beach at Tampa, where the American troops who were to wrest Cuba from the Spanish rule, set out for the harbor of Santiago, in the summer of 1898. All were cheerful and happy, eagerly looking forward to the not far distant time when they would find rich and populous cities to be sacked and looted in the same manner that they had despoiled the Peruvian and Mexican strongholds.

Fearing no enemy, about three hundred of them went ashore and encamped near the beach. They christened the bay, The Bay of the Holy Spirit; and yet they were to find no Holy Spirit nestling behind the solemn palm trees which grew almost down to the sand, for, as they lay in fanciful security, suddenly the thicket rang with the wild war-whoops of the native Floridians, and a horde of dusky forms rushed in among them, shooting arrows and striking with sharp, stone tomahawks.

All was now a scene of terror and confusion. A few of the Spaniards ran to the water's edge, shrilly blowing upon their trumpets in order to attract those left upon the ships. Others cried loudly for help, and, piling into the longboats, their comrades hastened to their assistance, leaped upon the sand, and, with a fierce battle-cry, drove the Indians pell-mell into the sheltering palms. Thereafter the Castilians were most careful to establish a picket-post around their encampments, for they had suffered severely in this first encounter.

The boats were now unloaded, many of the larger vessels were sent back to Cuba, while the smaller craft, or caravels, were kept for the service of the army. A number of men were left on guard at Tampa, while the remainder set off into the forest, heading towards the northeast. They had not gone far before they came upon a white man, who was none other than a lonely survivor of a previous expedition, led by a Spaniard called Narváez. His name was Juan Ortiz. He had been with the Indians for a long time, as he had been very young when captured by the natives. They had spared his life because of the intercession of a chief's daughter. Since this lucky proceeding, which was quite similar to that of Pocahontas and John Rolfe, he had lived with a neighboring tribe. The Spaniards were delighted to secure his services as a guide and interpreter. When the followers of Pizarro had reached Peru they had immediately found gold among the natives. You know that this is what they were after and what they seized upon with greedy fingers. Not so in palm-studded Florida. For, as the mail-clad invaders pushed into this barren and sandy country, they found no gold and no splendid cities with temples filled with jeweled images. After marching for hours through interminable pine forests and floundering through dense swamps, where the natives shot at them with poisoned arrows from behind trees, and harassed and slew them as they splashed through the mire and deep water, they found nothing but deserted villages and a few aged Indians who were too decrepit to make their escape.

This naturally angered the adventurers. Those who had sold their property in order to join in this hazardous expedition, began to be sorry that they had ever left the peaceful soil of old Castile. Those who had sacrificed good positions to take a chance in the search of this El Dorado, began to bewail their coming, and to bemoan the fact that they had listened to the sweet strains of romance which had been woven over these expeditions into the unknown.

The fabled El Dorado could be no gilded chieftain, he was a gilded fool. Alas that they ever left the gray cobbled streets of ancient Seville!

Yet on, on, they toiled wearily, ever hoping to find the gold which never came to view. They finally approached a native village which was filled with warriors of mettle, for they were furiously attacked. A shower of arrows fell among them, but, little heeding these missiles, the Spaniards discharged their guns, and, rushing upon the patriotic Indians, easily routed them. Many of the poor redskins took refuge in a pond and swam out so that they could not be reached. The Spaniards immediately surrounded the water and awaited developments. A historian of the period says:

"Nine hundred Indians took to the pond, and, all day long, continued to swim around shouting defiance and mounting on each other's shoulders in order to shoot their arrows. Night came, and not one had surrendered; midnight, and still not one. At ten o'clock the next day, after twenty-four hours in the water, some two hundred came out, all stiff and cold. Others followed. The last seven would not give up, but were dragged out unconscious by the Spaniards, who swam in after them, when they had been thirty hours in the water, without touching bottom. Then the humane invaders exerted themselves to warm and restore to life these unfortunate people."

In spite of this kind treatment, the men from Castile put irons on many of these natives, and took them along with them, so that they would have slaves to transport their baggage, pound their corn, and serve them when in camp. A soldier, who has written of this journey, says that, upon one occasion, the enslaved prisoners rose against their masters and tried to massacre them, but the Spaniards crushed this attempt, brought the helpless Indians to the village square, and caused them to be hacked to pieces by their halberdiers, or swordsmen. You can readily see that these invaders were making no happy impression upon simple-minded Americans.

The Spaniards were now in the country of Apalachee, which was then, as it is to-day, a land of agriculture, with well-tilled fields of corn, of pumpkins and beans, and with a farm-loving population of red men. The Castilians seized all the provisions which they needed for their journey, and, when the Indians objected, slew them mercilessly, but not without the loss of many of their own people.

Figure 11. de Soto in the Florida Wilderness.

Although the majority of the party were much dissatisfied with the fact that they had not discovered gold, de Soto seemed to be satisfied with the outlook. A few men were sent to the south in order to find the ocean, and came back with the report that they had run upon a magnificent harbor: the Bay of Pensacola. They had also seen the skulls of horses on the beach, these being the remains of those killed by the Spanish explorer, Narváez, who had fed the flesh to his men while engaged in building boats for their departure from this country. De Soto ordered a vessel to set sail for Cuba, stating that he had met with great success, was much pleased with the outlook, and wished more men and horses.

This was all very well for the provisional Governor, but still no gold had been found, and the soldiers were discouraged and disgusted with this lack of success. Eagerly they listened to the tales of two Indian boys who undertook to guide them to a region where they would find gold in abundance; the land of the Cofachiqui. It was towards the northeast, said the lads, so the Spaniards set out in that direction, expecting to find a city similar to Tumbez in Peru, and also El Dorado, the golden man, sitting upon a throne of solid golden ingots. Accordingly, they set out to cross the territory which is now the State of Georgia. It was a pleasant, fruitful land, inhabited by a peaceable and kindly people, who entertained them hospitably in their villages, and furnished them generously with food. The Spaniards had no need of resorting to their usual cruel methods, and the chiefs gave them guides and porters so that they could more easily pass on.

But see how crafty and keen these old Indians were!

A certain chieftain offered to furnish the travelers with guides and with porters. The Castilians eagerly accepted the offer, but so many armed warriors assembled in order to go with them, that the Spaniards suspected them of meditating treachery, and thus watched them very closely. The Indians seemed to travel along peacefully enough; but, when the village of Cofachiqui was reached, and the Spanish soldiers had gone to sleep, their redskinned guides and porters fell upon the unsuspecting natives, who lived there, and massacred all upon whom they could lay their hands. This, indeed, had been a war-party in disguise, which had taken a clever method of invading the territory of a tribe which was hostile to them, and which heretofore they had been afraid to attack. The affair took place at a distance of between thirty or forty miles below the present city of Augusta, Georgia.

Still the travelers kept on and on. Ever were their thoughts upon gold, and yet no gold seemed to appear, nor did the natives seem to possess any of the precious metal. After they had crossed a broad river, they found a well-to-do race of natives in a well-tilled country, governed by a young woman who received them with great kindness and gave them corn, pork, and sweet potatoes. She also presented them with pearls, of which she had a great quantity, as they were found in the shell-fish in the streams. De Soto saw little value in these stones, and, although he was invited to carry away all that he could, he refused to take more than fifty pounds, as a sample to show to the Cubans when he should return. He was also presented with a herd of hogs, which he drove off before him towards the west.

The climate was not unhealthy, and so the Castilians had an easy time of it. They wandered through upper Georgia, across the mountains into lower Tennessee, and then into the present State of Alabama. As vessels from Cuba were expected to meet them with re-enforcements and supplies, they now headed for Pensacola Bay.

At a place called Choctaw Bluff, not far from the present city of Mobile, they came to an Indian town presided over by a fierce chieftain by the name of Tuscaloosa, which means Black Warrior. This village had the sweet-sounding name of Mauvila. It was surrounded by a high palisade, which was chinked and plastered with mud, and, besides this, there were slits in the sides of the walls, so that those who defended it could shoot through at an attacking party.

De Soto rode ahead of the main body of Castilians with about a hundred horsemen. They were clad in doublets and trousers, with steel caps, breast plates and greaves upon their legs. As it was warm, most of this armor was slung to their saddles with cords, while the cavaliers trotted along joyously, chanting many an old Spanish song, and laughing and jesting with one another, for they were having a pleasant journey, even though no gold had been discovered. Reaching the sleepy little village of these southern Indians, they were met by the chief, Tuscaloosa, who appeared to be most friendly and asked them to enter and have a feast. Fearing nothing, and remembering the pleasant reception which they had received while marching through Georgia, they trotted gayly forward, while de Soto chatted with the chief by means of a native interpreter.

They rode to a position near the palisade, and then, dismounting, went inside in order to greet the inhabitants. Here was a large Indian town and hundreds of women, who greeted them in a friendly manner and waved their hands. Almost immediately a blow was struck. The Spaniards say that they were enticed into the palisade on purpose, and in order that they might be slaughtered by thousands of warriors who were hidden behind the wigwams, and had been summoned thither from the surrounding country. This is hardly probable, for, had the Indians contemplated a battle, they would certainly have first removed their children. No doubt a hot-headed Castilian started all the trouble. At any rate the soldiers from Seville were soon engaged in a fierce hand-to-hand encounter with a vast concourse of howling savages.

There was a fearful battle. The cavaliers had fortunately donned their armor, after dismounting from their horses, and it was well, for a shower of sharp-pointed arrows fell amongst them. A horde of Indians swarmed from their houses and swept the invaders before them, driving them in a struggling mass through the narrow entrance to the palisade. The Castilians ran to their horses and hastily mounted, but some were so hard-pressed by the natives that they were unable to get into their saddles, while their patient steeds, struck with a shower of arrows, broke away and ran frantically into the woods. In spite of the confusion and uproar, the Spaniards kept cool, and, although driven to a distance, formed a battle line and came back, pressing the native bowmen before them. With fixed lances they charged into the yelping mob, only to be met with splendid courage by the native soldiers.

De Soto bore himself right valiantly and led his men, using his long, sharp lance with deadly effect. His soldiers, too, were not laggards in the attack, and followed him closely, shouting the Spanish battle cry: "St. Iago and at them!" Many were sorely wounded. De Soto himself, as he leaned forward to make a lance thrust, received an arrow in the exposed portion of his thigh. This made it impossible for him to sit down, so, throughout the remainder of the day, he rode, standing in his stirrups.

Several of the more prominent Castilians were shot dead. The Spanish leader's brother, Diego de Soto, was pierced through the eye by an arrow, which came out at the back of his neck. A young cavalier, called Carlo Enriquez, who had married the Governor of Florida's niece, leaned over the neck of his horse in order to pull out an arrow from the animal's breast, and thus exposed his throat, which was instantly pierced by an Indian barb, so that he fell prostrate. Thus the battle raged furiously, while shrill trumpets blared out the distress of the Spaniards and summoned their easy-riding comrades to come speedily to their assistance.

The greater portion of de Soto's troop were jogging peacefully along in the sunshine, little realizing into what a desperate strait their advance guard had fallen. Late in the afternoon they approached the Indian village and were much surprised to see dense volumes of smoke rising to the sky. Those in advance sent back word to hurry on, while they galloped forward in order to see what was amiss. All hurried towards the sound of battle, and, now, realizing that their comrades were in a desperate fight, they rushed to their assistance, cheering wildly as they did so. The black smoke was pouring from the thatched Indian houses, which the Spaniards had set on fire, and a bloody hand-to-hand engagement was in progress around the smoking débris. The main body of cavaliers had now arrived. They charged vigorously, cutting down both women and men, and, amidst the shrieks of the women and wailing of little children, Tuscaloosa's people were annihilated. At last all had been dispersed or butchered.

The Spanish histories of this bloody affair say that at last only a solitary warrior was left. Seeing that all his friends and companions had either perished or fled, he sprang upon the palisade, and, finding that he was surrounded on all sides by vindictive steel-clad Spaniards with menacing swords, he twisted off his bow-string, and, making a slip-noose, hanged himself to the stout limb of a tree.

The battle of Mauvila had left de Soto in a sorry state, for eighty-two of his followers had been killed, and so many of the men had been wounded that the surgeon could not give them proper attention. In fact, so broken up were the cavaliers, and particularly the horses, which had suffered badly from the numerous arrows which had been fired into them, that de Soto was forced to tarry in the vicinity of the ruined Indian village for three weeks. The Spanish accounts of the battle say that eleven thousand natives fell before the swords, lances, and clumsy muskets of the Castilian invaders of this peaceful country.

De Soto was only a few days' journey from Pensacola, where the ship, which he had sent to Cuba for supplies, was to reach him. Yet, instead of heading for the ocean, he decided to march towards the north, evidently hoping to find some city where was gold and silver, similar to that which he had seen in the table-lands of Peru.

The El Dorado seekers accordingly marched northwest, and passed through a flat country where was much game. The Indians were treacherous and constantly annoyed them by attempting to steal their horses, and by attacking any parties which traveled at a distance from the main column. It was now December. As the weather grew chill, de Soto determined to spend the winter in some convenient spot, and, as he now came upon a well-built Indian town, which had recently been deserted, he reached the conclusion that this was the very place for which he had been in search. Accordingly, his cavaliers made themselves comfortable in the thatched huts of the Chickasaws, for such was the name of the redskins who had settled here.

Trouble was still in store for the adventurous gold-seekers.

After their many battles and long journeys, the men enjoyed themselves in hunting and in taking life easy. There was an abundance of corn stored here, so their horses grew sleek and fat, while their masters chased rabbits and other small game. All was peaceful. Apparently not an Indian was in the vicinity, so the guards relaxed their vigilance, grew somewhat careless, and unsuspectingly offered a tempting opening to any redskins who might wish to attack them.

One night the Chickasaws made good use of their opportunity to get even with the invaders of what they considered to be their sacred soil. It was towards the end of January and a fierce north wind was blowing. While the men were sleeping in their huts, suddenly a wild war-whoop welled upon the night air, and, as the wind howled dismally, the roofs over their heads burst into a crackling blaze. Fanned by the high breeze, the flames leaped into the air, and, in a moment the whole camp was red with fire. The Spaniards sprang to arms and rushed forth to the fray, some in their shirts, and many without their armor on.

What had happened?

Under cover of the darkness, and unheard, because of the blustering wind, the vindictive Chickasaws had approached their abandoned town and had furiously attacked it. They had poured in a volley of arrows with burning wisps attached to them, which quickly ignited the thatched roofs and sent a reddening glare over the scene of confusion. De Soto leaped upon his horse, but did so hurriedly and without tightening the girth. It turned with him and he pitched to the ground, falling upon his chest. Immediately the howling savages surrounded him and attempted to put an end to his life, but his men rushed to his assistance, beat off the shrieking Chickasaws, and dragged him by the feet to a position of safety. Leaping again to the saddle, with a mighty cheer, he led his men into the fray with such impetuosity, that the Indians disappeared into the blackness. Forty of the Spaniards had been killed, fifty of their precious horses had been prostrated by barbed arrows and flaming brands, while the larger part of their clothing, arms, their saddles and their provisions, had been consumed. They were also houseless, and the wind was bitterly chill. Fortunately, the Chickasaws did not again attack.

But the hostile savages did not leave them alone. When spring came and the horsemen resumed their march, they were repeatedly harassed by the red men, who crept near them on every side, and cut down any unsuspecting Spaniard who wandered from the column.

Pursuing a northwesterly course, the cavaliers at length came upon a great force of the natives, who, stripped to their waists and painted with various colors, yelled their defiance and brandished their spears and arrows at the invaders. Nearby was their stronghold, a palisade surrounding their huts, which had three entrances. The Spaniards advanced in three columns to attack these openings.

What could these half-clad redskins do against men in steel armor, and with sword, buckler, and arquebusier? The Castilians drove them into their fortification like sheep, and there massacred them as they had the fierce warriors under Tuscaloosa. According to old accounts, two thousand of the Indians were slain, although the native warriors inflicted quite a loss upon their attackers. The invaders secured provisions, corn, and female slaves, which they transported with them in their journey towards the northwest.

The Spaniards took their battles lightly, for they considered it all a part of the day's work. They resumed their march, but now they must have been pretty sure that no El Dorado could exist in this flat and somewhat marshy country. Still, they were cheerful, and when, a few weeks later, they came upon a great muddy river which was so wide that they could not see a man upon the other bank, they felt that certainly their trip, their many discomforts, and their losses, had not been in vain. When they viewed the turbid current of the Mississippi they were filled with silent awe, and a priest, holding the cross of Christ high in the air, blessed the surging flood, while de Soto cried out: "I take you in behalf of the King of Spain, and shall call you mine own from henceforth!"

This gallant cavalier was a man of resource. He set his soldiers immediately to work constructing boats, and, gradually moving up the river in order to find a place where it would be possible to cross—for the little army was upon high bluffs (now called the Chickasaw Bluffs)—he transported all in safety to the other side and into the land of Arkansas, the seventh State of the present Union, upon whose soil these restless explorers had set their feet.

They wandered towards the setting sun. Here were vast plains filled with herds of buffalo and roving bands of hostile redskins, from whom they learned that other white men had preceded them, although rumors of the adventurous Coronado's march had traveled eastward by word of mouth among the native inhabitants of the plains. This Spaniard had traveled thither from Mexico, and, could the two parties have met each other, there would have been great rejoicing. But there was to be no such good fortune, and de Soto's men found only simple, but treacherous natives. The Spaniards lost some of their horses. The escape of these was fortunate for future generations of pioneers, as many an emigrant in later years was able to cross the plains by capturing and taming one of the descendants of these fugitives from the bit and the saddle.

The adventurers wandered about for many months, wintered in a well-provisioned village near the Red River, within the present State of Louisiana, then, to the great joy of the now well-seasoned veterans, de Soto told them that he was about to return to the great, turbid Mississippi. He informed the wanderers that he intended to build boats, send them down the stream and across the Gulf of Mexico, to Cuba, and to transport thither many other men and a plentiful supply of provisions, so as to establish a colony in his Kingdom of Florida.

The conception was a grand one. Yet the imaginative and jealous Castilian had not reckoned with one powerful enemy, that cruel and unrelenting persecutor called Death.

The active brain of this gallant explorer was busy with perfecting his plans for the founding of a settlement in the wilderness. He carefully selected the officers and crews who were to take charge of the vessels which he proposed to build. He chose those who were to remain with him upon the banks of the rolling Mississippi. Some were set to work cutting timbers; others collected gum from pine trees; while still others put up forges and made nails from bits of iron which they had carried with them. All were busy and active in preparation both for the stay of those who were to colonize this country, and the departure of those who were to leave. Yet the fever was in the veins of our venturesome Castilian and his customary vigor was slackened. De Soto grew so weakened that he had to be carried to his tent and was delirious.

While upon the Red River, one of the malaria-breeding mosquitoes had driven his tiny sting into the flesh of the brave adventurer. He had sickened from the poison, yet refused to give up to the disease, until the fever was raging in his veins. He now sank rapidly. Yellow fever had doubtless assailed him, and his system, already weakened by much exposure and by shock of battle, could not throw off the inroads of the dread disease. He sank day by day. When he knew that the end was approaching, he called his officers together, asked their forgiveness for any wrong which he might have done them, and named Moscoso de Alvarado to succeed him to the command of the expedition. Officers and bluff soldiers all swore allegiance to their new leader. The dying explorer begged his followers to carry out his ideas in the settlement of the vast country of Florida, and this they promised him that they would do.

One warm, sultry morning, when the mocking bird was trilling a beautiful melody from an overhanging sycamore, which jutted over the bank of the slow-moving, yet turbulent Mississippi, the spirit of the bold adventurer departed. His hardened and sunburned companions were dewy-eyed when they gazed upon the still countenance of their friend and kindly adviser. They wrapped him in a sheet, rowed him to the center of the swirling stream, dropped him overboard, and left him amidst the silence of the great, wild country where the "golden man" had never been found.

So perished de Soto, a cavalier of Spain in a day when Spain had great warriors and noble- minded, yet adventuresome men. As a horseman he had few superiors; as a soldier he could bear as many privations as any man. Towards his own cavaliers he was merciful and just; towards the hostile natives of silent Florida he was merciless and cruel. He was a man of learning, of imagination, of iron will, as is exhibited by the fact that he held his gold-worshiping supporters to their journey long after many had sickened of the affair and had wished to go home. At one time worth a million dollars, the companion of Kings and of Princes, he died in the wilderness of the New World. His followers drifted back to Mexico, broken in both health and in spirit, so his ambitious dream for a colony in the land of the fanciful El Dorado was never consummated.

Chapter 11

SAMUEL DE CHAMPLAIN

EXPLORER OF THE CANADIAN WILDERNESS, (1567-1635)

>Where the hemlock bends her tufted head;
>Where the beaver breeds in the pool;
>Where the moose-bird chatters his mimic song;
>And the willowy grilses school;
>'Neath the feathery arch of the drowsy larch,
>The birch bark floated and swayed,
>As the rhythmic paddles dipped and swung,
>And splashed with the slap of the spade.
>On the rocking waves of the foaming lake,
>The Frenchman turned and gazed,
>For he saw a land which was new, which was grand,
>And his spirit shrank amazed.
>So he planted the flag of King-cursed France,
>As he waved his sword above,
>And the waters were called the Lake de Champlain,
>
>—'Twas the lake which the redskins love.

Upon the north side of the river St. Lawrence, in Canada, and five hours' journey by steamer from the quaint old city of Quebec, nestles the little village of Murray Bay. It is a picturesque, peaceful collection of houses, where many of those who have wealth and leisure journey in summer to enjoy the champagne-like air and the rugged scenery. Now a great, modern hotel rises majestically from the hemlock-covered riverbank; but if some of the fashionable guests who frequent it had stood there one brilliant day, many years ago, they would have seen two pigmy vessels holding their course up the lovely St. Lawrence. On board was a pair of venturesome Frenchmen: the Seigneur de Chastes and Samuel de Champlain, the latter a youthful and energetic explorer, who looked forward to adventures in the land of the treacherous redman, the broad-antlered moose, and the moon-eyed caribou.

This brave son of France had been born in the year 1567 in the little town of Brouage, some twenty miles south of the seaport of La Rochelle. Little is known of his family or of his early life. His father, doubtless the son of a fisherman, was a Captain in the navy, and one of his uncles was a sea-pilot of some renown.

In youth Champlain became an excellent seaman, but, as his country was soon embroiled in civil and religious wars, his energies were engaged in martial exploits upon the land, and not upon the foaming Atlantic. Joining Henry of Navarre, he fought for the King with zeal and enthusiasm, although he, himself, was a Catholic, and his sovereign championed the Huguenot or Protestant cause. Champlain, in fact, loved country more than religion, and struggled to save her from dismemberment. His purse was small, his want great, and thus Henry the Fourth, from his own slender revenues, gave him a position as Captain.

The war was finally over, and the youthful Champlain conceived a design which was quite in harmony with his adventurous nature. He would, indeed, visit the West Indies and bring back a report of those wondrous regions where was much peril, and where every intruding Frenchman was threatened with death. Here was adventure enough for any young fellow who had the stomach for a fight.

No sooner conceived than executed! The hot-blooded Frenchman was quickly on board a vessel bound for Vera Cruz. He stopped at the West Indies, made plans and sketches of them all, then landed upon the Mexican

Coast. He penetrated inland and was struck with amazement at what he saw in the beautiful City of Mexico, where Cortés had battled, bled and conquered. He visited Panama, and,—what think you!—even at this early date conceived the plan of shipping freight across the Isthmus, where to-day the United States has dug a great canal to expedite the commerce of the world.

"I believe that a ship-canal, if constructed, would shorten the voyage to the South Sea by more than fifteen hundred miles," he has written.

Oh, valorous Frenchman, had you but lived to see your wayward dream come to be a living reality!

The adventurer now returned to the French Court, that Versailles of which has been truthfully said: "It cost one billion of francs and it took one billion drops of the peasants' blood to build it!" Where, also, is the portrait of the famous soldier whose epitaph reads: "He was invincible in peace, invisible in war." Here was the center of frivolity and fashion, exactly what would weary the blood of such a backwoods soul as Champlain. He soon tired of it and longed to plunge again into the wilderness of the unknown West, for there, forsooth, would be danger and hardship enough for any man.

Good fortune was to be with him. At court was a gray-haired veteran of the civil wars, who wished to mark his closing days with some notable achievement for France and for the church. This was Aymar de Chastes, commander of the order of St. John, and Governor of Dieppe. He longed to sail for Canada, or New France—would Champlain go with him? Well, I should think so! They embraced, shook hands upon it,—they would seek adventure and hardship together.

So this is how they happened to be sailing past the hemlock-clad hills of Murray Bay, upon that bright, clear morning, and I'll warrant that, if you ever play golf upon the course far above the town, as many of you doubtless have often done, and you will look out upon the great, turbid and raging river, where perhaps you can see the bobbing back of a white porpoise, you will think different thoughts than those which are connected with a sliced drive or a miserable putt.

Like veritable gnats upon the surface of the tide-swept stream, the vessels kept upon their way, passing the trading-post of Tadoussac (once a flourishing settlement, but now abandoned), the channel of Orleans, and the spuming falls of Montmorenci. They drifted by the brown rocks of Quebec, on, on, up the blue and charging river, until they came opposite that rounded mountain which lifts its head high above the present city of Montreal. All was solitude. Sixty-eight years before this Jacques Cartier, the navigator, had found a numerous savage population, but now all had vanished, and only a few wandering Algonquin redskins peered at them from the edge of the forest.

Here are the fiercest of rapids, which, if you pass through to-day, you will find to be dangerous and an exciting adventure. The vigorous Champlain endeavored to paddle up them with a few of the childlike Algonquins. His courage was greater than his ability to stem the whirling foam and tempestuous waves. Oars, paddles, poles, and pikes could not force the thin birch-bark canoes up the swift-moving St. Lawrence, and he was forced to return, acknowledging himself beaten. When he mounted the deck of his vessel, the redmen made rude sketches upon the planking of what he would find above, and spoke of a mighty water-fall (Niagara Falls) where the river plunged downward in a mass of tempestuous spray. Champlain listened with pleasure to these stories of what lay beyond, but he had to return, as De Chastes so willed it. After an uneventful voyage the adventurers reached the shores of France.

The gray-haired De Chastes, worn out by the rigors of the voyage, now passed to the great beyond, leaving his title to the great land of New France to Sieur de Monts, who immediately petitioned the King to allow him to colonize Acadie, a region defined as extending from Philadelphia to Montreal. Truly these early adventurers had magnificent ideas of distance, quite in keeping with their ambitious designs of conquest! The King readily gave him what he desired, so, with one vessel, he sailed from Havre de Grace upon the seventh day of April, 1604.

But how about the adventure-loving Champlain? He remained at home not only for that year, but for five full years, while de Monts and his men were having plenty of hard knocks and experience in the bleak land of New France.

The good seaman, in fact, quietly resided in Paris, but his unquiet thoughts were ever turning westward. He was enamored with the strange, hemlock-wooded country whose rugged hills and blue rivers were mirrored upon his memory and continually urged him to "come back and explore!" Even as Commander Peary has said that he pined for Arctic ice and snow, so, with restless longing, the noble-hearted Frenchman ever sighed for days upon the broad surface of the St. Lawrence, with starlit nights filled with the balsamy odors of the forests. Upon the banks near the mountain of Montreal he had determined to lay out a settlement, from which, as a base, the waters might be traced back far into the vast interior of the continent. With eager and tempestuous thoughts, he yearned to be once more scudding by the two peaks, which held high their heads as the Saguenay discharged its swift-moving current into the rushing St. Lawrence, far, far beneath them.

The danger-loving de Monts returned after four years of adventure. To him Champlain expressed his views, which met with a ready response. Yes, indeed, they would go forth together, would trade with the Indians, bring back a cargo of furs, and would found a town by those whirling rapids, neath the mountain of Montreal.

On April the 16th. 1604, they sailed in a ship of 150 tons from Havre de Grace, with a mixed company of priests, Huguenot ministers, impressed rogues, and honest settlers. Another vessel, under one Pontgrave, had preceded them by eight days, for she was laden with goods for the Indian trade at Tadoussac.

By the third of June the adventurous Champlain neared the mouth of the Saguenay. The robust Frenchmen eagerly breathed in the clear air of the St. Lawrence, tinged with the faint smell of the spruce and the balsamy hemlock. The little vessel, swept by the tide and eddies, held its course up the stream until the Island of Orleans was reached. Then it was run towards the northern bank and was anchored beneath the high cliffs of Quebec. The men went ashore, axes rang against the tree trunks, and soon a number of wooden buildings arose on the brink of the St. Lawrence, not far from the present market-place of the Lower Town. A settlement had been founded in the wilderness, which was to exist for centuries.

It was now the eighteenth day of September. Pontgrave set sail for France, leaving Champlain with twenty-eight men to hold Quebec throughout the winter. October was soon upon them, October with its crystal air, shriveling leaves and laughing sun; but it soon passed away, and the chill of frosty winter settled upon the little colony. It was to be a cold and cheerless stay, and, as is always the case when men are in need of fresh vegetables, the scurvy broke out among the adventurers, killing many and seriously crippling the remainder. By the middle of May, only eight men out of the twenty-eight were alive, and of these half were suffering from the dreadful disease. Champlain, however, seems to have been an iron fellow, and successfully withstood the lack of that which it is necessary to eat in order to ward away the awful pestilence.

But every lane has its turning, and spring at last put in an appearance. Ice and snow melted under the genial rays of the sun, the honk! honk! of the wild geese was heard as they winged their way towards the north, and the bluebirds warbled from the budding maple trees. Great was the joy of the survivors of this awful winter when they saw a sail-boat rounding the Point of Orleans, and cheers greeted the French explorer Marias as he cast anchor in the ice-freed river. He brought good news. Pontgrave had been to France and back again. He was then at Tadoussac, waiting to speak with Champlain, and to talk of further explorations into the wilderness.

The hardy explorer hastened to confer with his friend and companion, for, in spite of the pestilence, his giant constitution had defied the scurvy. Sailing down the St. Lawrence, they soon met, and it was determined between them, that, while Pontgrave remained in charge of Quebec, Champlain should at once enter upon his long-meditated explorations, by which, he foolishly had hope of finding a way to China.

Now was to be a series of great adventures. Late that autumn a young chieftain from the banks of the Ottawa River had come to visit the half-starved colonists at Quebec, and had begged Champlain to join him, in the spring, in an expedition against his enemies. These were the Iroquois, or dwellers in fortified villages within the limit of the present State of New

York, who were a terror to all those tribes who lived north of them. They were not only warriors of fierceness and bold endeavor, but were also tillers of the soil, living at ease and affluence when compared with the Indians who fished, camped, and hunted game, near the waters of the blue St. Lawrence. About the middle of the month of May, Champlain set forth to paddle up the river, accompanied by a band of the Montagnais redskins. As he proceeded, he saw the lodges of an Indian encampment thickly clustered in the bordering forest, and, landing, found there his Huron and Algonquin allies. The red men were amazed to see a person with a white skin, and gathered about the steel-clad strangers (for he had several other Frenchmen with him) in astonished awe and admiration.

"I would speak with your chieftain," said Champlain.

The staring natives led him towards a great lodge where sat not one chief, but two, for each tribe had its own leader with them. Now there was much speech-making, feasting, and smoking of the peace pipes; then, all paddled down the river to Quebec, for the redskins were anxious to view that town, the fame of which had been borne to them in their distant habitations of the forest.

The native Canadians were much interested in the wooden houses built by the white men. They yelped in consternation at the explosions of the French guns, and the roar of the iron cannon. After they had examined everything to their satisfaction, their camps were pitched, they bedecked themselves for the war dance, and, when night fell, leaped about, howling and singing in the yellow glare of a huge bon-fire. Next morning they were ready for their expedition into the wilderness, where their enemies, the fierce Iroquois, had dragged unfortunate members of their tribe, who had fallen into their hands, to be beaten and tortured with horrible indignities. No wonder they longed to have these white men as their allies, so that they could revenge themselves upon their enemies.

It was now the twenty-eighth day of May. The air was balmy, yet cool, so the expedition started under pleasant auspices. Entering a small sloop, the Sieur De Champlain pointed her nose up stream, and, accompanied by eleven companions, and surrounded by hundreds of redskins in birch bark canoes, set sail for the mouth of the Rivière de Iroquois, which connects the swirling waters of the St. Lawrence with that beautiful lake which was to subsequently bear the name of this venturesome explorer. The members of the famous war-party crossed the Lake of St. Peter, threaded the crooked channels among its many islands, and at length started down the winding stream towards the dreamy, gray expanse of the tempestuous lake,—afterwards to be known as Lake Champlain,—and the country of the Iroquois.

As the canoes advanced, many of the warriors went ashore, and, spreading out, hunted for game in the leafy forests. A provision of parched corn had been brought along; but this was only to be used, when, owing to the nearness of the enemy, no game could be secured. The river widened as they went on, and they passed great islands, many miles in extent, and finally debouched into the rocking waters of the glittering lake, which was ever afterwards to bear the name of this adventurous Frenchman. He, himself, was amazed, startled, pleased with this, his first view of the great body of water. To the left the forest ridges of the Green Mountains raised themselves against the blue horizon; while to the right, the Adirondacks stretched, themselves above the swaying spruces and hemlocks, jutting above the woodland fringe in height quite equal to their sister hills across the wave-tossed water.

But now they were in the country of the ferocious Iroquois. They must use caution in their advance, for they might be attacked at any moment. They changed their mode of travel, lay all day hidden in the depth of the forest, sleeping, lounging, smoking tobacco, while at twilight they again entered the canoes and paddled down the side of the lake until the flush of dawn began to redden the eastern skyline. At the very end of the water was a rocky promontory where Fort Ticonderoga was afterwards built, and this was their objective, their intention being to carry across into a small lake lying to the south (Lake George) and thence to paddle southward in search of hunting parties of the Iroquois, or of the more southern, but equally ferocious Mohawks. They even intended to carry their canoes to the upper reaches of the Hudson River, should no enemies be met with, and thus penetrate into the very heart of the Mohawk country. They were to be spared this lengthy journey.

At ten o'clock in the evening of the twenty-ninth day of July the flotilla approached the end of the wave-tossed lake, and, as the shadows descended, an advance scout saw dark objects in motion upon the water before them. They drew nearer, and, as paddles flashed to the straining arms of the braves, suddenly a wild, unnerving war-whoop sounded above the splashing of the water. An Iroquois war-party was before them.

The hostile warriors yelled derisively, and, turning about, paddled furiously for the shore, as they had no desire to engage in a hand-to-hand struggle upon the surface of the lake. They landed, rushed into the forest, and soon the hack! hack! of their stone hatchets and iron axes, captured in warfare, showed that they were busily preparing a fortification. The Canadian redskins remained upon the lake, with canoes lashed together by means of poles, and, floating to within bowshot of their enemies, yelled derisively at them.

Night descended. Those upon the lake danced in the bottoms of their frail canoes, yelling derisively and singing songs of defiance. Those on shore hacked away at their fortifications, yelping dismally and boasting of their prowess in battle. Champlain slept uneasily, and, as day dawned, put on his breast and back plates, his steel thigh protectors, and upon his head his plumed casque. In his hand was his gun or arquebus, loaded with four balls. An ammunition-box hung over one shoulder and a long sword was by his side. Thus he stood, respectfully gazed upon by his redskin allies, who took him for a sort of god, come from the Great Spirit in order to rescue them from their enemies and bring victory to their painted braves.

Daylight soon came. With yells of defiance the allies now approached the shore, and, without opposition from the Iroquois, landed upon the beach, where they drew up in battle array. The Iroquois defiled from their barricade, and, as Champlain looked upon them, he saw that they were all tall, strong men, about two hundred in all, the fiercest and most able fighters of North America. In the center of the line were several chiefs, who had great headdresses of eagle and heron plumes, and, as they advanced through the forest, all set up a vigorous yelping, similar to a pack of wolves in full cry. Some had shields of wood and of deerhide, others were covered with a kind of armor made of tough twigs interlaced together. Stealthily and steadily they bore down upon the northern host, while afar off, on the roughened water of the lake, a blue and white loon screamed discordantly.

Figure 12. Champlain in the Indian Battle.

The stout-hearted Sieur de Champlain stood in the rear of the Canadian redmen; but, as the Iroquois drew near, his friendly braves called loudly for him to come out in front in order to lead them on to the fray. The good knight was eager to do so. Yet, as he stood forth, with the sun gleaming upon his armor, the Iroquois remained stock still and gazed at him in mute astonishment. The Frenchman leveled his arquebus at a gaudy chieftain, and fired. At the discharge, the red man leaped high into the air, uttered a gurgling yell, and fell prostrate upon the green moss. Bang! A second redskin lurched upon his face. Then arose a wild, alarming scream from his allies, and the air was filled with whizzing arrows.

The Iroquois were no cowards and returned the barbs with some equally as good, but, as the guns of the other Frenchmen spoke, and numerous redskins fell to the earth in mortal agony, they saw that here was a death-dealing instrument which they had never met with before. This brought confusion to their ranks. They stood for a few moments, then broke and ran in uncontrolled terror, while, with wonderful leaps and bounds, the allies started in pursuit. Many of the Iroquois went to the Happy Hunting Grounds; but many others were captured; while camp, canoes, provisions and weapons were all abandoned. Terrorized and dismayed by Champlain and his arquebus, these denizens of the forest had been signally defeated. Thus the scientific knowledge of the white man triumphed over the ignorance of the Indian, and thus New France, for the first time, rushed into contact with the renowned warriors of the Five Nations.

The allies held a three hour dance in commemoration of their victory, and when it was completed, they started homeward, first torturing the prisoners, and killing the majority of them. At the Falls of Chambly on the river Richelieu, the Hurons and Algonquins went their ways, and Champlain paddled down the St. Lawrence with the friendly Montagnais at the rate of seventy-five, to ninety miles, a day. At length he reached Tadoussac, where the wives and daughters of the redskins greeted them with a feast and war dance. All rejoiced at the signal victory over the hated Iroquois and sang and yelped in commemoration of the famous battle near the rocky promontory of far distant Crown Point.

The adventurous Champlain had much enjoyed this little trip, yet, eager to report his explorations to the French King, he sailed for France, and, after a month's voyage, found himself at Fontainebleau. The King was much pleased with the news which was brought of happenings across the wide Atlantic. He also was delighted with a belt of porcupine quills, as a present from the Canadian wilds, with two skins of the scarlet tanager, and the pointed skull of a gar fish, unknown in France and much appreciated.

By spring the daring voyager was again upon the ocean, headed for Tadoussac and the hills of the Laurentian Mountains. The colony at Quebec had spent a good winter, and had not been visited with the scurvy, so he felt that France at last had her grip upon the New World.

As he went up the river he was met by his old friends, the Montagnais Indians, who were again upon the warpath. Would he join them? Why, nothing suited his fancy better! He was soon to be in a battle more ferocious than that skirmish away off upon the bank of the great Lake Champlain.

The redskins were encamped upon an island in the river, where they were to meet the Algonquins and proceed against a band of Iroquois, who had come there from the south in order to have revenge for the slaughter of the previous year. All were busy felling branches and trees for a barricade, when suddenly an Algonquin paddled up, crying,

"Arm yourselves! Get ready! The Iroquois are not far away and have thrown up a fortification. If you do not attack them, they will attack you!"

With a wild yelp of eager anticipation, the Montagnais took to their canoes, paddled up the stream, leaped to the shore, and were soon running through the woods in the direction of the camp of the hated invaders. As for Champlain, and some Frenchmen whom he had with him, they could come along as best they might. This they did, and, as they advanced through the forest, they heard loud shouts and battle cries. The fight was on in earnest.

The Sieur de Champlain, in armored breast plate and with greaves and arquebus, soon came into a clearing, where he viewed a strong, log fortification. Behind this, the Iroquois were raising an ear-splitting din. They were firing at the attacking party of Montagnais and Algonquins, who were afraid to advance. The Frenchman soon saw how to bring the matter to a successful issue.

"Here, my friends!" said he to the redskins. "You must make a breach in yonder fort. As I and my companions shower bullets at a certain point, you must rush forward, must tear down the logs with this rope, then all can enter and put an end to these invaders."

The Indians followed his advice. As the Frenchmen advanced and commenced firing, the redskins rushed forward, tied ropes to the logs, and, wrenching them away, soon made a breach in the fortress. Champlain was hit in the ear by an arrow, but he tore it away, although it had buried itself in his neck, and continued the fight. As the redmen worked willingly, a fresh band of Frenchmen approached and began to fire upon the fort from the other side. They had come from a trading pinnace, which had followed

Champlain's shallop, and, hearing the sound of gun-fire, had hurried forward in order to take part in the fray.

Crash! The logs at last gave way. With a wild, discordant war-whoop, the allies rushed forward, brandishing their knives and tomahawks, and followed by Champlain with his men. The Iroquois, frightened at the awful effect of the firearms, made but a slight resistance. Some were shot upon the spot, others ran and were killed at once, still others plunged into the St. Lawrence, where they were drowned, while fifteen were taken prisoners. Not one escaped the fury of the allied assault. It had been a second glorious victory.

Champlain had no further battles with the redmen, at this time; but, a few years later, made a journey up the Ottawa River which brought him in contact with many of them. This was then, of course, an unknown country, inhabited only by bands of Indians, who lived by fishing and by hunting. The Frenchman was the first white man to venture among the native Canadians, so you can well imagine what must have been their surprise and interest in viewing a warrior with a "stick which spoke with the voice of thunder." They marveled at his ability to travel up the river, which was rapid and treacherous, saying, "You must have fallen from the clouds as you are so far from the great river (St. Lawrence)." They gave him food, showed him their gardens, planted with Indian corn, and sent him on to other Indian villages, with an escort.

"We live here because we fear the Iroquois," said one chief. "But, if our white brothers will but settle upon the great, blue river to the south of us, so that we may be protected from these fierce warriors, we ourselves will come down there to live."

After spending some time in exploring this wild and beautiful country, the adventurer erected a great cross, decorated with the arms of the King of France.

"You must preserve this," he said to the savages, "for it belongs to my Great Father beyond the sea."

Then, turning about, he began the journey to Montreal. It was June, the woods were radiant with the flush of new foliage, deer, moose, and beaver were seen in abundance, and even the lean, sneaking timber wolves howled at the interlopers. The trip down the Ottawa was swifter than the ascent and, about the middle of June, the voyager arrived beneath the mountain of Montreal. He bought all the furs that he could from the Indians, and, after feasting with the French traders and dusky sons of the forest, embarked in one of the trading ships for France, promising to return on the following year.

He did as he had said, and, addressing the redmen, told them that it was his aim to get them to live at peace with one another and to form a league which would have as its object the extermination of the Iroquois. Champlain had great ideas for New France. He wished to have the Indians as his allies and friends. French soldiers were to fight their battles for them. French traders were to supply their wants. French priests would baptize them and lead them in the ways of the true Christian faith. It was to be an alliance of soldier, priest, and trader.

The Indians were well treated by the French explorers, who were kinder than the English and far more hospitable. Champlain was anxious to gather twenty-five hundred of them so as to attack the Iroquois. The redskins promised to collect at Montreal at a stated time, and, believing them, the great-hearted Frenchman traveled to Quebec for needed supplies. When he returned, he found, to his dismay and chagrin, a perfect solitude. The wild concourse of Algonquins, Ottawas, and Hurons had vanished, and nothing remained but the smoke of their fires, the skeleton poles of their tepees and the débris from their feasting. Impatient at the delay in waiting for him, they had set out for their villages.

Nothing daunted, but greatly chagrined, Champlain determined to journey up the Ottawa to the land of the Hurons, of whom he had heard much, but had never seen. With two canoes, ten Indians, and two Frenchmen, he therefore pushed up the stream, reached Lake Nipissing, and, hearing that a still larger lake was beyond, pressed onward to the country of the Hurons. The scenery delighted him, for here were deep woods of pine and of cedar, thickets full of brown rabbits and partridges, wild grapes, plums, cherries, crab apples, nuts, and blackberries.

The Hurons were soon met with; noble-looking, well-fed savages, who took him to their tents, feasted him on corn, pumpkins and fish, and welcomed him as the great hero who was to lead them successfully in battle against their hated enemies, the Iroquois.

At length many warriors had gathered, and, with many cries of defiance, they put boldly forth upon the broad bosom of Lake Ontario, crossed it safely, and landed near a bay called Hungry Bay, within the borders of the State of New York. The canoes were hidden in the woods, and the warriors walked single file for ten or twelve miles down the edge of the lake. Then they struck towards the south, and, threading a tortuous way through the forest, were soon deep within the country of the Iroquois: their deadly and hated enemies.

It was the month of October, the month of the harvest and the month of crisp, joyous days. The rustling leaves were just turning to gold and to crimson as the warriors crept onward upon their mission of death. On, on, they went, until they had approached a fortified town of the enemy, surrounded by plowed fields, in which were pumpkins and stalks of corn. In advance were some young Huron braves, whose zeal out-weighed their common sense. Seeing some Iroquois at work among their crops, they made a rush upon them, uttering a wild yell as they did so.

The hot-headed Huron warriors had counted without their host, for, as they raced forward, the Iroquois seized their bows and arrows, shot into their midst, and killed and wounded a half dozen of the oncomers. The rest were driven back, hotly pursued. But Champlain and his Frenchmen stopped their onrush at the border of the wood, sending them yelping to their stockade, bearing their dead and wounded with them.

The battle was a three hour affair. Truly the Iroquois were noble fighters, for, in spite of an equality of numbers, they easily were the victors of the day, wounding Champlain in the knee with an arrow, while another pierced the calf of his leg. The Hurons, in fact, had a sufficiency of battle, and, withdrawing to their camp, waited five days for a detachment of Algonquins which had promised to appear. They did not come, and, in frequent skirmishes with the Iroquois, the invaders were given all the fighting that they wished for. At length, disheartened, the Hurons retreated to the place where their canoes lay hidden, pursued by parties of the

Iroquois, who shot great quantities of arrows at their retreating forms. They embarked, paddled across the lake, and were again in their own country.

The Sieur De Champlain was not quite the hero which he had been before this affair, for he had not been found to be invulnerable. The man of iron breastplate, fluttering plumes, and "stick which spoke with the voice of thunder" was, after all, a common mortal. Some of the redmen even treated him disdainfully, for they were angered at the reception which they had received.

In spite of this, the French empire-builder spent the winter with his redskinned allies. When spring came, he turned homeward, and, accompanied by an Indian chieftain, again paddled down the Ottawa, at length reaching Montreal, where he was welcomed as one risen from the dead. Launching his canoe, he journeyed to Quebec, where he received a royal welcome. The chief was amazed at the houses, ships, and barracks, and, after admiring all that he saw, returned to his wigwam in the forest, bewildered and astonished at the possessions of these fair-skinned strangers.

The rest of Champlain's life was troublous, indeed, and quite different from those venturesome experiences in the wilderness. He had dedicated himself to New France, he loved the great surging St. Lawrence River, the wooded hills, the glorious lakes, the hemlock forests, the spruce, the fir, and the wonderfully clear air. He craved the wild life among the redskins, the battles in the silent forest, the war-dance and the shrill yelpings of victory. He reveled in the woodland scents and sounds, the chatter of the moose-bird, the scream of the loon, the plaintive meow of the lynx, the grunt of the brown, bull moose, and the quavering wail of the great northern diver. His eye responded to the view of bogs, morasses, waterfalls and plunging rapids. He was—in fact—a lover of the beautiful in nature. In a period of unbridled license his was a spotless life, and, like the good Chevalier Bayard, he was a warrior without fear and without reproach.

A British fleet, sailing up the St. Lawrence, found the little town of Quebec, which the good Chevalier had built, with a garrison of but sixteen, and these half famished. They were ordered to surrender, were captured, were convoyed to their own country (each soldier with furs to the value of twenty crowns with him) and the cross of St. George of England was planted upon the crumbling walls of the citadel. Yet Champlain was again to return, for, by a treaty between France and England, at this time, New France was restored to the French crown. The founder of this struggling colony reassumed command of Quebec in the following May.

Two years now passed, years of pleasurable toil, among the Indians, for priests and soldiers of the crown. A mission was established amongst the Hurons, a trading post at Three Rivers, and the authorities in France begged for troops with which to attack the vindictive Iroquois. But Cardinal Richelieu, who governed the destinies of the nation, had enough to do at home and cared little for the affairs of this far-distant wilderness colony. Harassed by anxieties, Champlain became more pious, grave and stern, as the years passed on. He had married, but his wife remained in Europe, where she became a nun; so the bold explorer made his will, leaving all of his little property to the Church.

Christmas day, 1635, was a bright day overhead, and the sun shone brilliantly upon the snow, but it was a dark day in the annals of New France. For in a chamber of the old fort at Quebec, breathless and cold, lay the hardy frame of the great explorer, the man of the sea, the wilderness, the palace, and the wigwam. The grave, the valiant Champlain was dead at the age of sixty-eight. His labors for his beloved New France were over and he had ceased to watch over the destinies of his struggling people. He was buried with a simple ceremony, which was attended by Jesuits, officers, soldiers, traders, Indian braves, and the few settlers of the quaint, little town. A tomb was erected to his honor and his remains thus rested near the scenes of his explorations, his adventures, and his dreams of empire for his beloved country.

THE SONG OF CHAMPLAIN

This is the song which the loon sang,
Sang as he swam on the glimmering lake,
Sang to the splash and thud of the waves,

As the hills reëchoed his wild, laughing call,
This is the song of Champlain!

***

The day was bright, and the sun was warm, as I rocked on the waters I love,
And the scent of the hemlocks blew fresh from the shore, and the coo of the gray, mourning dove.
Afar down the lake came the voice of my mate, as he heard my laughing refrain,
And we laughed at each other, like sister and brother, then dove, and laughed once again. But see, down the lake comes a strange, thrilling sight, 'tis a sight fit for gods to behold,
A swarm of red warriors in birch bark canoes, their prows threading silver and gold.
Algonquins and Hurons, Montagnais as well, bedaubed with yellow and red,
While the plumes of the heron and eaglet wave forth, like flags from each clean-shaven head.
In front of them all sits a warrior white, with breastplate and greaves of hard steel;
As the paddles flash keenly, he gazes serenely, and smiles as the warriors wheel.
They wheel into line with yells and with cries, as another wild party draws near,
From the southward they come, while the weird, moaning drum booms forth a death-slogan clear.
"The dread Iroquois! The bad Iroquois!" reëchoes from stem and from stern,
While loud, yelping cries ascend to the skies, as Algonquins and fierce Hurons turn.
They turn and they wheel, form in battle array; but the Iroquois dart to the shore,
Where they rush to the forest to cut down the trees, and hasten as never before.

Night comes; as the smothering blackness creeps on, there are dances and songs on the lake,
While on shore the deep drum makes a low, whining hum, e'en as branches and war-bonnets shake.
Day breaks at last, and the shrill trumpet's blast—wakes the stillness in forest and glade,
'Tis the dawning of death, for the grim specter's breath has blown o'er the host unafraid.
The paddles dip deep, as the warriors sleek drive onward to white, gleaming sand,
They leap to the beach, with arrows in reach, advance to the uprising land.
A yell of defiance is hurled at their heads, as the Iroquois rush to the fray,
Then the keen, whizzing barbs rush swift through the air; they advance in battle array.
But, see, there steps forth a warrior white,—'tis Champlain in casquet of steel,
A sword by his side, in his hand a long gun, he sights as the Iroquois wheel.
Crash! bang! and the bullet is speeding along, it reaches the breast of a chief,
One despairing wail and the lean body, frail, has gone to the Kingdom of Grief.
Ahah! what is this, for the Iroquois turn, they have met with their masters at-last,
The warriors fierce, who can slaughter and burn, now wince at the steel bullet's blast.
The Montagnais are yelping and dancing with glee, their enemies fear them at length,
For many years past they have kept them in awe; now they wince at the arquebus' strength.
A wild mêlée now, and the green balsam bough, sways o'er the carnage of hate,
And night shadows cover the rioting braves, the Iroquois meet with their fate.

***

See! the Hurons, Algonquins, are paddling away, and northward they turn with a will,
As war songs and yelpings ascend to the sky, of torture the braves have their fill,
Calm and quiet there sits that warrior white, who has won them the stirring lake fight,
And the breeze sighs, "Champlain!" while the stirring refrain clarions forth like the wild eagle's flight.

This is the song which the loon sang,
Sang as he swam on the glimmering lake,
Sang to the splash and thud of the waves,
As the hills reëchoed his wild, laughing call;
This is the song of Champlain!

WHISKEY JACK
(Canadian Blue Jay)

I was the first to see the redskin, I was the first to view Champlain;
Flitting in the hemlock branches, I fly South, then North again;
Up among the gray brown mountains, down amidst the soggy waste,
I am ever on the lookout, never worry, never haste.

Yes, I'm called old Whiskey Jack, gray and black, along my back,
Beady eye and slender tail, I can spy out any trail.
Old bull moose and caribou wink their eyes as I fly through,
Yelling, crying, "Chank! chank! chank!"—
Trappers call me "awful crank!"

Away up where the brook trout gather, away off by the blue St. John;
O'er broiling falls of foaming lather, where splashing jumps the muscallonge,
Where otters mew and spruce grouse flutter, where brown bears dig the honey tree,

That is where I spend the summer, where hunts the "sport" and half-breed Cree.

All men call me Whiskey Jack; I don't have to tote a pack;
Beady eye and slender tail, I can spy out any trail,
Old bull moose and caribou wink and blink as I fly through,
Yelling, crying, "Chank! chank! chank!"—
Trappers call me "awful crank!"

I don't have to hunt for foodstuffs—no! I fly right into camp,
Seize a piece of bread and butter, grab a muffin—then decamp,
Ha! the trappers try to hit me! Ho! they throw their spoons and knives,
But I dodge them by and chuckle, they can't hit me for their lives.

So, I'm called old Whiskey Jack, nice old Whiskey,—gray and black.
I was here in Indian days, know their customs, know their ways,
I was here when Marquette came, saw Quebec when it began,
Saw the hemlock forests falling, lowered by the hand of man.

Yes, I've seen some doings surely, seen the redskins on Champlain,
Seen them fight on land and water, seen the bodies of the slain,
Seen the waves of Lake George glisten, heard the yells on Richelieu,
Heard the scalp dance, seen the torture, viewed the crackling flames,—"A-hoo!"
Yes, I'm just old Whiskey Jack, plain old blue jay, gray and black,
Canadians know me, for I bring news of game and coming Spring,
What's a woodland camp without me? what's a fire without my call?
True, I'm just a plain old ranger, but—Egad—I'm loved by all!

Chapter 12

HENRY HUDSON

DISCOVERER OF HUDSON BAY AND EXPLORER OF THE MAGNIFICENT RIVER WHICH BEARS HIS NAME, (15??-1611)

"Oh! See there, redskinned brother, where the winding river parts,
Where the shadows glance and glisten, where the silvery salmon darts.
See that hulk approaching,—floating without a sound,
With white clouds riding up above and sides so dark and round.
Come! Let us paddle to it. Ha! See the pale-skinned men;
They beckon, smiling on us.
They must be friendly, then."

We had been plowing along over the great Atlantic on a clear and starlit night. The Mauretania was as steady as a pier in the East River, so we were expecting no disaster, yet, when we tumbled from our cots upon the day following, we were startled to see that the great, steel hulk had ceased to move with her accustomed vigor. The resounding poom, poom, of her giant propeller-shaft was no longer heard, and she was only just drifting along through the gray-green waters. Every now and again her massive fog-whistle would roar out its leonine warning:

"O-o-o-o-o-m! O-o-o-o-o-m!"

We stumbled to the deck, only to be chilled and dampened by a shroud of mist, which had shut down upon our steel-clad home like a giant pall. It curled, rolled and settled upon us as if it were a blanket saturated with dank sea-water; it cut off the view, so that one peered at the swishing ocean in vain; and it benumbed one, so that one's voice was stifled and choked, as if a huge overpowering hand were grasping at one's throat. And even from above came that soul-deadening roar of the steam siren:

"O-o-o-o-o-m! O-o-o-o-o-m!"

In the blinding mist I bumped into a sailor.

"Avast there, my lad," said he. "Can't you get your sea legs?" "No," I replied. "Where are we?"

"Off the banks."

"And the fog?"

Usual thing. She'll burn off in a couple of hours. We have to go easy because of the Gloucester fishing fleet. Hear them!"

Indistinctly, in the murky pall, I seemed to hear the thin whining of numberless, tin fish-horns. "Pretty weak fog-whistles, aren't they?"

I laughed.

But just then something happened.

The mist seemed to part as if rent by a strong and virile hand. We could see the great, combing, green billows go careening and bobbing by, as the cloud-bank shifted like a veil, and there, tossing restlessly on the waves, was a long, brown boat! A number of men were in her, all huddled together in a heap. They were dressed in old-fashioned garments and their faces were drawn, haggard, pinched. In the stern sat a bearded man holding fast to the tiller, at his feet lay a slender youth.

The vista lasted but for a moment or two and then the fog-bank rolled in again, hiding the picture from our startled, yet eager visions.

"Who are they?" asked I, breathlessly, as the sailor lurched against my side. "Henry Hudson and his crew," he answered, with a hoarse chuckle.

And as I stumbled below, I thought that perhaps the weather-beaten sea-dog might be correct.

If you had happened to be sitting upon the beach of Manhattan Island, near the spot where is now the Battery, upon the eleventh day of September, 1609, you would have seen a curiously shaped vessel floating, lazing, along near the shore, and you would have also seen a number of weather- scarred navigators who were anxiously peering at the beach. The name of this boat, with a high poop and a curving prow, was the Half Moon, and her captain was Henry Hudson, or Hendrick Hudson, as he is sometimes called.

He was not only pleased, but also interested to see a land where was a goodly lot of timber, lovely islands and broad harbors, pearly beaches and dusky-bodied inhabitants, who seemed to be peacefully inclined.

And who was this fellow Henry, who had dared to come to explore that island of Manhattan, where the mighty Woolworth Building was to rise up in all its splendor, as if to laugh at the former simplicity and quiet of the brush-covered strip of sandy soil?

Of the early history of the bold mariner hardly anything is known. He was a native of England, a contemporary and friend of the famous Captain John Smith, the settler of Virginia, and, like him, was a professional navigator and intrepid adventurer. He resided in London, was married, and had a son, to whom he was devotedly attached.

When Hudson was living in London, there were a great many merchants there who were anxious to learn of a northern and westward route to the East Indies, from which they imported teas, spices, and many other articles. The commerce of this country was now brought partly over land and then floated through the Mediterranean Sea. It was a slow and laborious route for trade, so those nations farthest removed from the advantages of that route (such as Spain, Portugal, and England), became restless, and most desirous of finding a new and a shorter passage to the East Indies.

In the year 1499, a celebrated Portuguese navigator, called Vasco da Gama, had doubled the Cape of Good Hope, and, passing onward, had appeared upon the coast of Hindustan. He had brought back word of the southern route, but it was such a long and dangerous passage, that the nations of Europe were not satisfied with it. They desired a shorter highway to the wealth of the East, and began to think that they might find it by sailing through the Arctic Ocean, and, passing northwestwardly around the coast of North America, might journey around the shore of Asia to the Indies with their marvelous wealth.

A number of rich men who lived in the city of London joined themselves together as a London Company in the year 1607, and raised sufficient money to purchase a ship and supply it with provisions for a journey to the northwest. Knowing that everything depended upon the skill of the commander, they chose, as their leader, Henry Hudson, who readily accepted the position.

Upon a bright day in April, the Captain and crew went to the church of Saint Ethelburge in Bishopsgate Street, and there received the sacrament of the Lord's Supper. There were eleven seamen in all, among whom was John Hudson, son of the daring sea captain. It was a pious and beautiful custom of those ancient times for seamen to thus act before entrusting themselves to the mercy of the seas, where they were to meet with unknown perils.

Strange as it may seem to us now, the object of this voyage was to find a passage directly across the North Pole to Japan and China. Imagine these brave fellows setting out in one of the small vessels of those days to sail to the Pole! It seems absurd, for, even with a vessel specially constructed to meet the ice packs, Commodore Peary had great difficulty in keeping his vessel, the Roosevelt, from being crushed. Yet, with their flimsy craft, these adventurers started out in quest of the much-desired North West passage.

On May 1st. 1607, the navigators weighed anchor at Gravesend, and, taking a northerly course, in twenty-six days reached the Shetland Isles. Leaving these wild, rocky shores behind them, they now steered northwest, and, in a week's time, although they discovered no land, they had the satisfaction of seeing six or seven whales near the ship. Two days later, at 2 o'clock upon a foggy morning, land was seen ahead of them. It was high, covered with snow, and, at the top, it looked reddish; underneath a blackish color, with much ice lying about. There were also great quantities of ducks and other wild-fowl along the coast, and a whale spouted near the shore. This was the peninsula of Greenland.

Thick fogs now shut down upon the mariners, accompanied by storms of rain and of snow. The vessel was sometimes driven before a heavy gale of wind; at other times becalmed. Yet, in spite of this, Hudson still held on in a northeasterly course, hoping to sail around the land in front of him and thus to reach the passage across the North Pole. At last, discouraged at his slow progress, he determined to steer in an easterly direction, hoping to find an island which was called Newland upon the charts.

After sailing about sixteen miles, the ship came within sight of land and many birds were seen flying over it with black and white stomachs, and in form like a duck. Fogs again set in and much floating ice was encountered, yet the vessel was headed onward in a northeasterly direction. Land was seen at different intervals and the weather was both temperate and pleasant. So, again steering eastward, the ship struggled on against hard winds and heavy fogs until it had reached the coast of Spitzbergen.

Great numbers of whales were playing around in a bay which they ran into, and, while one of the men was amusing himself with a hook and a line overboard, in order to try for a bite, one of the monster fish dove under the vessel and caught upon his line. All the sailors feared that they would be upset, but the big, black fellow made off without doing them any serious damage.

"By God's mercy," says Hudson, in his diary, "we had no harm but the loss of the hook and three parts of the line."

After sailing along the coast for some time, again the mariner headed for Greenland, hoping to steer around it, towards the north, and then return to England. But fogs, storms, and floating ice interfered with his journey, to such an extent, that he was forced to turn around and head for the place from which he had started.

Thus, after a hard voyage of four months and a half, he sailed up the river Thames, beaten in his effort to find the North West passage, yet with the news of many lands which no Englishman had yet seen. His employers greeted him warmly and were sufficiently well pleased with his success to trust him with a second adventure, for he had been farther north than any navigator who had preceded him, and had opened the commerce of the whale fishery to his countrymen. He was also the re-discoverer of Spitzbergen, which had first been seen by one William Barentz, a Dutch navigator, in the year 1596.

Spring had no sooner opened, in the year following, than Hudson commenced making his preparations for a second voyage. This time he was to endeavor to seek the passage for the East Indies by passing between Spitzbergen and Nova Zembla. Thus, with a crew of fifteen persons, and his son John, he set sail from London on the twenty-second day of April, heading north, where lay the region of ice and snow.

At one time the vessel would meet large quantities of drift-wood driving by in a confused mass; then large numbers of whales and porpoises would be met with, and the sea would be covered with multitudes of birds. Then again the mariners would come across numbers of seals lying about upon cakes of ice, and polar bears would lumber away over the glistening ice-pack. Two of the sailors, also, said that they saw a mermaid close to the side of the ship, but a big wave came along and overturned her. As she went down into the surging brine they saw her tail, which was similar to the tail of a porpoise, and was speckled like a mackerel.

After sighting land, and exploring numberless bays and harbors, Hudson finally reached a great sound, into which emptied a stream. The vessel was anchored, and five men were sent forward in a boat to explore this river, in order to see whether or not the water-course dipped to the south and led to a passage through to Asia. But the water became very shallow, as the explorers proceeded, so they came back and reported that the vessel could not venture farther upon its way. As the provisions were now getting somewhat low, Hudson decided to steer for England. This he did, entering the peaceful Thames, after an absence of about four months. He was not received with the same cordiality which had greeted him after his first voyage. His employers had grown discouraged by these two unsuccessful attempts to find a shorter route to Asia.

The members of the London Company, in fact, refused to lend any more money or supplies to Mr. Henry Hudson, so that gallant gentleman took a jaunt to Holland in order to offer his services to the Dutch East India Company. His fame had preceded him, and he was greeted with cordial respect. A small ship was given to him called the Half Moon, and he was requested to go forth once more and discover the North West passage, upon which his heart was set. With a crew consisting of twenty Englishmen and Dutchmen, among whom was the same mate who had served with him upon his last voyage, he was now ready to brave again the ice and storms of the Arctic seas.

Upon March the 25th, the experienced navigator left New Amsterdam, and was ere long upon the coast of Nova Zembla, when he met with so much ice and fog, that he gave up any hope of reaching India by this route.

But Hudson was made of no common clay, and, although beaten by the elements, which denied him a northern route, determined to sail to America, that land about which every one in Europe was hearing such wonderful stories. Furthermore, he had with him some maps which had been given him by his old friend, Captain John Smith, on which a strait was marked, south of the fair land of Virginia, by which he might reach the Pacific Ocean and the East Indies. Then, too, he might gain a passage through to the northwest, by means of Davis Strait. Why not? He asked his crew about it, and they voted, to a man, to sail westward. Many of these bronzed sea-dogs had been trained in the East Indies service, were accustomed to sailing in warm, tropical climates, and therefore chose to sail south, rather than to meet the fog, the ice, and the chill tempests of the northern seas.

Heading towards the West, the Half Moon soon reached one of the Faroe Islands, where the casks were filled with fresh water, and then the sails were again hoisted, and a course was set towards Newfoundland. Early in July the Grand Banks were reached, where was a great fleet of French fishing smacks, which had come this great distance in order to catch cod and haddock. As the Half Moon was now becalmed for several days, the crew was sent to the banks to try their luck, and, in one day, one hundred and thirty cod-fish were captured. The wind now freshened, so the mariners sailed towards the west. They soon cleared the banks, passed the shore of Nova Scotia, and, on the morning of the 12th, saw the coast of

North America before them. Clouded by fog banks, but brown, rock-ribbed, pine-clad, lay the wonderful country which was inhabited by the deer, the beaver, the moose, and the red Indian.

The Half Moon careened along for several days at some distance from the land, as the fog was so thick, that Hudson feared to approach. Finally the sun burned through the mist and the mariners ran into a goodly harbor at the mouth of a large river. It was Penobscot Bay, upon the coast of Maine, as beautiful then as it is now.

As the ship was lying-to off the harbor, unable to enter because of the fog, two birch-bark canoes had approached them, with six natives of the country, who seemed delighted to see the mariners. Captain Hudson gave them some glass beads and other trinkets,—then they ate and drank with him. One of the natives could speak a little French and told them that the French people were in the habit of trading with them, and that they had gold, copper, and silver mines near by.

When the Half Moon entered Penobscot Bay, great numbers of the redskins paddled out to the vessel, climbed on board, and eagerly gazed upon the sailors, as they mended the sails and made a new foremast. Some of the mariners went ashore to get a needed supply of water, while others amused themselves by catching lobsters,—not in a lobster-pot, you may be sure, but in a small net baited with fish.

Hudson's men seemed to have had a foolish distrust of the redskins. The Indians were friendly and wished to trade beaver-pelts and fine furs for hatchets, beads, and knives; yet the mariners were so suspicious that they kept a strict watch upon the ship in order to see that no natives approached under cover of the darkness. At last, their mast being ready, these navigators manned a boat with twelve men armed with muskets, and, landing upon the shore, made a savage attack upon the peaceful red men, whom they drove from their houses. It is to the disgrace of Hudson that he allowed this to happen, the only excuse that can be offered being that he had under his command a wild and ungovernable lot of uneducated Dutch and Englishmen.

Having perpetrated this act of cruelty, the adventurers set sail, steering southward along the coast of America, and, in a short time came within sight of Cape Cod. They sounded and found the water quite deep within bowshot of the shore, and, proceeding to the land, discovered grapes and rose-trees, which they brought on board their ship. The Half Moon was now sailed towards the shore and was anchored there. Here Hudson heard voices calling to him from the beach, and, thinking that they might be the cries of some poor sailors who had been left behind, he immediately sent a part of the crew in a boat to land. Upon jumping out upon the sand, it was found that the calls had been made by Indians, who appeared to be greatly rejoiced to see them. The men returned to the ship, bringing one of the natives on board with them, whom they fed, presented with a few glass buttons, and then put ashore in the boat. When the redskin reached the land, he gave every manifestation of great joy, by dancing, leaping, and throwing up his hands. Then letting out a wild and uncouth yell, he disappeared into the brush.

Amused and interested, Hudson now steered southeast, and soon passed the southern point of Cape Cod, which he knew to be the headland which Bartholomew Gosnold had discovered in 1602, seven years before. He sailed by Nantucket and Martha's Vineyard and kept upon his course due south, until, upon the 18th. day of August, he found himself at the entrance of Chesapeake Bay, where, two years before, the first English settlement had been made in America. Hudson was filled with great admiration for these broad waters, and, keeping on, reached the thirty-fifth degree of latitude, or a position which made him certain that there was no passage to the South Pacific Ocean, as John Smith had said. So, retracing his course, he passed the shores of Maryland and discovered the great bay of Delaware.

"It is a good land to fall in with, and is a pleasant land to see," writes Hudson in his diary, transcribed as the Half Moon was sailing off the shore of Long Branch, New Jersey. The weather was dark and misty, so, sending some men inshore in order to find out the depth of the water, the vessel was headed inland, and, upon the morning of September third, was anchored within Sandy Hook, in five fathoms of water. The next morning, this bold navigator saw that there was "good anchorage and a safe harbor," so he steered his little vessel within the bay of Sandy Hook, at a distance of two cable lengths from the shore, resting in the famous harbor of New York.

Figure 13. Henry Hudson in New York Harbor.

Could Henry Hudson have looked forward through the years and have seen the city of tall buildings, wharves, cobbled streets and rolling elevated-trains which was to cover the island of Manhattan, then lying tranquilly before his gaze, he would doubtless have passed a night of restless nightmare. But he had no forward vision, and, as he feasted his eyes upon a long beach of white sand, behind which were low scrubby bushes, plum trees, grape vines, and twisted oaks, he peacefully smoked a long pipe which an Indian brave had given him, and dreamed of discovering a passage to Asia.

The ship lay drowsily at anchor, and, as it swung upon its chain, many redskins came paddling out from the shore, clambered on board, and seemed to be delighted to see these strange visitors. They were dressed in well-cured deer-skins, which hung loosely over their shoulders, and had many ornaments of copper scattered upon their persons. They brought ears of corn with them and also tobacco, which they wished to exchange for beads, for knives, and for other trinkets. The sailors had much fun in bartering with them and in smoking their stone pipes.

The ship rode snugly at anchor, but during the night a gale sprang up, which was of such fury, that the anchor dragged, and the Half Moon was soon high and dry upon the Jersey beach. But she was not even strained, as the bottom was "soft and oozy," and when flood-tide came along she was easily towed into deep water. Yet, this was of great interest to the native inhabitants, who crowded eagerly to the shore: men, women and children. They were also very kind, giving the sailors presents of dried currants and green tobacco. Notwithstanding this, the mariners suspected them of treachery and kept continually upon their guard.

Henry Hudson saw that a large river emptied into this bay, where lay the Half Moon, so he sent five men in order to explore and discover how far he could go. They passed through what is now known as the Narrows, found the land to be covered with trees, grass, and flowers, the fragrance of which was delightful, and, after going six miles into New York Bay, turned back. Now an unhappy event was to occur, yet one which showed that the distrust of the natives was a well-founded prejudice.

The boat was being driven along toward the ship, just at dusk, when it was attacked by two canoes containing twenty-six redskinned warriors of old-time New York. Rain was falling, so it was impossible to use the ancient muskets, or match-locks, which were touched off by means of a lighted fuse. The white men could therefore make no defense and rowed off as fast as they could, while a shower of Indian arrows fell into the boat, striking three of the explorers in the body. One of them, John Colman, was killed by an arrow which struck him in the neck. He had been with Hudson in his first voyage and was greatly loved by the brave and resolute navigator.

In this, the first boat race in New York harbor between the redskins and the whites, the white men were victorious, for they escaped into the darkness and wandered around all night. In the dim gray of the early morn they found the ship; climbed thankfully on board, and told of their experience with some show of anxiety, for they feared a general attack from the red men. None came, however, and the dead body of Colman was taken ashore at Sandy Hook, where it was buried in the soil at a place called Colman's Point.

Just as soon as the burying party had returned to the ship, the boat was hoisted in, and bulwarks were erected upon the sides in order to repel the expected Indian attack. But none came. The night was quiet, only the lapping of the water around the ship's bow could be heard, and, when day dawned, numerous redskins paddled out to the vessel in the most friendly manner, bringing corn and tobacco to trade with the sailors. From their actions, it appeared that they knew nothing of the battle upon the previous day, and they left in good humor, promising to return next morning with more provisions and many beaver-skins for trade.

In the flush of the early dawn, two large canoes came off to the Half Moon, one filled with men armed with bows and arrows, who seemed to be in war paint. Hudson was suspicious of treachery, so only allowed two of the braves to come on board, whom he dressed up in red coats. The remaining savages returned to the shore, and presently another canoe approached in which were two lone warriors. One of them was allowed to come on deck, Hudson intending to keep him as a hostage to insure the good behavior of his fellow citizens on the Isle of Manhattan.

The redskins, however, did not seem to like their fair-skinned brothers, and one immediately dove into the sea and swam hastily ashore. Expecting an immediate attack, Hudson weighed anchor and floated the Half Moon off into the channel of the Narrows, where he again anchored for the night. He expected an assault, but none came, so he set sail, next morning, for the Bay of New York, which he says that he found to be "an excellent harbor for all winds." He again anchored, and the Half Moon was soon surrounded by the Indians, who were apparently friendly "making a great show of love, and giving tobacco and Indian wheat." The navigators, however, were afraid of an attack and kept continually upon their guard, yet the red men departed to the shore, and all was peace and quiet, save for the mewing of the sea gulls and the squawking of a great blue heron, as he winged his way to the inland marshes.

The dreamy haze of September hung over the swirling, blue river as Henry Hudson gazed up the stream which was to ever afterwards bear his name, and, upon the morning of the twelfth, he weighed anchor, and steered towards the northwest. Twenty-eight canoes had visited him that morning, filled with redskinned men, women and children, who had brought oysters and clams to trade for blue beads and glass trinkets. The braves smoked great tobacco pipes of yellow color and their cheeks were smeared with red ochre, so that the mariners were suspicious of them, and, although they traded with them, allowed none to come upon the deck.

The wind was unpropitious, so the Half Moon only sailed about two leagues, when it anchored for the night. Yet, next day, the wind was fresher, so the vessel proceeded to travel about eleven miles, until it came opposite the present town of Yonkers, where the anchor was again let down. The redskins immediately crowded around the boat, but none were allowed to come on board, as the navigators feared treachery.

The weather continued to be fair, so the Half Moon proceeded upon her way, and, driven by a strong breeze, finally anchored in a region where the land was very high and mountainous, evidently the neighborhood of the Highlands and near the present site of the West Point Military Academy. No cries of "Battalion, Attention!" "Squads, Right!" or "Forward, March!" then echoed from the peaceful shore; instead of this, the mariners heard the hooting of a great, brown owl, while far off upon the mountain-side glimmered the camp-fire of a straggling band of Indians. As night descended upon the wilderness, the scream of a panther reverberated from the dense foliage of the high hills, which were beautiful with the first changing colors of autumn. The stream was narrowing, instead of expanding, so, thought Hudson, could it be possible that, after all, there was no passage to the East Indies?

A filmy mist hung over the rippling waters of the stream, next morning, but as the sun shone, a clear wind arose which seemed to blow it away. As Hudson gave orders to his men to haul up the anchor, a sudden splash near the vessel's side made him run to the gunwale and look eagerly into the water, expecting to see a small whale, or a porpoise. Instead, the head of a redskin bobbed up in the ripples of the stream, as with furious strokes, one of the braves who had been held prisoner, swam towards the shore. Another head appeared. The two red men, who had been held as hostages, had escaped through the port hole.

The Indians soon reached the banks of the stream, climbed out, and standing there with clenched fists, shook them vindictively at the white men, making loud and angry cries. Not at all worried at the happening, Hudson kept on up the now narrowing river, passed by high mountains upon either side, and finally came in sight of other mountains, about fifty miles from his former anchorage. Here the redskins came out to view the curious vessel, and, says Hudson in his journal, they were "very loving people and very old men, who treated us very kindly." The anchor was cast and a boat was sent off with sailors to catch fish, of which there was a great abundance.

Going ashore, next day, the brave navigator there met an old chieftain who lived in a circular house and was surrounded by forty men and seventeen women. The aged redskin was hospitably inclined and begged the white man to come and feast with him, an invitation which Hudson readily accepted. Two mats were immediately spread for him to sit upon and food was brought forward in large, red bowls made of wood. Several natives were meantime dispatched into the woods in search of game.

After awhile the braves returned with a pair of pigeons which were roasted upon the fire. A feast was now held, consisting of corn, beans, pigeon and fat dog, after which Hudson was requested to spend the night. "I must return," said the mariner, but this seemed to worry the chief redskin, so that his people took all of their arrows, and, breaking them in pieces, threw them into the fire, as they supposed that the explorer was afraid of them. However, Hudson would not remain in the wigwam, preferring to sleep among his own compatriots.

After trading with the red men, who brought Indian corn, pumpkins and tobacco to the ship, the Half Moon was again steered up-stream, until the water was found to be very shoal. This was probably near the spot where the city of Hudson has grown up. The weather was warm and enervating, but the vessel was kept upon her course until she reached several small islands in the middle of the river, and also very shallow water, which made it impossible to proceed. As night came on, the vessel drifted near the shore and grounded. But she was floated off by means of an anchor, and again lay peacefully in the stream.

Hudson had now proceeded about as far as he could go, and saw that it was impossible to reach the East Indies by way of the winding watercourse upon which his vessel lay. His men who had been sent up-stream to explore, in the small boat, brought back word that there was nothing but still shallower water above. So it was apparent that the vessel must return to the sea again, and another passage must be sought for. Yet, before he returned, he determined to make an experiment with some of these many Indians who were crowding about his vessel, in order to learn if they were really treacherous, or were peacefully inclined. This experiment was to be by means of the famous Holland gin, or "fire water" of the white men, and it was decided to place some of the red men under its influence.

Next day, several of the Indian braves were invited down to the broad cabin of the Half Moon, where gin and brandy was given them, until they were all as merry as a marriage bell.

Their squaws looked innocently on as their lords and masters betook plentifully of the cup that cheers, and saw all of them become, first merry, then boisterous, then drowsy. Finally one Indian brave became so deeply intoxicated that he fell asleep upon a bench, snoring with right good will. All of his companions now arose in great fright, for they feared that he was poisoned. Taking to their canoes, they cried out with some show of anger: "You pale faces have sent our brother to the Land of the Great Spirit. Ugh! Ugh! You have poisoned him!" They did not, however, forget their poor companion, and several soon returned, bringing with them long strings of beads which they offered to Hudson, saying: "Take these, brother, and let us have our miserable friend. He has gone to the Land of the Hereafter!" But the mariner declined, answering:

"Let your brother sleep. He is safe with us and will get well. The Great Spirit is watching over him and you need fear nothing."

The redskin slept peacefully all night, and, when his frightened countrymen came out to see him, next day, they were rejoiced to find him alive and smiling. Crying out, "Ugh! Ugh! The white man was right. The

Great Spirit has looked carefully after our brother," the red men paddled him joyfully to the shore, but soon returned, bringing beads and tobacco, which they gave to Hudson. They also presented him with a large platter of venison. "Pray take this, brother," said a bronze-skinned chieftain. "We love our brother, for he has let no harm come to our beloved friend who has loved the fire water far too well. Ugh! Ugh!"

Disappointed in not finding the passage to the Far East, Hudson now prepared to return. But how far had he gone? Writers seem to disagree upon this point, yet, when one considers that the Half Moon was a small boat, not as large as many of the stone sloops which now sail in the North River, it is reasonable to suppose that it went up the Hudson to a place about in the neighborhood of where Albany now stands, while the boat which was sent on ahead to explore the stream, advanced as far as the town of Waterford.

It was now the twenty-seventh day of September, the weather was balmy, and the leaves of the forest were turning with the first chill of autumn. The Half Moon drifted slowly down the broadening river, passing the home of the hospitable, old chieftain, near Catskill's Landing. The redskin came out in his canoe, begging Hudson to come ashore and eat with him; but the wind was too fresh for the navigator to listen to his invitation, so the boat kept on down-stream, leaving the old chief "very sorrowful for their departure." Toward night the vessel anchored near what is now known as Red Hook Landing, where the sailors had splendid fishing in the blue depths of the magnificent water- course.

Now, detained for a day by head winds, the ship dropped slowly down the river, passing the famous highlands of the Hudson where the mountains looked as if there were some metal, or mineral in them. "The hills seemed to be all blasted, some of them barren with few or no trees on them." The Indians still crowded around the boat, several of them bringing a stone on board which was like emery, for it would cut iron or steel. On the 1st day of October, with a fair wind behind, the Half Moon sailed through the highlands, and, reaching a point opposite Stony Point, was becalmed, and cast anchor.

No sooner had the pronged holding-iron touched bottom than the redskins came crowding around, astonished at everything they saw, and desirous of trade. They offered pumpkins, beaver skins, and dried plums for exchange, but apparently could not procure all that they wished, for one fellow was prompted to steal. Paddling his birch bark canoe near the stern of the Half Moon, he crawled up the rudder into the cabin window and made off with a pillow and some clothes. Jumping stealthily into his canoe, he paddled away as fast as he was able, but was seen by the Mate, who shot and killed him. As he dropped lifeless into the stern of his canoe, the remaining red men fled in terror, some even leaping overboard to swim for it. Meanwhile the ship's boat was manned and a number of sailors were sent to rescue the stolen articles, which were easily obtained. As the boat headed for the Half Moon, one of the swimming redskins took hold of the stern and endeavored to overturn her. When he did this, the cook drew a sword, and, making a vicious blow at him, cut off his hand. Shrieking with pain, the poor creature sank to the bottom, never to rise again. The sailors hastened their rowing, were soon on board the ship, and, fearing an attack, hoisted sail in order to drop down the stream to the mouth of the Croton River.

The next day was a clear one, with a fair wind, so the Half Moon sailed twenty-one miles to a position somewhere near the head of Manhattan Island, where there was quite a deal of trouble in store for these valiant navigators. As you remember, on the way up the stream, Hudson had held two red men captive, who had escaped through the porthole. These had returned to their fellows, angry and indignant at their captivity, and had raised their compatriots to a revengeful spirit against these white interlopers. The warriors had assembled along the shores of the river, and, as the Half Moon approached, a canoe neared the vessel, in which was one of those who had escaped, and many others, armed with bows and with arrows. Although they attempted to come on board, the wise Hudson would not allow this to be done. Showing anger by their gesticulations, the redskins withdrew, but presently two canoes filled with armed warriors dropped under the stem and began to attack the vessel by showering arrows at her. The mariners fired six muskets at the red men and three of them fell dead in the bottom of their birch-bark canoes.

The Indians who were on the shore, and had been keeping a keen watch upon the affair, now moved down to the beach in a solid body (there were about one hundred in all) and shot arrows at the ship, as she floated by. A cannon was now loaded with ball and was discharged among them, whereby two of them fell mortally wounded. The remainder fled into the woods, with the exception of nine or ten desperate men, who, resolved upon revenge, jumped into a canoe and advanced to fight the ship at close quarters. But the cannon was again discharged, the canoe was pierced by the ball, and three or four redskins were killed by musket shots. The rest swam to shore.

The ship was sailing slowly onward, and, after skirting the shore for about two miles, dropped anchor beneath the cliffs at Hoboken. The day following was a stormy one, but the fourth of October was clear, with an excellent wind, so the Half Moon weighed anchor, passed through the bay, and, with all sails set, shoved her nose into the swirling billows of the broad Atlantic, leaving the noble river far astern.

The mate was in favor of wintering in Newfoundland, and of then seeking a passage to the Far East by means of the Davis Strait, but Hudson opposed this. The course of the Half Moon was kept in a line for England, where, on the seventh day of November, after an absence of a little more than seven months from Amsterdam, she glided into the harbor of Dartmouth. The crew, as you doubtless remember, was composed partly of English, partly of Dutch sailors, and, it is said that the Englishmen refused to allow their Captain to sail into a Dutch harbor. Dutch historians declare, that, as the English King was jealous of the bold mariner's enterprises, he was not allowed to sail to Holland. At any rate, Hudson remembered his duty to his employers, and sent them a journal and chart of his discoveries, pointing with great pride to what he called "the Great River of the Mountains." The Dutch soon came over to settle the new-found country, and named the stream the North River, to distinguish it from the Delaware, or South River. The Indians called it Cahohatatea, Mahackaneghtue, and sometimes Shatemuck.

This successful voyage had now given Hudson a great name, and his discoveries fired his old employers of the London Company with enthusiasm. So they again called him into their service, determined to make an effort to find the North West passage by examining the inlets of this wonderful continent of America,—more particularly Davis Strait, through which it was supposed a channel might be found into the "Great South Sea." Hudson was furnished with the ship Discovery, of fifty-five tons, which, equipped and manned with twenty-three men, set out for the Far West. This journey was to be his last one.

Upon the 17th. of April, 1610, the Discovery passed out of the mouth of the Thames, and, sailing near the coast of Scotland, the Orkney, Shetland and Faroe Islands, left the coast of Ireland astern, and headed for the barren shores of Greenland. Great numbers of whales were encountered, and two of these sea monsters dove underneath the ship, but did the craft no harm. It was soon evident that there was a turbulent and mutinous disposition among the crew,—Robert Juet, the Mate, being the chief offender, for he had remarked to one of the sailors that there would be bloodshed before the voyage was over, and he was evidently plotting to seize the vessel, even at this early date.

The history of this journey is very similar to that of most of the Arctic explorers. Hudson and his men met great, floating fields of ice; were chilled by the perpetual frost and snow; and were finally starved into a submissive recognition of the fact that there could be no passage to Asia through the desolate region of the frozen North.

Yet, the adventurous mariner discovered the great bay which bears his name and also the strait which is known as Hudson Strait. Forced to winter upon the land near Cape Digges, he soon discovered that his food supply was so low, that, should not succor come to him, he and his men would die of starvation. Luckily, there were many white partridges, or ptarmigan, near the ship, which supplied them with provender, and, when spring came, great numbers of swans, of geese, ducks and other water-fowl came soaring by. Unfortunately they went farther North to breed, so the poor explorers were forced to search the hills, the woods, and the valleys for anything which might afford them subsistence, even eating the moss which grew upon the ground.

About the time when the ice began to break up, a brown-skinned savage, doubtless an Eskimo, put in his appearance, and, as he was treated well, returned in a day or so, bringing beaver and other skins, which he gave to Hudson and his men, in return for presents which he had received the day before. He went away, promising to visit them again, but, as he did not do so, it is evident that he did not think that the white men had given him good treatment.

The ice had now begun to melt, so the ship was headed southward. It was the middle of June, yet there were still great quantities of floating ice, so much, in fact, that the vessel was obliged to anchor. The food supply was about exhausted and all that was left was a little bread and a few pounds of cheese. Hudson now told one of the crew to search the chests of all of the men in order to find any provisions which might be concealed there. The sailor obeyed and brought the Captain thirty cakes in a bag. When the crew learned this, they were greatly exasperated, and plotted open mutiny against the famous navigator.

The vessel had been detained about a week in the ice when the first signs of mutiny appeared. Two sailors, called Greene and Wilson, the latter being the Boatswain, came one night to another mariner called Pricket, and told him that several of the crew had resolved to seize Hudson and set him adrift in a boat with all those on board who had been disabled by sickness.

"There are only a few days' provisions left," said Greene, "and the master seems to be entirely irresolute which way to go. I, myself, have eaten nothing for three days, so our only hope is to take command of the ship, and, after escaping from these regions, we will go back to England."

Pricket remonstrated with them, saying: "If you stain yourselves with so great a crime you will be banished from England forever. Pray delay your intention for four or five days, when we will be free of the ice and can doubtless get plenty of fish in our nets."

Upon this Greene took up the Bible which lay there and swore that he would "do no man harm, and that what he did was for the good of the voyage and nothing else."

There were many poor fellows who were ill and it was determined to maroon them in the boat with Hudson, so that the mutineers could do as they wished with the Discovery, and would not be hampered by either their master or any one who could not work the ship. It was decided to put the plot into execution at day-break.

As Hudson came up from the cabin, next morning, after eating a scanty breakfast, he was immediately seized by two sailors and his arms were bound fast behind him.

"What does this mean, men?" cried he, with great indignation.

Only sneers of defiance greeted his question. He now called upon the ship's carpenter to help him, telling him that he was bound, but, as this poor fellow was also surrounded by mutineers, he could render him no assistance.

The boat was now hauled alongside, and the sick and the lame were made to come up from below. They were told to get in, and Hudson's little son was forced to clamber over the steep sides of the vessel, and to lie upon the bottom of the boat. The sails were now hoisted upon the Discovery, and she stood eastward with a fair wind, dragging the poor fellows in the boat, astern. In a few hours, being clear of the ice, the rope leading to the shallop was cut, and soon afterwards the mutineers lost sight of Henry Hudson forever.

The hardy adventurer was never heard of again. As for the mutineers, although they steered for Ireland, before they reached the coast they were so weakened that no one was found strong enough to stand by the helm. When only one fowl was left for their subsistence and another day would be their last, they abandoned all care of the vessel and prepared to meet their fate. Suddenly the joyful cry of "a sail" was heard, and a fishing vessel came alongside which took them into a harbor of Ireland. They arrived in London after an absence of one year and five months.

The English people were horrified to learn of the treatment which the mutinous crew had administered to Henry Hudson and sent out two vessels, the next spring, in the hope of learning something of the fate of this brave navigator. Yet nothing was ever seen or heard of the unfortunate discoverer, who perished amidst the fogs and the ice of that bleak, northern ocean. Hudson was brave, resourceful, and resolute. He has been accused of cruelty to the Indians, and of want of high principle in causing their general intoxication when sailing upon the great river which was to be named after him. Yet you must remember that he had a mutinous body of men under his command, and could not easily restrain them from returning insult for injury, when their redskinned friends shot arrows at them. The death of the nine Indians killed at the head of Manhattan Island may be said to have been caused in a war of self-defense. As for the charge of heartlessness in getting the redskins intoxicated, you must also remember, that, like his men, he was suspicious and alarmed, and therefore was determined to learn the honesty or treachery of the Indians by any means whatsoever. In England, they grieved deeply for the death of such a gallant countryman, and in the new world he has perpetual monuments to his memory, for here a great bay, a city, and a mighty river, all bear the name of this brave yet unfortunate navigator.

THE WIND FROM THE NORTHLAND

The wind blew from the northland, as the frozen bergs went by,
And it sobbed a song through the grizzly murk, to the bobbing siren's cry.
It sang of men of daring, and it whined of maids of the mist,
Who burnish the shields of their men-at-arms, where the ice with the sunset's kissed.
Ah! it told of Leif the Lucky, with his sword and his Vikings bold,
Who hounded the bear to his cavern in the land where the penguins scold.
We heard the clang of their axes; we were jarred with the crash of their swords,
As the blaring bugles shrilled their notes in thin, transparent words.
And the wind sang of brave Hudson, and it sobbed for his starving son,
As, adrift in a boat, they were chilled by the glut of that night without a sun.

And the blast sobbed out its tale of death, of Baffin, Franklin, and Kane,
Of Marvin, de Long, and Parry; of the days of sorrow and pain.
Yet, the blinding sea-mew caroled with joy, as it whined by the loitering fleet,
Which cruised where the cod and the haddock shoal, at the rock-ribbed island's feet.
And it shouted and roared a pæan, to the heroes who'd carried a flag,
A bit of a piece of red, white, and blue, to the spot where the ice-drifts sag,
As it southward flew, it grew and it grew, 'til it roared out a rollicking psalm,
To Peary, MacMillan, Borup; brave travelers, silent and calm.
Southward it sang its slogan, where the tossing palm groves sway,
And it rolled out a cheer of three times three, for "Uncle Sam and the U. S. A.!"

Chapter 13

Pierre-Esprit Radisson

First Explorer of the West and Northwest, (1651-1710)

>Where sheldrakes dart on Lake Niege,
>Where the lazy beaver swim,
>He drove his blade and packed the trail,
>By the icy snow lake's rim.
>From the shores of Athabasca,
>To the caves of Saguenay,
>From the sleepy Mistassini,
>To the marsh of Hudson Bay;
>From the steppes of old Fort Caribou,
>From the glades of Fond du Lac,
>He slept and dwelt with redskins,
>And followed the unknown track.

It was at the trading post of Three Rivers on the St. Lawrence River, the year 1662, and the time, early in the morning, when the wood thrush had just begun his call. Strange things happened then, but these were frontier days when strange things used to happen, so do not be surprised when you learn what befell Pierre Radisson, son of a French emigrant to Canada, and then a youth of about seventeen years of age.

With two companions, young Pierre had gone out from the stockade to shoot ducks on Lake St. Peter, not far from this first home of the French emigrants to Canada.

The sportsmen were all young, for only young boys would have left the shelter of the fortification at this time, as all the Canadians knew that the dreaded Iroquois had been lying in ambush around the little settlement of Three Rivers, day and night, for a whole year. In fact, not a week passed but that some settler was set upon in the fields and left dead by the terrible redskins. Farmers had flocked to the little fortification and would only venture back to their broad acres when armed with a musket.

But these were only boys, and, like all boys, they went along, boasting how they would fight when the Indians came. One kept near the edge of the forest, on the lookout for the Iroquois, while the others kept to the water in quest of game. They had gone along in this manner for about three miles, when they met a fellow who was tending sheep.

"Keep out from the foot of the hills!" he called to them. "The Iroquois are there! I saw about a hundred heads rising out of the bushes about an hour ago."

The boys loaded their pistols and primed their muskets.

In a short time they shot some ducks, and this seemed to satisfy one of the young men. "I have had enough," said he. "I am going back to the stockade where I can be safe." "And I will go with you," said the second.

But young Radisson laughed at them.

"If you are afraid to go forward," said he, "I will go ahead by myself."

So the wild youth went onward, shooting game at many places, until, at length, he had a large number of geese, ducks, and teal. There were more than he could possibly carry, so, hiding in a hollow tree the game that he could not bring back, he began trudging towards Three Rivers. Wading swollen brooks and scrambling over fallen trees, he finally caught sight of the town chapel, glimmering in the sunlight against the darkening horizon above the river. He had reached the place where his comrades had left him, so he sat down to rest himself.

The shepherd had driven his sheep back to Three Rivers and there was no one near. The river came lapping through the rushes. There was a clacking of ducks as they came swooping down to their marsh nests and Radisson felt strangely lonely. He noticed, too, that his pistols were water-soaked. Emptying the charges, he re-loaded, then crept back to reconnoiter the woodland. Great flocks of ducks were swimming on the river, so he determined to have one more shot before he returned to the fort, now within easy hail.

Young Pierre crept through the grass towards the game, but he suddenly stopped, for, before him was a sight that rooted him to the ground with horror. Just as they had fallen, naked and scalped, with bullet and hatchet wounds all over their bodies, lay his comrades of the morning. They were stone dead, lying face upward among the rushes.

Radisson was too far away from the woods to get back to them, so, stooping down, he tried to reach a hiding place in the marsh. As he bent over, half a hundred tufted heads rose from the high grass, and beady eyes looked to see which way he might go. They were behind him, before him, on all sides of him,—his only hope was a dash for the cane-grown river, where he might hide himself until darkness would give him a chance to rush to the fort.

Slipping a bullet and some powder into his musket as he ran, and ramming it down, young Pierre dashed through the brushwood for a place of safety. Crash! A score of guns roared from the forest. He turned, and fired back, but; before he could re-load, an Iroquois brave was upon him, he was thrown upon his back, was disarmed, his hands were bound behind him with deer thongs, and he was dragged into the woods, where the Indians flaunted the scalps of his friends before his eyes. Half drawn, half driven, he was taken to the shore where a flotilla of canoes was hidden. Fires were kindled, and, upon forked sticks driven into the ground, the redskins boiled a kettle of water for the evening meal.

The Iroquois admired bravery in any man, and they now evinced a certain affection for this young Frenchman, for, in defiance of danger, they had seen him go hunting alone. When attacked, he had fired back at enough enemies to have terrified any ordinary Canadian. This they liked, so his clothing was returned to him, they daubed his cheeks with war paint, shaved his head in the manner of the redskinned braves, and, when they saw that their stewed dog turned him faint, they boiled him some meat in clean water and gave him some meal, browned upon burning sand. That night he slept beneath a blanket, between two warriors.

In the morning the Indians embarked in thirty-seven canoes, two redskins in each boat, with young Pierre tied to a cross-bar in one of them. Spreading out on the river, they beat their paddles upon the gunwales of their bateaux, shot off their guns, and uttered their shrill war cry,—"Ah-oh! Ah-oh! Ah-oh!"

The echoes carried along the wailing call, and in the log stockade the Canadians looked furtively at one another as the horrid sound was borne to them by the gentle wind. Then the chief stood up in his canoe, signaled silence, and gave three long blood-curdling yells. The whole company answered with a quavering chorus like wolf barks, and, firing their guns into the air, the canoes were driven out into the river, past the nestling log-stockade of Three Rivers, and up the current of the rushing stream. By sunset they were among the islands at the mouth of the river Richelieu, where were great clouds of wild-ducks, which darkened the air at their approach.

Young Pierre bore up bravely, determined to remain with his captors until an opportunity to escape presented itself. The red men treated him kindly, saying: "Chagon! Chagon! Be merry! Cheer up!" He was given a paddle and was told to row, which he did right willingly. Another band of warriors was met with on the river, and the prisoner was forced to show himself as a trophy of victory and to sing songs for his captors, which he did to the best of his ability. That evening an enormous camp-fire was kindled and the united bands danced a scalp-dance around it, flaunting the scalps of the two dead French boys from spear heads, and reënacted in pantomime all the episodes of the massacre, while the women beat on rude, Indian drums.

Pierre was now a thorough savage. He was given a tin looking-glass by which the Indians used to signal by the sun, and also a hunting knife. The Iroquois neared Lake Champlain where the river became so turbulent that they were forced to land and make a portage. Young Radisson hurried over the rocks, helping the older warriors to carry their packs. As night came on, he was the first to cut wood for the camp-fire.

It was now about a week since the redmen had left Lake St. Peter and they entered the gray waste of Lake Champlain. Paddling down its entire length, they entered the waters of beautiful Lake George, and, beaching the canoes upon its western bank, abandoned them: the warriors striking out through the forest for the country of the Iroquois. For two days they thus journeyed from the lake, when they were met by several women, who loaded themselves down with the luggage of the party, and accompanied the victorious braves to the village. Here the whole tribe marched out to meet them, singing, firing guns, shouting a welcome, dancing a war-dance of joy.

It was now time for young Pierre to run the gauntlet. Sometimes the white prisoners were slowly led along with trussed arms and shackled feet, so that they could not fail to be killed before they reached the end of the line. With Radisson it was different. He was stripped free and was told to run so fast that his tormentors could not hit him. He did this and reached the end of the human lane unscathed.

As the white boy dashed free of the line of his tormentors, a captive Huron woman, who had been adopted by the tribe, caught him and led him to her cabin, where she fed and clothed him. But soon a band of braves marched to her door, demanded his surrender, and took him to the Council Lodge of the Iroquois for judgment.

Radisson was led into a huge cabin, where several old men sat solemnly around a central fire, smoking their calumets, or peace pipes. He was ordered to sit down. A coal of fire was then put into the bowl of the great Council Pipe and it was passed reverently around the assemblage. The old Huron woman now entered, waved her arms aloft, and begged for the life of the young man. As she made her appeal, the old men smoked on silently with deep, guttural "ho-ho's" meaning "Yes—yes. We are much pleased." So she was granted permission to adopt Radisson as a son. The nerve and courage of the young French boy had thus saved his life. He must bide his time,—bye and bye, he would have an opportunity to escape.

It was soon autumn, the period of the hunt, so young Pierre set out into the forest with three savages in order to lay in a supply of meat for the winter months. One night, as the woodland rovers were returning to their wigwams, there came the sound of some one singing through the leafy thicket, and a man approached. He was an Algonquin brave, a captive among the Iroquois, and he told them that he had been on the track of bear since day-break. He was welcomed to the camp-fire, and, when he learned that Radisson was from Three Rivers, he immediately grew friendly with the captive white boy.

That evening, when the camp-fire was roaring and crackling so that the Iroquois could not hear what he said, the Indian told Radisson that he had been a captive for two years and that he longed to make his escape.

"Hist! Boy!" said he. "Do you love the French?" Pierre looked around cautiously.

"Do you love the Algonquins?" he replied.

"As I do my own mother," was the answer. Then, leaning closer, the warrior whispered: "Brother—white man—let us escape! The Three Rivers, it is not so far off! Will you live like a dog in bondage, or will you have your liberty with the French?" Then he lowered his voice. "Let us kill all three of these hounds to-night, when they are asleep, and then let us paddle away, up Lake Champlain, again to the country of our own people."

Radisson's face grew pale beneath his war paint. He hesitated to answer, and, as he looked about him, the suspicious Iroquois cried out:

"Why so much whispering?"

"We are telling hunting stories," answered the Algonquin, smiling.

This seemed to satisfy the Iroquois, for, wearied by the day's hunt, they soon dozed off in sleep and were snoring heavily: their feet to the glowing embers. Their guns were stacked carelessly against a tree. It was the time for action.

The French boy was terrified lest the Algonquin should carry out his threat, and so pretended to be asleep. Rising noiselessly, the captive redskin crept up to the fire and eyed the three sleeping Mohawks with no kindly glance. The redmen slept heavily on, while the cry of a whip-poor-will sounded ominously from the black and gloomy forest.

The crafty Algonquin stepped, like a cat, over the sleeping forms of the braves, took possession of their firearms, and then walked to where Radisson was lying. The French boy rose uneasily. As he did so, the Indian thrust a tomahawk into one of his hands, pointing, with a menacing gesture, to the three Iroquois. Radisson's hand shook like a leaf.

But the captive red man's hand did not shake, and, lifting his own hatchet, he had brained one of the sleeping redskins without more ado. Pierre endeavored to imitate the warrior, but, unnerved with the horror of it all, he lost hold of his tomahawk, just as it struck the head of the sleeping Iroquois. The redskin leaped to his feet, uttering a wild yell, which awakened the third sleeper. But he had no chance to rise, as the Algonquin felled him with one, swift blow, while Radisson, recovering his hatchet, hit the second red man with such force, that he fell back, lifeless.

Hurray! Radisson was free!

The Algonquin did not waste precious moments; but, hastily scalping the dead, he threw their bodies into the river, then, packing up all their possessions, they placed them in the canoe, took to the water, and slipped away towards Lake Champlain.

"I was sorry to have been in such an encounter," writes Radisson. "But it was too late to repent." The fugitives were a long way from Three Rivers, on the St. Lawrence, and they knew that many roving Iroquois were hunting in the country between them and the French settlement. They must go carefully, be perpetually on their guard, and then,—they would be among their own people again! Only, caution! caution! And never a sound at any time!

Traveling only at night, and hiding during the day, the fugitives crossed Lake Champlain, entered the Richelieu, and, after many portages, finally swept out upon the wide surface of Lake St. Peter, in the St. Lawrence. They paddled hard and were soon within a day's journey of Three Rivers, yet they were in greater danger then than at any time in the hazardous trip, as the Iroquois had infested this part of the St. Lawrence for more than a year, and often lay hidden in the rush-grown marshes and the wooded islands, waiting for some unsuspecting French Canadian to pass by. It was four o'clock in the morning when the Algonquin and white boy reached the side of Lake St. Peter. They cooked their breakfast, covered the fire, and lay down to sleep.

At six o'clock, the Algonquin shook Pierre by the shoulder, urging him to cross the lake to the Three Rivers side.

"The Iroquois are lurking about here," the French boy answered. "I am afraid to go. Let us wait until dark. Then, all will be well."

"No, no," answered the brave. "Let us paddle forward. We are past fear. Let us shake off the yoke of these whelps who have killed so many French and black robes (priests). If you do not come now, I will leave you, and I will tell the Governor that you were afraid to come."

Radisson consented to take a chance at getting to the stockade, although his judgment told him to wait until dark. So the canoe was pushed out from the rushes, and, with strong strokes, the flimsy boat was driven towards the north shore. They were half way across, when Pierre called out: "I see shadows on the water ahead."

The Indian, who was in the stern, stood up, saying:

"It is but the shadow of a flying bird. There is no danger."

So they kept on; but, as they progressed, the shadows multiplied, for they were the reflections of many Iroquois, hidden among the rushes. The fugitives now saw them, and, heading their canoe for the south shore, fled for their lives.

On, on they went; but, on, on, came the Iroquois. The redskins came nearer and nearer, there was a crash of musketry and the bottom of the canoe was punctured by a ball. The Algonquin fell dead with two bullet wounds in his head, while the canoe gradually filled with water, settled, and sank, with the young Frenchman clinging to the side. Now a firm hand seized him, and he was hauled into one of the canoes of the Iroquois.

The victors set up a shrill yelp of triumph. Then they went ashore, kindled a great fire, tore the heart out of the dead Algonquin, put his head on a pike, and cast the mutilated body into the flames. Radisson was bound, roped around the waist, and thrown down upon the ground, where he lay with other captives: two Frenchmen, one white woman, and twenty Hurons.

In seventeen canoes, the Iroquois now paddled up the Richelieu River for their own country, frequently landing to camp and cook, at which times young Pierre was pegged out on the sand, and left to be tortured by sand-flies and mosquitoes.

When they reached the village, Radisson was greeted with shouts of rage by the friends of the murdered Mohawks, who, armed with rods and skull-crackers (leather bags loaded with stones) rushed upon him and beat him sorely. As the prisoners moved on, the Hurons wailed the death dirge. But suddenly there broke from the throng of onlookers the Iroquois family that had adopted young Pierre. Pushing through the crowd of torturers, the mother caught Radisson by the hair, crying out: "Orimba! Orimba!" She then cut the thongs that bound him to the poles, and shoved him to her husband, who led the trembling young Frenchman to their own lodge.

"Thou fool," cried the old chief, turning wrathfully upon the young man. "Thou wast my son! Thou lovest us not, although we saved thy life! Wouldst kill me, too?" Then he shoved him to a mat upon the ground, saying: "Chagon —now be merry! It is a fine business you've gotten yourself into, to be sure."

Radisson sank to the ground, trembling with fear, and endeavored to eat something. He was relating his adventures when there was a roar of anger from the Iroquois outside, and, a moment later, the rabble broke into the lodge. He was seized, carried back to the other prisoners, and turned over to the torture. We will draw a veil over what now befell him.

After three days of misery the half-dead Frenchman was brought before the council of the Mohawk Chiefs. Sachem after sachem rose and spoke, while tobacco was sacrificed to the fire- god. The question to be decided was, could the Mohawks afford to offend the great Iroquois chief who was the French youth's friend? This chieftain wished to have the young man's life spared. Would they do so?

After much talk and passing of the peace-pipe, it was decided that the young man could go free. The captive's bonds were cut, he was allowed to leave the council chamber, and, although unable to walk, was carried to the lodge of his deliverer. For the second time his life had been saved. Spring came at last and the young Frenchman was taken on a raid amidst the enemies of the Iroquois. Then they went on a free-booting expedition against the whites of the Dutch settlements at Orange (Albany), which consisted, at that time, of some fifty thatched log-houses surrounded by the settlements of one hundred and fifty farmers. The raid was a bloodless one, the red warriors looting the farmers' cabins, emptying their cupboards, and drinking up all the beer in their cellars. Finally they all became intoxicated, and, as they wanted guns, the Dutch easily took advantage of them in trade.

Radisson had been painted like a Mohawk and was dressed in buckskin. For the first time in two years he saw white men, and, although he could not understand the Dutch language, it gave him great pleasure to see some one of his own race again.

As the white Mohawk moved about the fort, he noticed a soldier among the Dutch who was a Frenchman, and, at the same instant the soldier saw, that, beneath all the paint and grease, was a brother. They spoke to each other, threw their arms around one another's necks, and from that moment Radisson became the lion of Fort Orange.

The Dutch people crowded about him, shook his hand, offered him presents of wine and of money. They wished to ransom him at any price; but he was pledged to return to his Indian parents and he feared the revenge of the Mohawk braves. So he had to decline the kind offer of the white men, returning to his lodge in the Indian country, far more of a hero in the eyes of his Indian allies than ever before.

Young Pierre had not been back among the Iroquois for more than two weeks when he began to pine for the log fortress at Three Rivers. He loathed the filthy food, the smoky lodges, the cruelties of the Mohawks, and he longed to be once more among his own people. Hidden beneath all the grease and war paint was the true nature of the white man, and he determined to escape, even if he had to die for the attempt.

The white Indian left his lodge, early one morning in the month of September, taking only his hatchet, as if he were going to cut wood. Once out of sight of the Mohawk village, he broke into a run, following the trail, through the dense forests of the Mohawk Valley, towards Fort Orange. On, on, he ran until the morning, when, spent with fatigue, he fell exhausted to the ground. After a short sleep, he again arose, pressed forward through the brush, and finally came to a clearing in the forest where a man was chopping wood. He found that there were no redskins in the cabin, then, hiding in it, he persuaded the settler to carry a message to the Fort. While he was absent, he hid behind some sacks of wheat.

The frontiersman had been gone about an hour, when he returned with a rescue party, which conducted the young Frenchman to the Fort. Here he hid for three days, while a mob of Mohawks wandered through the stockade, calling for him by name, but they could not find him. Gifts of money from a Jesuit priest enabled him to take a ship to New York, then a settlement of five hundred houses, with stores, barracks, and a stone church. After a stay of three weeks the ex- Mohawk set sail for Amsterdam, where he arrived in January, 1674.

He took a ship for Rochelle, but alas! He there found that all of his relatives had moved to Three Rivers in New France. Why remain here? In a week's time he had embarked with the fishing fleet which yearly left France for the Great Banks, and came, early in the spring of 1675, to Isle Percée, at the mouth of the St. Lawrence. He was a week's journey from Three Rivers, but Algonquin canoes were on their way up the blue St. Lawrence for a fight with the Iroquois. He jumped into one of them, and, in a very short time, once more sprang ashore at the stockade of Three Rivers where he was welcomed as one risen from the dead.

Not long after this, we find Radisson at the stockade of Onondaga, a French fort built upon a hill above a lake upon the Oswego River. Here the French had established a post, the farthest in the wilderness; and here about sixty Frenchmen were spending the winter, waiting for the spring to break up the ice so that they could return to Quebec. The redskins seemed to be friendly; but, early in February, vague rumors of a conspiracy against them came to the ears of the white men. A dying Mohawk confessed to a Jesuit priest that the Iroquois Council had decided to massacre half the garrison, and to hold the other half captive until their own Mohawk hostages were released from Quebec. These were held there by the French to ensure good treatment of their own people at this far-distant fortress.

What were the French to do? Here they were, miles and miles from Three Rivers, surrounded by hostiles, with winter at hand. How could they escape? Radisson was quite equal to the emergency and proposed a way to outwit the savages, which was as cunning as it was amusing. He would invite all of the braves to a big feast, he would get them stupefied with food and with drink, then, when all were asleep, the sixty Frenchmen would take to their boats and would make a break for it down the river. A bold idea—this. Let us see how it worked out?

Radisson told the redskins that he had had a "big dream," a dream to the effect that the white men were to give a great feast to the Iroquois. They greeted the news with joy, and, as couriers ran through the forest, bidding the Mohawks to the banquet, the warriors hastened to the walls of Onondaga. To sharpen their appetites, they were kept waiting outside for two whole days. Meanwhile, inside the fort everything was made ready for a hasty departure. Ammunition was scattered in the snow; guns which could not be taken along were either burned or broken; canoes were prepared to be launched; all the live stock, except one solitary pig, a few chickens, and the dogs, was sacrificed for the feast. The soldiers cooked great kettles of meat and kept the redskins from peering into the stockade, lest they discover what was going on.

The evening of the second day arrived, and a great fire was kindled in the outer inclosure of the fort, between the two walls, where blankets were spread for the redskinned guests. Now the trumpets blew a deafening blast, the Mohawks shouted, and the French clapped their hands wildly. As the outer gates were thrown open, in trooped several hundred Mohawk warriors, who seated themselves in a circle around the fire, saying:

"Ugh! Ugh! We much hungry!"

Again the trumpets blared, and twelve enormous kettles of mince-meat were carried around the circle of guests. All dipped deeply into the steaming dish, while one Mohawk chieftain arose solemnly, saying:

"The French are the most generous people on earth. The Great Spirit has indeed blessed the French, to make them so kind to the Mohawks. We are truly glad to be at the feast with our white brothers."

Other speakers arose, proclaiming the great virtues of the French; but, before they had finished talking, there came a second and a third relay of kettles. Here were plates of salted fowl, of venison, and of bear. The

Indians gorged themselves, each looking at his neighbor to see if he could still eat.

"Cheer up! Cheer up!" cried Radisson, as he circled among the braves. "If sleep overcomes you, you must awake! Cheer up! Cheer up! Beat the drum! Blow the trumpet! Cheer up!"

The eyes of the Indians began to roll, for never before had they had such a banquet. Some shook their heads and lolled backwards, others fell over in the dead sleep which comes from long fasting, fresh air and overfeeding. By midnight all were sprawled upon the ground in deep slumber. The moment for action was at hand.

The French retired to the inner court, while the main gate was bolted and chained. The Indians were all outside the French quarters, so they could not see what was going on inside, even if they had been awake. Through the loop-hole of the gate ran a rope attached to a bell which was used to summon the sentry, and to this rope Radisson tied the only remaining pig, so that, when the Indians would pull the rope for admission, the noise of the disturbed porker would give the impression of a sentry's tramp, tramp on parade. Stuffed soldiers were placed around the palisades, so that, if an Indian should climb up to look into the fort, he would still see Frenchmen there.

The baggage was now stowed away in flat boats, and dugouts were brought out for the rest of the company. The night was raw and cold, while a thin sheeting of ice had formed upon the margin of the river. The fugitives were soon on board their craft, had pushed out into the stream, and were off; while, behind them, the redskins still lay around in a circle of stupid insensibility. Only the barking of a dog disturbed the quiet of the evening.

Piloted by the crafty Radisson, the French left Onondago on the 20th. day of March, 1678. On the evening of April 3rd. they came to Montreal, where they learned that New France had suffered intolerable insolence from the Iroquois all winter. On the 23rd, they moored safely under the walls of the citadel of Quebec, where all laughed heartily at the good trick which they had worked upon the bloodthirsty Mohawks.

When spring came and canoes could venture up the river, couriers brought word that the Mohawks at Onondago had been greatly deceived by the pig and the ringing bell. The stuffed figures had led them to believe that the French were there, for more than a week. Crowing of cocks had come from the chicken yard, dogs had bayed in the kennels, and whenever a curious brave had yanked the bell at the gate, he could hear the measured march of the sentry.

When seven days passed by, and not a white man came from the fort: "The black robes must be at prayers," whispered the Mohawks.

But they could not pray on for seven days. Suspicions of trickery flashed on the minds of the Iroquois, and a warrior climbed to the top of the palisade. It was empty, and the French had gone! Two hundred Mohawks immediately set out in pursuit, but there was much ice and snow, so that they had to return, cursing their stupidity, and the cleverness of Pierre Radisson.

Radisson did more than this, he discovered the Great Northwest. When a captive among the Mohawks, he had cherished boyish dreams of discovering many wild nations; and, when his brother-in-law, Groseillers, asked him to take a journey with him far to the westward, he only too readily acquiesced. Late one night in June, Groseillers and he stole out from Three Rivers, accompanied by Algonquin guides. They went as far as Green Bay, spent the winter there, then, when the spring sun warmed the land, they traveled westward, passed across what is now the State of Wisconsin, and reached a "mighty river rushing profound and comparable to the St. Lawrence." It was the upper Mississippi, now seen for the first time by white men.

The spring of 1679 found the explorers still among the prairie tribes of the Mississippi, and from them Radisson learned of the Sioux, a warlike nation to the West, who had no fixed abode, but lived by the chase and were at constant war with another tribe to the north, the Cree.

The two Frenchmen pressed westward, circled over the territory now known as Wisconsin, eastern Iowa and Nebraska, South Dakota, and Montana, and back over North Dakota and Minnesota to the north shore of Lake Superior.

Then Radisson made a snow-shoe trip towards Hudson's Bay and back again, living on moose meat and the flesh of beaver and caribou. Finally, after adventures exciting and hair-raising, he and Groseillers found their way to Three Rivers.

Although Radisson was not yet twenty-eight years of age, his explorations into the Great Northwest had won him both fame and fortune.

So this is the way that he spent his life. Voyaging, trapping, trading, he covered all this great, wild country, paddled up her rivers, fished in her lakes, smoked the pipe of peace in her settlements. In ten years' time he brought half a million dollars' worth of furs to an English trading company which employed him.

Yet, with all his explorations, all his adventures, all his trading, as he grew old, he remained as poor as one of the couriers de bois who used to paddle him up the streams of New France. Until the year 1710 he drew an allowance of £50 a year ($250) from the English Hudson Bay Trading Company, then payments seemed to have stopped. Radisson had a wife and four children to support, but what happened to him, or to them, is unknown to history.

Somewhere in the vast country of New France the life of this daring adventurer went out. And somewhere in that vast possession lies the body of this, the first white man to explore the Great Northwest. Oblivion hides all record of his death, and only the cry of the moose-bird, harsh, discordant—the true call of the wilderness—echoes over the unknown spot where lie, no doubt, the bones of this trickster of the Mohawks and explorer of the wastes of New France.

Memorial tablets have been erected in many cities to commemorate La Salle, Champlain, and other discoverers. Radisson has no monument, save the memory of a valiant man-of-the-woods, reverently held in the hearts of all those who love the hemlock forests, the paddle, the pack, and the magnetic call of the wilderness.

Chapter 14

FATHER MARQUETTE

TRUE MAN OF GOD, AND EXPLORER OF THE MIGHTY MISSISSIPPI, (1637-1675)

> The wild goose honked its message of fear,
> As it winged away o'er the marshes sere,
> And the little brown teal went, "quack, quack, quack,"
> it fled from the man all dressed in black.
> But he, a priest, had a smile on his lips,
> For he saw a stream with the sunset kissed,
> And he raised aloft his hand, with a cross,
> And blessed the waves, which the wild winds toss.

Many, many years ago, when the Indian tribes inhabited the wilderness of North America, a good priest came among them to teach them the ways of Christ. He was a Frenchman called Père, or Father Marquette, and he had been born at Laon, France, June 1st, 1627.

Early choosing the profession of priesthood, he entered the Jesuit College at Nancy, where he finally graduated, a man of saintly character, accurate learning and distinguished culture. Yet, disdaining to remain in France, he eagerly looked forward to adventure in the wilderness of North America, and was consequently overjoyed to receive an order to proceed to

Canada, then termed New France. He set sail, arrived at the struggling village of Quebec, September 20th, 1666, and, in October of that same year, was sent to Three Rivers, to begin the study of the Indian language and to obtain some knowledge of the life of a missionary.

Some of you have doubtless camped in the Canadian wilderness, where you have seen the Indians, trappers, and guides, who hover around the outfitter's store, where one buys his food for a canoe trip into the woods. The Canadian wilderness, then, was much wilder than it is now. In those days there were thousands of redskins, where now there are only a few, and in those days the red men were really ferocious, often engaging in great battles with each other, and torturing their prisoners with fire-brands and also making them run the gauntlet.

The French were very kind to the redskins and sent many Jesuit missionaries among them, so the red men liked the Frenchmen, even as they disliked the English. The Englishmen treated them like some inferior sort of dogs, whereas the French priests endeavored to help them in every way possible; taught them medicine, cooking and house-building, and looked after them when they were ill.

Father Marquette was accustomed to the refinement and culture of the France of his day, so it must have been a curious experience for him to be suddenly thrown into the wilderness life. Yet he settled down to his career of a missionary with zeal and enthusiasm, taking up a residence with one Father Drulettes, who lived in a log hut. Here he spent two years of hard study and still harder life, eagerly learning woodcraft, canoeing and the Indian language, which was to be of great assistance to him in later years.

Time passed pleasantly by. Finally it was agreed that young Father Marquette knew sufficient "Indian talk" to make himself understood by the redskins, so, in April, 1668, he was sent forth among the Ottawas. With several others he left Three Rivers for Montreal, traveling by canoe, and from this small settlement journeyed to the Sault de Sainte Marie, a trading post built where the waters of Lake Superior rush tumultuously through boiling rapids towards Lake Huron. Here was the mission of St. Mary, the headquarters of the Jesuit fathers who labored among the Ottawa Indians.

Here also were many white fur traders, who wished to barter with the red men.

The Indians were many. The Ottawa tribe consisted of the Chippewas, Beavers, Creeks, Ottawas, Hurons, Menomonees, Pottawattomies, Sacs, Foxes, Winnebagoes, Miamis, Illinois and the Sioux. The natives lived along the shores of Lake Superior, Lake Huron, and through the woods of Michigan and Wisconsin, near the banks of the many rivers in this region.

The "Soo" or Sault Ste. Marie is a busy place to-day, and it was a busy place then, for it was the heart of all Indian activity, being the place from which all the redskins set out upon their trips to the wilderness and to Quebec and Montreal. Now the great locks make continuous travel by water possible between Buffalo and Detroit. In our times as many ships pass this point as did birch-bark canoes in the year of 1600. Yet then, there was as much trade and barter at the "Soo," in comparison to the Indian and white population, as there is now, with the vast population which surrounds it.

Father Marquette enjoyed himself greatly among the redskins, and particularly loved the long canoe trips in the beautiful rivers and lakes. He was much respected by the Indians, who called him, "the good brother," and so successful was he in converting them to Christianity that he was sent from Mission Sault Ste. Marie to Mission La Pointe, on Lake Superior, where he arrived in September, 1669. Here he labored among the peaceful red men until the post was abandoned in 1671, because the warlike Sioux had determined to fight with the Hurons.

For the poor Hurons to accept the gauge of battle would have meant their utter destruction, so they fled to the south, taking up their residence at Michillimackinac, on Lake Huron. Thither went the noble Father Marquette, and, seated among them in his black robe, took part in all their many deliberations. He baptized their children, married their young braves, and taught the gospel of Jesus Christ. Here he established the Mission St. Ignace and built a beautiful chapel, to which, years later, worn out and exhausted by his serious labors in the wilderness, his body was carried by the redskins for burial.

As the good priest lived among the red men, he heard stories of a great river which lay to the westward, so he determined to discover and explore it. Wandering trappers brought him news of this stream, and, as he now knew how to talk with these wild men of the north, he easily learned all that they could tell him about it. His heart and mind were stirred with the fever of the adventurer. He must, he would go and see what lay far to the westward where were ferocious redskins, wild beasts, and unknown watercourses.

As dreams of exploration floated through the pure and boyish mind of the good Jesuit missionary, a Frenchman, called Joliet, arrived from Quebec. Ah, but he was a roving dog, this Joliet, and, when he heard that the priest was contemplating a trip of exploration and adventure, up went his hands, a smile came to his face, and he exclaimed, "Oh, my good Father Marquette, I am the man to go with you! I, and I alone, shall be your companion in this venture into the wilderness. Here's my hand upon it!"

So the two adventurers clasped hands, then set about to secure five stout canoemen with backwoods experience, to paddle with them to the great unknown. It was not difficult to find such fellows (couriers de bois, they were called).

On May 17th., 1673, Marquette and Joliet, with five as staunch Frenchmen as ever lifted a pack and poled a canoe, started upon an ever-memorable journey of exploration. They went in but two canoes—big birch-bark fellows to be sure—and carried with them guns, clothing, food, robes, books, and scientific instruments. 'Twas a good load to stow away in such small bateaux, but they must have been larger canoes than we use to-day, where only three can comfortably travel. There were two brave men at the head of this expedition; they loved God; they loved France, and they strove to do something for God and Fatherland. They succeeded in both.

From the little mission of St. Ignace the party of explorers followed the right shore of Lake Michigan in a westerly and southerly direction. They first stopped at Green Bay, where they visited the tribe of Menomonees, so

Figure 14. Marquette and Joliet Discovering the Mississippi River.

called after the wild rice which there grew luxuriously in the rich mud bottoms and swamplands. The red men were very hospitable and begged the good priest in his black robe not to proceed farther. "You will meet a nation which never shows mercy to strangers," said one chieftain. "They will break your heads with their stone hatchets. The great river which you look for is very dangerous. It is full of horrible monsters which will devour your canoes. There is a big Demon in the path which swallows all who approach him, and the heat is so great that you will all die."

To this the Jesuit missionary replied,

"I do not fear these things, my red brothers. My God is with me and he will protect me from all these demons."

So the voyagers bade the doubting redskins good-bye, turned the bows of their canoes towards the setting sun, and went forth upon their journey.

The paddles drove the light birch-bark boats along the shore of Lake Michigan. Many times the voyagers gazed at the magnificent scenery with rapt attention, for they were in the heart of the wilderness, and, as lovers of nature, they enjoyed the magnificence of wooded shore-line and wave-tossed water. On, on, they went, passing from Green Bay to the southern end, and down this into Lake Winnebago: blue, forest-hidden, and shimmering in the rays of the brilliant sunlight. At the end of this beautiful sheet of water was an Indian village, where now is the town of Oshkosh. Here were many redskins, Mascoutens, Miamis and Kickapoos, some of whom had migrated thither from Virginia and Ohio. Pere Marquette was greeted hospitably, for many of these Indians were Christians and had erected a handsome cross in the center of their town, adorned with skins of the fox and the beaver, with red belts, bows and arrows, all offerings to the Great Manitou, or God of all Gods.

The wandering priest conducted religious services, then asked his hearers for two guides to pilot them to the mighty river, which he heard was to the westward. Joyfully the red men gave him two Miami braves, who, leading him to the branches of the upper Fox, showed him where to take to the land and portage across country to the head-waters of the Weskonsing, now the Wisconsin River. The birch-bark boats were soon floating past virgin forests, in which robins and cat-birds caroled songs of welcome to these, the first white men who had ever sailed past upon the surface of the stream, The Miami guides now departed and the adventurers went forward alone.

For seven days the paddles drove the shallow canoes down the slow-moving Wisconsin, and then, upon the morning of the eighth day, the waters widened and the couriers de bois with their venturesome man-of-God suddenly paddled into the muddied current of the mighty Mississippi, or Great River. It was a point where the Father of Waters was a mile across and was fifty-three feet deep, so, as Pere Marquette gazed upon the turbid current, he had "a joy which he could not express." For days he had journeyed westward to view the fabled river, and now he saw that wonderful stream of which the wandering fur traders and redskins had told him at the far distant mission of St. Ignace.

It was the tenth of June. Marquette had left the quiet mission on May the seventeenth, nearly a month before this; the journey, so far, had been pleasant, but what lay beyond? Hostile Indians, fever, treacherous currents, death in the stream and death upon the shore! Yet, on, on, went Pere Marquette until he had reached the mouth of the Arkansas. Here he halted, for he believed that he was within three days' journey of the ocean. The good priest was feverish, for the malarial mosquito hovered over the yellow current of the Mississippi then, even as he does now. Yet, what cared he? His work had been well done and he had added much to the glory of France and to the renown of the Jesuit brotherhood.

Again and again, as they descended the stream, the canoes had struck the backs of monster fish, the sturgeons, which looked and felt like great tree trunks in the water. The boatmen had landed, every day, and had shot wild turkeys, ducks and prairie hens. Near the spot where is now the town of Rock Island, they saw great herds of bison, or buffalo, and they marveled at their stupidity and their ugliness. Whenever the explorers landed they kept a strict guard, for fear of an Indian attack, and as each evening came on, they made a small fire on shore to cook their meals, then entered the two canoes, paddled into the stream, and slept as far from the bank as possible.

As the French adventurers came down the mighty Mississippi, there were, of course, many meetings with the various Indian tribes which had their homes upon its banks. On the 25th. day of June, they saw the tracks of men upon the water's edge and a narrow, beaten path across the prairie. "It must be a road leading to a village," said Marquette; "we will reconnoiter it and see what is there!"

Recommending themselves to God, Marquette and Joliet undertook to investigate, and silently followed the narrow path. They walked onward for about two miles and then heard voices. Before them was an Indian village. They halted, and then advanced, shouted with all their energy. The redskins swarmed from their huts, much excited, but, seeing the Black Robes, of whom the traveling Hurons had told them, they quieted down, sending four of their old men to meet the white voyagers.

As the Indians approached, they bore, in their hands, tobacco pipes, finely ornamented and adorned with various feathers. They walked slowly, with the pipes raised to the sun and said nothing at all. These were calumets, or peace pipes, which they carried. As Marquette and Joliet walked towards the village, with an Indian on either side, they saw before them an old man standing before a lodge, with his hands outstretched and raised towards the sun. Looking intently at the priest and his companion, he said:

"How beautiful is the sun, O Frenchmen, when you come to visit us! All our town awaits thee, and thou shalt enter all our cabins of peace. Welcome to the land of the Illinois. Welcome, thrice welcome!"

The visitors entered the cabin, where was a crowd of red men, who kept silence, but eagerly gazed upon the strangers. Finally several spoke, saying:

"Well done, brothers, to visit us!"

Now all sat down, the peace pipe was passed around, they smoked, and then conversed in sign- language. But soon messengers arrived from the Grand Sachem of the Illinois, inviting the Frenchmen to visit his town, where he wished to hold a council with them.

So the seven explorers started for the village of the Grand Sachem, attended by a vast crowd of red men, who, never having seen a Frenchman before, could not apparently see enough of them. At length they reached the lodge of the Grand Sachem, who stood in his doorway holding his calumet, or peace pipe, towards the sun.

"Welcome, my white brothers," said he. "Welcome to the land of the Illinois."

Marquette stepped forward, and, presenting the old man with four separate gifts of beads and of knives, said:

"With this first gift, O Sachem, do I march in peace to visit the nations on the great river, which courses to the sea. With this second, I declare that God, the mighty creator, has pity on you, and it is for you to acknowledge and obey him. With this third, I declare that the Great Chief of the French informs you that he has spread peace everywhere, and has overcome the Iroquois, the enemies of you all, and has put them down forever. With this fourth I beg you to tell me the way to the sea, so that I can reach it without having trouble with the nations which I must pass in order to reach it."

This speech pleased the Great Sachem mightily, and rising, he laid his hand upon a small Indian child, saying:

"I thank thee, Black Gown and thee, Frenchmen, for taking so much pains to come and visit us. Never has the earth been so lovely nor the sun so bright as to-day. Never has our river been so calm or so free from rocks, for your canoes have removed them as they passed. Never has our tobacco had so fine a flavor, nor our corn appeared so beautiful as we behold it to-day. Here is my son that I give thee, so that thou mayest know my heart. I pray thee to take pity on me and all my nation. Thou knowest the Great Spirit who has made us all, then speak thou to him and hear thou his words; ask thou him to give me life and health, and to come and dwell amongst us, that we may know him."

Saying this, he gave the little Indian boy to Marquette and then presented him with a calumet, or peace pipe. He then urged the Frenchmen to proceed no farther and not to expose themselves to the dangers that would meet them with hostile tribes:

"I would esteem it a great happiness to lose my life for the glory of Jesus Christ,—he who has made us all," replied Marquette.

The old Sachem marveled much at this answer.

After several days of pleasant intercourse with the Illinois, the voyagers again took to their canoes and sailed southward towards the mouth of the Mississippi. Marquette left the little Indian boy behind him, for he did not wish to take him from his father. They had not gone very far, when they passed a rocky promontory where two great monsters had been painted upon the brown stones by some Indian artist.

"They are as large as a calf," says Marquette in his diary. "They have horns on their heads like those of a deer, a horrible look, red eyes, a beard like a tiger, a face somewhat like a man's, a body covered with scales, and so long a tail that it winds all around the body, passing above the head and going back between the legs, ending somewhat like a fish's tail. Green, red, and black are the colors composing this picture."

Fortunately there were no monsters in the country similar to these awful pictures, and the worst that the explorers encountered were dangerous masses of fallen trees, through which the canoes had a difficult time to wend a tortuous passage.

Near the mouth of the Ohio River the Frenchmen passed a part of the shore much dreaded by the redskins, who thought that an evil Manitou lived there, who devoured all travelers. The Illinois had warned the good priest to avoid the place. Yet the evil monster turned out to be a small bay full of dangerous rocks, through which the current of the river whirled about with a furious commotion, driving the canoes through a narrow channel filled with frothing spray and whirling spume. The couriers de bois sat tight, paddled hard, and pulled away from this peril.

Yet death soon stared the navigators in the face, for, when they reached the mouth of the Arkansas, armed warriors saw them, plunged into the river, and approached the two canoes, uttering fierce battle cries. Others came from the bank in wooden boats, hurling wooden clubs at the Frenchmen. Many redskins on the shore seized bows and arrows, pointing them at the explorers in a menacing manner. It was certainly a ticklish position and one that called for all the presence of mind that brave Pere Marquette possessed.

Rising in his canoe, the good priest held up the calumet, or peace pipe, which the Illinois had given him.

It apparently had no effect on the young braves, and they came swimming along, knives held in their teeth, ready and eager for a hand-to-hand battle in the muddy water.

Again the good priest raised the pipe of peace.

This time it had some effect, for some old men on the bank called to the young braves to desist in their attack, saying:

"Brothers, our young men shall not hurt you. Come ashore and we will have a big feast. Ugh! Ugh! You are welcome here."

So the voyagers heaved sighs of relief, paddled ashore, and had a grand banquet. Next day, ten of the men of this tribe guided them farther down the stream, and introduced them to the next tribe, which lived opposite the mouth of the Arkansas River.

They seemed to like good eating as well as do the natives of Arkansas in our day, for they had a noble banquet at which was served boiled dog, roast corn, and watermelon.

As I have said before, Father Marquette was suffering much with fever. As for his companions, they wished to return, for, said one: "If we go farther south, some Spaniards will capture us, or we will be killed by fiercer Indians than we have yet met with."

So they started to ascend the muddy river, toiling terribly against the current, but ever watchful of a night attack, and careful to sleep in the canoes, well away from the bank. Yet on, on, they went towards the north until the mouth of the river Illinois was reached. Into this they turned, paddled to its source, portaged into gray Lake Michigan, and soon were homeward bound for the busy post of Sault Ste. Marie. Marquette was quite ill with the fever and worn out with the exertion of the long journey, so at Green Bay he remained at the Jesuit mission of St. Francis Xavier, established there some years before. Joliet, on the other hand—apparently an iron man—was feeling splendidly. He had traveled only 2,767 miles in a birch canoe and was as well and hearty as when he had started. A true athlete, this Joliet, and one who must have had muscles of steel!

It was now September, and the explorers had been away for five months. It was also the time of stress and of storm on the Great Lakes, so it was thought best to pass the winter quietly at the little mission, there to write up the report of this wonderful journey. Both adventurers, therefore, sat down to rest, busying themselves in editing their journals. Marquette's alone has been preserved; as for Joliet's, his was upset in his canoe, when returning to Quebec in the following Spring, and all of his papers were lost in the frothing current of the raging La Chine rapids of the Ottawa River, near Montreal. Marquette's account, with maps drawn from memory, reached his superiors in the Jesuit mission at Quebec, and they are to-day of great interest to historians, geographers, and antiquarians.

On the way to Green Bay, the good priest had promised the Illinois Indians that he would return to them in the spring, in order to preach the gospel. Although much shattered in health, because of the fever which had fastened itself upon him, he again started south in October, 1674. Dismissing his great accomplishment from his mind, again he turned to teach the savages the words of Christ. Reaching the Chicago River, he found it covered with ice, so he remained at a poor log cabin, near the shore of Lake Michigan. He was ill, but brave, and, when the warm breath of spring again brought tassels to the willows, this noble priest of God pushed southward to the country of the friendly Illinois.

The redskins loved the peaceful soldier of the cross and welcomed him, "as an angel from Heaven." Easter time soon came, and a great service was held for the red men and their wives and children. First the priest presented the chiefs with gifts of wampum to attest his love and the importance of his mission, then he explained the doctrine of Christianity and his reason for journeying to this wild and distant land. "I cannot stay longer," he said, in conclusion, "but the peace of God be with you."

The children of the forest listened to him with great joy and appreciation, and, at the conclusion of his address, begged him to return to them again. They escorted him to his canoe with great pomp and ceremony, many of the warriors accompanying him for thirty miles. Then they waved "good-bye" saying: "Come again to us, good father, for we love you right well. Come again, for you are truly a brother of the Great Spirit."

Alas! The good priest's strength now began to fail him and he became so ill and weak that he had to be carried by his faithful attendants. The season was stormy, and, as the Frenchmen paddled northward towards Green Bay, they had to wait in the land-locked harbors of the St. Joseph River, the Kalamazoo, the Grand, and the Muskegon. The white-caps raged on Lake Michigan, so that it was not safe for the frail birch-bark canoe to venture upon the tossing waves.

Poor Father Marquette! Your journeys are almost over! Ill, weak, exhausted, the gentle priest had to be carried upon the shoulders of his faithful couriers de bois.

"Take me to the shore," he said, weakly. "Build me a cabin and let me there give up my soul to Christ. I cannot live much longer and it is well. God's will be done."

Near the present city of Ludington, upon a plot of rising ground, the expiring Marquette selected a place to die. His companions made a rude, log cabin, laid him upon a bed of evergreens, over which were stretched his blankets, and, as the white-breasted woodthrush sang a soft cadence from the branch of the wild apple tree, the gentle soul of the explorer and Jesuit Missionary went to the Great Beyond. His rough boatmen clustered about him with tears in their eyes, and they have said that, as the noble man-of-God awaited Death, his countenance beamed and was aglow with the spark of a curious and brilliant radiance.

Spring came. Some Huron Indians, whom Marquette had instructed at his mission at La Pointe, heard of his death and burial as they were returning from a hunt in the vast woods of northern Michigan. They sought the grave of this good man, whom they had so tenderly loved. With reverent hands they removed him from his forest sepulchre, carried him to their canoe, and started back to the little chapel which he had built at St. Ignace.

Thirty canoes formed a funeral procession which passed along the Great Lakes for nearly two hundred and fifty miles. When the mission was reached, the cortége approached the land, where a vast concourse of Indians, trappers, soldiers, priests, and half-breeds, paid reverence to this sweet-souled Jesuit missionary. Here, in the little church, he was laid to rest, and here, in 1877, a splendid monument was erected to the memory of that noble Christian gentleman, who had floated down the turbid current of the Mississippi in a memorable journey of exploration. Pax vobiscum, Pere Marquette!

THE BURIAL OF GOOD FATHER MARQUETTE.

Lift him gently, redskinned brothers, let no voice disturb his rest,
Peace is here, the great blue heron wings his way from out the West.
The tiny wren is gently trilling; the swallow dips and darts around,
As the veery carols sweetly: "True! His equal ne'er'll be found."

Softly, softly, tread so lightly, to the border of the lake;
Bow your heads and keep the silence, as the bending branches shake.
Place him in the birch barque's bottom, cover him with blankets fine,
Paddle gently, oh, so gently, as the wind sobs through the pine.

Yea! the wind speaks, and it whispers, as the cortége wanders past,
"Marquette! Marquette! Son of Jesus! You have reached the land of rest!

In the Kingdom of the Blessed, in the Vale of shadows dim,
Marquette! Marquette! Son of Jesus! You will rest at last with Him."

And the wild goose—Old Shebogah—honks a pæan from the sky,
Saying: "Farewell, farewell, brother, would that I, myself could die,
So that I could wander with you through the vale of shadowy tears,
Would that I could traverse with you, through the mist of golden years!"

And the squirrel—little Ooquah—chatters shrilly from the glade;
"Farewell! Farewell! Father, when you are gone I'll be afraid.
Yea, I'll hide from men and maidens, for my friend has passed away,
Farewell! Farewell! Father! Sad the scene and sad the day!"

And the beaver, sleek and square-tailed, casts his brown eyes on the lake,
Sobbing, mutt'ring; "Farewell! Father! All my kin obeisance make.
You, a good man, never harmed us; you, a brave man, never killed;
Farewell! Farewell! Father! Man of God in kindness skilled."

And the blue jay—bad Mootsito—scolding cries out from the oak,
"Good night! Good night! Father!
Would that I could be your cloak,
Would that I could travel with you, would that I could shield from harm,
Good night! Farewell! Father! The woods are cold. They've lost their charm."
Gently! Gently! Paddling northward, past the shallow pebbled bays,
See the cortége wanders slowly, near the scenes of other days,
When the good priest taught the Hurons how to live in peace and love,
Taught them how to like each other, true to Him who is above.

So they journey, while the forest echoes with the psalm of Death,
So they journey, sad and lonely, 'midst the balsam's balmy breath.
Then, at last, they reach the Mission, here sad rites they chant for him

Who has led them gently onward, through the glades of ignorance dim.

Trappers, soldiers, priests and redskins, bare their heads at St. Ignace,
Weeping, sobbing, bid him "Farewell!" he, the leader of their race.
Weeping, sobbing, cry out: "Vale!" While the heron wings away,
Croaking: "Good night, good night, Father! Sad the scene and sad the day!"

Chapter 15

ROBERT DE LA SALLE

FRENCH ADVENTURER, AND EXPLORER OF THE VALLEY OF THE MISSISSIPPI, (1643-1687)

> From Tadoussac the eagles scream; their wild cries sound alarming,
> As up the stream a vessel sails, her steersman a Prince Charming.
> A man of iron—valiant, strong, his name the Sieur La Salle,
> Who loved the hemlock forests from Lachine to Roberval.
> Alas! he ventured to the West where redskins wish to kill,
> There left his bones—'neath barren stones—where Frenchmen wander still.

While good Father Marquette was gliding over the muddied waters of the Mississippi, gazing at wonderful sights which no Frenchman had dreamed of heretofore, a man lived upon the banks of the St. Lawrence who brooded over projects of peril and adventure and gazed wistfully towards the Far West. This was no other than Robert, Chevalier de La Salle, a Frenchman who had come to Canada about the year 1667. He had been born at Rouen, in Normandy, of a noble family, and had been well educated in a Jesuit seminary.

Urged onward by a desire for both adventure and money, this vigorous young blade emigrated to Canada. Here he traveled up and down the great river St. Lawrence from Tadoussac to Sault Ste. Marie, and busied himself in trading European merchandise for beaver, bear, and other skins. He built houses for the storage of furs and merchandise, made excursions among the Indian tribes bordering on the shore of Lake Ontario, and penetrated as far as the Huron country in the north, where he lived for some time among the redskins, learning their life, their manners, and their language.

Perhaps some of you have taken the steamer at Toronto, have threaded your way among the beautiful Thousand Isles, and have shot through the foaming spray of the Lachine rapids, before reaching the city of Montreal. This seething cataract was named by the adventurous La Salle, for he hoped to find the St. Lawrence leading into the China Sea, and, to commemorate this anticipation, called the trading station, upon the Island of Montreal—La Chine (or the China) a name which has fastened itself to the rapids, and a name which it has borne to the present day. Here the adventurous Frenchman was resting when word was brought to him of the expedition of Marquette and Joliet. He felt certain that the Mississippi discharged itself into the great Gulf of Mexico, a fact which inflamed his desire to complete the discovery of that mighty watercourse. He wished to found colonies upon its banks and to open up new avenues of trade between France and the vast countries of the West. Nor did he lose his visions of China and Japan. From the head-waters of the Mississippi, he still hoped to find a passage to those distant countries, and thus, stirred with ideas of conquest and glory for his beloved France, he made a voyage to his native shores towards the end of the year 1677, hoping to gain assistance from the King for his ambitious designs.

The French monarch gave a ready ear to the talk of the venturesome Canadian. He was authorized to push his discoveries as far as he chose to the westward, and to build forts wherever he should think proper. In order to meet the large expense of his labors he was given the exclusive traffic in buffalo skins. Yet he was also forbidden to trade with the Hurons and other Indians, who usually brought furs to Montreal, for fear that he would interfere with the established traders and incur their jealousy and displeasure.

La Salle had the true love of adventure, a passion for exploring unknown lands, and an ambition to build up a great name for himself which should rival that of the early discoverers and conquerors of the New World. He wished, in fact, to die great. Let us see how he succeeded!

Two months after receiving this patent, the adventurer sailed from the shores of France, accompanied by the Chevalier Tonty, the Sieur de La Motte, and a pilot, ship-carpenters, mariners and other persons, about thirty in all. He had also a quantity of arms and ammunition, with a store of anchors, cordage, and other materials necessary for rigging the small vessels which he had determined to construct for the navigation of the lakes.

He arrived at Quebec near the end of September; but here he remained no longer than was necessary to arrange his affairs, for he hastened forward, passed up the dangerous rapids of the St. Lawrence in canoes, and at length reached Fort Frontenac, which he had erected at the eastern extremity of Lake Ontario, where the St. Lawrence issues from that great, blue inland sea. La Salle was eager for exploration. Busily he prepared to build and equip a vessel above the Falls of Niagara, so that he could navigate the upper lakes. His men worked hard and had, before long, fitted out a brigantine of ten tons in which they stowed away everything needed for the construction of a second vessel. This barque had been made at Fort Frontenac, the year before, with two others, which were used for bringing supplies. It was a small boat, but was suitable for the purpose.

In order to have any success in building a fort and a ship on the waters of the Niagara River, it was necessary to have the good will of the red men who lived in the surrounding country. The Senecas here had their hunting grounds, and they were a powerful tribe, excellent in the hunting field, bloodthirsty on the field of war. So La Motte had orders from La Salle to go on an embassy to this nation, to hold a council with the chiefs, explain his object, and gain their consent.

With some well-armed men, La Motte consequently traveled about thirty miles through the woods, and came, at length, to the great village of these redskins. Before a roaring council fire, around which the Indians gathered with their usual grave and serious countenances, both white men and red delivered many speeches. The French promised to establish a blacksmith at Niagara, who should repair the guns of the red men, and, as a result of this guarantee, the Senecas gave them permission to establish a trading place and fort in the wilderness. Well satisfied with the mission, La Motte and his companions went back to Niagara.

La Salle soon arrived, sailing thither from Fort Frontenac in one of his small vessels, laden with provisions, with merchandise, and materials for rigging the new ship: the first to glide over the waves of these great western lakes. In person he visited the Seneca Indians, and, by soft speech and flattering words, secured their friendship and good-will.

Yet he had enemies, too, for the monopoly which he had gained from the government and the large scale upon which he conducted his affairs, raised, against him, a host of traducers among the traders and merchants of Canada. In order to thwart his designs, they told the Indians that his plans of building forts and ships on the border was in order to curb their power. Agents were sent among the redskins in order to sow the seeds of hostility to this ambitious Frenchman.

These moves against him were well known to La Salle, yet it did not put an end to his plans. About two miles above the Falls of Niagara, he selected a place for a dock-yard at the outlet of a creek, on the western side of the Niagara River. Here the keel of the new vessel was laid, and, in a very short time, her form began to appear. An Indian woman brought word that a plot had been hatched to burn the vessel, while it was on the stocks, yet the redskins did not molest it, and soon she proudly glided into the water. She was called the Griffin, in honor of the Count de Frontenac, who had two griffins upon his coat of arms.

It was the month of August, a time of softness and mellow sunlight in the Canadian wilderness, when, bathed in a flood of radiance, the sails of the Griffin were spread to the winds of Lake Erie. Heretofore, only birch-bark canoes had floated upon the surface of this wind-tossed sheet of water, now a real vessel was plowing a westward course over the rocking billows. The voyage was a prosperous one, and, on the 27th. day of

August, the little company of explorers, thirty-four in all, reached the Island of Mackinac, where the redskinned denizens of the forest looked with wonder and amazement upon this ship, the first which they had ever seen, calling her the great wooden canoe.

The Sieur de La Salle dressed himself in a scarlet cloak, in order to make an impression upon the redskins, and, attended by some of his soldiers, made a visit of ceremony to the head men of the village. Here his missionaries celebrated mass, and here he was received and entertained with much civility by the red men. Yet, although the redskins showed him much courtesy on the surface, their minds had been poisoned by the lies which had been circulated among them by his enemies, and for the same reason several of his followers had deserted. Not deterred by this happening, La Salle again entered his ship, hoisted sail, and soon was coasting along the northern borders of Lake Michigan.

After a voyage of about a hundred miles the Griffin reached Green Bay, where anchor was cast before a small island at its mouth. This island was inhabited by Pottawattomies, and here La Salle found several Frenchmen, who had preceded him in birch canoes, had gathered a supply of stores, and had also collected a vast quantity of furs. With these he loaded his vessel; sent it back to Niagara, for the purpose of satisfying his creditors; and ordered his navigators to return as soon as possible, and to pursue their voyage to the mouth of the Miami River at the south-eastern extremity of Lake Michigan.

The adventurers now remaining consisting of fourteen persons, who were soon paddling down the west shore of Lake Michigan in four bark canoes, laden with carpenters' tools, a blacksmith's forge, merchandise, and arms. After a stormy passage, they reached the mouth of the Miami River, since called the St. Joseph. Winter was approaching, hostile natives were near, so La Salle determined to build a fort. A hill was selected as the proper position for the stockade, the bushes were chopped down and logs were cut and hewn, so that a breastwork could be constructed, inclosing a space about eighty feet long, by forty broad. It was surrounded by palisades and was called Fort Miami.

All hands were thus kept busy during the month of November. In spite of this occupation, the men were very discontented, for they had no other food but the flesh of bears, which some Indian hunters killed in the woods. The Frenchmen did not like this, and wished to go into the woods in order to hunt deer and other game. This permission was refused by La Salle, as he saw that they were more bent upon desertion than upon assisting in improving the larder.

As they thus grumbled and worked at the edge of the wilderness, the Chevalier de Tonty came down the lake with two canoes well stocked with deer which he had recently killed. Hurrah! Here was a different kind of meat, at last, and this cheered the spirits of all the company. Yet there was bad news, also, for the good Chevalier brought word of the total loss of the ship which had brought them hither. No sight had ever been had of her, and, although the red men, who lived along the shores of Lake Michigan were closely questioned, no one brought any word of the ill-fated Griffin, which doubtless had been swallowed up by the waves of Lake Michigan, while on her way from the island of Mackinac. La Salle was much distressed, yet he had become accustomed to the buffeting of ill fortune in the wilderness, and, consequently turned again towards the wilderness with renewed courage and resolution to go onward, to explore, and to bring back news of these virgin forests and this interesting country.

An Indian hunter, who had been sent out to look for deer, came and told them where there was a portage to the head-waters of the Kankakee River. So, desirous of moving onward, they followed him down stream and paddled for a hundred miles on the muddy waters, which wound through marshes and a dense growth of tall rushes and alder bushes. The adventurers became much in need of provisions, for at this season the buffalo had traveled south; yet, they succeeded in killing two deer, several wild turkeys, and a few swans. Providence also came to their relief, for a stray buffalo was found sticking fast in a marsh, and it was therefore captured with ease.

At length the canoes floated upon the waters of the Illinois River, and, as they paddled onward, the voyagers came upon an Indian village where were great quantities of corn. The inhabitants had departed upon a hunt, so the ravenous Frenchmen appropriated a large store of grain for their own use. They kept on their way, reached a great lake, called Lake Peoria, and found a second Indian village upon the bank, the inhabitants of which met them with great friendliness and good will.

Here La Salle decided to build a fort. It was named Fort Crèvecœur, or the Broken Heart, so called because of the sadness which he had experienced at the loss of the good ship Griffin. The men also constructed a brigantine, forty-two feet long and twelve feet broad, in which it was hoped to make further discoveries in the Mississippi. When it had been completed, a priest, called Father Hennepin, was sent down the Illinois River to make further explorations, not in this boat, but in a canoe, accompanied by two Frenchmen and an Indian; while La Salle, himself, determined to begin an overland journey to Fort Frontenac, assisted by three Frenchmen and an Indian hunter. The Chevalier de Tonty was left in command of the fort, with sixteen men and two missionaries.

La Salle had quite an undertaking before him, but he did not quail. He was to travel over land, and on foot, through vast forests and through bogs and morasses, to Fort Frontenac, a distance of twelve hundred miles. He had to journey along the southern shores of Lake Erie and Lake Ontario, ford numerous rivers and cross others on rafts, all of this in a season when snow hid the ground and floating ice rendered traveling most fatiguing. Nothing seemed impossible to his strong heart and unbending resolution. Shouldering his knapsack and musket, he bade adieu to his companions of the wilderness, and set his face towards far distant Canada.

No record has been preserved of the incidents of his long and perilous journey from the slow- moving Illinois to the blue and sparkling St. Lawrence. At any rate, he arrived without mishap at Fort Frontenac, where he was chagrined and mortified to find his affairs in a condition of confusion that was deplorable. His heaviest loss, of course, was that of the Griffin, with her cargo valued at twelve thousand dollars; but, besides this mishap, he found that his agents had despoiled him of all the profits of his trade. Some of his employees, in fact, had stolen his goods and had run away with them to the Dutch of New York. A rumor had been circulated to the effect that he and his whole party had been drowned on their voyage up the lakes, so his creditors had seized upon his effects, and had wasted them by forced sales. All Canada seemed to have conspired against him. Many a less resolute heart than his own would have failed, but despair was never known to settle upon the mind of the Chevalier La Salle. He was the first Theodore Roosevelt of the United States.

The adventurer had still one friend left,—Count Frontenac, whose influence and authority was now exerted in his favor. They discussed together the Mississippi problem and determined to give up the plan of navigating this mighty water-course in a ship. Instead, La Salle decided to prosecute his explorations with canoes.

He engaged more men, left Fort Frontenac on the 23rd. day of July, 1680, and, although detained by head winds on Lake Ontario, reached Mackinac during the month of September. By offering brandy in exchange for Indian corn, he soon had enough to satisfy his needs, and, embarking on the rough waters of Lake Michigan, at length arrived at the mouth of the river Miami. The fort which he had left there had been plundered and dismantled!

Journeying south, La Salle reached the villages of the Illinois, which he found had been sacked and burned by the Iroquois during his absence. He saw nothing of Tonty and those Frenchmen whom he had left behind him, a proof that they had either been killed or dispersed. So he returned to the Miami River and here spent the winter, visiting the Indian tribes near Lake Michigan. Here he learned that the Iroquois had attacked the settlements of the Illinois with vindictive ferocity, during his absence, driving the red men far westward across the Mississippi. As for the Frenchmen, whom he had left behind him, no one seemed to know what had become of them. Towards the end of May, 1681, the vigorous explorer left the Miami River, and, after a prosperous voyage, once more entered the harbor of Mackinac. What was his joy to here find the Chevalier Tonty and those Frenchmen, whom he had last seen in the wilderness. They had passed through great dangers, but had at length escaped from the bloodthirsty Iroquois and had reached the French fortress, lean, haggard, but praising God that they had escaped with their lives. La Salle embraced them all, gave them presents of firearms and blankets, and begged them to accompany him again into the wilderness.

The Chevalier was now determined to journey down the entire length of the Mississippi, and, with this end in view, took into his service a company of Frenchmen, together with a number of eastern Indians, Abenakis, and Loups, or Mahingans, as they were called by the French writers. Putting Fort Frontenac in command of the Sieur de La Forest, he journeyed by canoe to Niagara, where a stockade had recently been built, called Fort de Tonty, and thence embarked with his entire company in canoes for the Miami River, which he reached in safety. Six weeks were now spent in making arrangements for the great trip down the river.

There were twenty-three Frenchmen in the party, eighteen savages, ten Indian women, and three children. The redskins insisted on taking these women with them to prepare their food, according to their custom, while they were fishing and hunting. When all was ready the adventurers started for the mouth of the Chicago River, which was found to be frozen.

Undaunted, the explorers passed down the water-course on sleds, down the Illinois to Lake Peoria, and thence to the muddy waters of the Mississippi. They had a peaceful passage southward, hunting much and fishing in the stream, and eventually arrived at the Chickasaw Bluffs. Here redskins were met with, who gave them kind treatment, and, pushing on, the little party soon arrived at a mighty village of the Arkansas Indians.

These redskins were a frank and open-hearted people of gentle manners, and very hospitable. The Sieur de La Salle was treated with marked deference and respect. He took possession of the country in the name of the King of France, erected a cross, and adorned it with the arms of his native country. This was done with great pomp and ceremony, the savages believing that it was a ritual for their amusement. Two weeks were pleasantly spent among the red men and then the voyagers kept on their way.

Figure 15. La Salle at the Mouth of the Mississippi River.

The journey to the mouth of the mighty water-course was easy and pleasant. Many Indian tribes were met with, but no battles occurred. Finally, on the 6th. day of April, the river was observed to divide itself into three channels, so the Sieur de La Salle separated his company into three divisions and, putting himself at the head of one of them, he took the western channel, the Chevalier de Tonty the middle, and the Sieur Dautray the eastern. The water soon became brackish, then salt, until, at last, the broad ocean opened up before them. La Salle encamped for the night about twelve miles above the mouth of the western branch, and the next day he and Tonty examined the shores bordering on the sea in order to ascertain the depth of the waters in the two principal channels. The day following was employed in searching for a dry place, removed from the tide and the inundation of the rivers, on which to erect a column and a cross. Next day this ceremony was performed.

All the Frenchmen were drawn up under arms, while a column was erected with this inscription: "Louis the Great, King of France and Navarre, reigns; the 9th. of April, 1682."

The Te Deum was now chanted and the soldiers discharged their muskets with shouts of Long Live the King! La Salle then made a formal speech, taking possession of the whole country of Louisiana for the French King, the nations and people contained therein, the seas and harbors adjacent, and all the streams flowing into the Mississippi, which he called the great river St. Louis. A leaden plate was then buried at the foot of a tree, with a Latin inscription, containing the arms of France and the date, and stating that La Salle, Tonty, Lenobe, and twenty Frenchmen were the first to navigate the river from the Illinois to its mouth. The cross was then erected with appropriate ceremonies. At the same time an account of these proceedings was drawn up, in the form of a Proces Verbal, certified by a Notary and signed by thirteen of the principal persons of the expedition.

La Salle felt happy, for he had seen, he had come, he had conquered!

Although the journey up the Mississippi was without danger, La Salle, when he reached the upper courses, was seized with a dangerous illness which made it impossible for him to go forward for forty days. The Chevalier de Tonty was dispatched to Mackinac in order to inform the Count de Frontenac of the particulars of the voyage, and then, by slow stages, La Salle reached the Miami River, where he arrived by the end of September.

Tonty was faithful and accurate in executing his orders, so faithful that, shortly afterwards, when La Salle was well enough to sail for France, he left him in charge of all his interests during his absence.

The explorer met with a favorable reception in the old world, and it was decided that an expedition should be fitted out, for which the Government should provide vessels, troops, munitions, and such other supplies as were wanted: the whole to be under his command. He was authorized to establish colonies in Louisiana, and to take command of the immense country and all of its inhabitants from Lake Michigan to the borders of Mexico. He was given four vessels and was furnished with two hundred and eighty men.

Certainly his own government thought well of him, even if other people did not, so he and his men started for the Gulf of Mexico, determined to there found a colony which would perpetuate the name of France for all time in the Western Hemisphere.

The history of this expedition is an unfortunate one. In four vessels the adventurers crossed the ocean, intending to land at the mouth of the Mississippi. There were about two hundred and eighty persons in all, including many missionaries and soldiers, the latter being an assemblage of vagabonds and beggars from the streets, some of whom had never handled a musket. The vessels touched at the island of Santo Domingo, then crossed over into the Gulf of Mexico, heading, as all thought, for the mouth of the Mississippi. But such was not the case, and the explorers touched land near the borders of Mexico, at the Magdalen River, where the soil was barren and sandy, and where there was little game.

At different times, parties landed, hunted the wild buffalo, and explored the flat and somewhat desolate country. They constructed a fort with the timbers and planks of one of their ships, which floated ashore after the vessel went to pieces, and also with drift wood from the beach. After this was done, the Sieur de La Salle, taking fifty men with him, set out on a tour of discovery, finding a flat game-filled country and a noble river which he called the Vaches, because of the great numbers of wild cows, or buffaloes, seen upon its banks. This name it still retains.

After a journey of considerable length, the Chevalier returned, built a new fort, and then set out upon another journey of discovery. Many of his men died of exposure and rattlesnake bites, but this never disturbed the even calm of his manner. He pressed on, found the great Colorado River, and crossed it, penetrating into the wilderness for many miles. After an absence of more than four months, La Salle was again received with joy by the colonists at the fort. His men were ragged in dress, some without hats, and all were haggard and worn by exposure.

The Indians had always shown themselves to be hostile and had murdered several of the French explorers when they had strayed away from their companies. Of the four vessels which had brought over the expedition, three had returned, and the last, the la Belle, had been destroyed by a storm. The Sieur de La Salle was thus cut off from all supplies in a new country, two thousand miles from any civilized settlement to which he could look for succor, and surrounded on every side by hostile savages. It is no wonder that many of his followers were dissatisfied and miserably unhappy, some even plotted to kill their great and gallant leader.

Of the many expeditions which I have taken into the wilderness, with parties of men, none has ever been tranquil throughout. There is always some evil dispositioned fellow along, who raises a disturbance, makes others unhappy, and, by his surly manner, creates uneasiness and distrust, so that all are happy when the settlements have been reached and the malcontents have been allowed to go their ways in peace. So it was here. There were several Frenchmen of a jealous and mean disposition, who, feeling ill-humored because of their hardships in the wilderness, felt it their duty to murder the only true man among them all: the valiant leader. It was easy to succeed in their evil design.

Somewhere on the Mississippi River was the Chevalier Tonty, the staunch friend and companion of La Salle, and a man who was as brave and as valiant as this courageous Frenchman. Why not go in search of him? The proposition was a good one, and La Salle determined to take only the bravest and the strongest; to travel eastward; to reach the Mississippi, and to there find, if possible, his brave and noble companion-in-arms.

This was a wonderful trip. The valiant Frenchman and his companions crossed unknown rivers, broad prairies, and flat plateaus. A crocodile seized one of the soldiers by the leg and dragged him to destruction, in one instance; in another, several of the French adventurers were badly gored by buffalo.

La Salle finally reached the land of the Cencis Indians, the future home of many a Daniel Boone, a perfect paradise for the sportsman and a land of noble rivers, beautiful valleys, and much wild game. He was charmed with it, he reveled in its scenery, its beautiful valleys, its wonderful water courses, yet, here it was that he was to meet his end, an event as sad and tragic as any of the great events of American history.

On the 15th. day of March, 1687, the adventurers came to a place where the Sieur de La Salle had buried a quantity of Indian corn and beans on his last journey, and he ordered his followers, Duhaut, Hiens, Liolot,

Larcheveque, Teissier, Nika, and his footman Saget, to go and bring it away. They found the place, but the corn and the beans were spoiled. Nika was fortunate in killing two buffalo, and the others dispatched Saget to inform the commander of this fact, and requested him to send horses for the meat. La Salle, consequently, directed Moraquet, De Marie, and Saget to return with horses and to send back one of them loaded with the flesh of the buffalo, for immediate use, and to wait until the rest was dried.

Moraquet arrived, found that the meat had been smoked, though it was not dry enough for this process, and Duhaut and the others had laid aside certain parts to be roasted for themselves, which, it seems, was the custom on similar occasions. Moraquet, in a passionate manner, reprimanded them for what they had done, and took away, not only the smoked meat, but the pieces which they had reserved, saying, in a menacing tone:

"Comrades, I will do with it as I please!"

This irritated the rest. Duhaut had an old grudge against Moraquet, and was quite ready to take revenge. He brought over Liolot and Hiens to help him accomplish his purpose, and finally the others, and they determined to murder Moraquet, Nika and Saget. In the night, when the unsuspecting victims were asleep, they were butchered with an ax.

The bloody work had commenced, why not let it continue? The conspirators laid a scheme, on the spot, to destroy the Sieur de La Salle. They would shoot him.

Meantime, the courageous leader of the expedition expressed anxiety at the long absence of Moraquet, and seemed to have forebodings of some unhappy event. He feared, indeed, that the whole party might have been cut off by the savages. He determined, finally, to go in search of them, leaving the camp on the 19th. day of March, in charge of Jontel. With Father Anastase, and two natives who had served him as guides, he started out to look for his companions in arms.

The valiant French explorer traveled for about six miles, when he found the bloody cravat of Saget, one of the murdered men, near the bank of a river, and, at the same time, two eagles were seen hovering over their heads, as if attracted by food somewhere on the ground.

La Salle thought that the party must be near, and fired his gun to draw the attention of those whom he wished to find. Duhaut and Larcheveque immediately came across the river and advanced to meet him. La Salle approached, saying:

"Where is the good Moraquet? Has anything happened to him?" "He is along the river," answered Larcheveque.

At that moment, Duhaut, who was concealed in the high grass, discharged his musket, and shot the unsuspecting Chevalier through the head. He fell forward upon his face, and Father Anastase, who was standing at his side, expected to share the same fate, until the conspirators told him that they had no design upon his life.

La Salle lived for about an hour, unable to speak, but continually pressed the hand of the good priest to signify that he understood what was said to him. Finally he passed away, and was buried by the kind father, who shed tears over the body of this brave and valiant adventurer.

Thus perished the wise Chevalier: generous, engaging, adroit, skillful, and capable of any accomplishment. He died in the full vigor of life, in the midst of his career and his labors, without the consolation of having seen the results of his great explorations. In some of the higher attributes of character, such as personal courage and endurance, undaunted resolution, patience under trials, and perseverance in contending with obstacles and struggling through embarrassments that might appall the stoutest heart, there is, I believe, no man who surpassed this Sieur de La Salle. He was cool and intrepid at all times, never yielding for a moment to despair, or even to despondency, and he bore the heavy burden of his responsibilities manfully until the end. To him and to good Father Marquette must be mainly ascribed the discovery of the vast regions of the Mississippi Valley and its subsequent occupation and settlement by the French. His name must therefore always hold a high position among those adventurous souls who struggled to conquer, to colonize, and to explore the vast American Continent, when it was a wilderness inhabited by wild men and wild beasts, and unknown to those of a white complexion.

A SONG OF THE MISSISSIPPI

Down where the muddied waters run and boil in a rushing flood,
On the banks of the stream, as if in a dream, a stalwart Frenchman stood.
And the mocking bird from a blossoming spray sang a song which was joyous and gay;
As the welcoming sun shone on cutlass and gun, these words he trilled through the day:

"La Salle! La Salle! O brave La Salle!
You're a man of France, I know,
La Salle! La Salle! O good La Salle!
You can shoot with the gun and the bow. La Salle! La Salle! O true La Salle!
I salute your courage and love,
For the lilies of France, may they wave, may they dance, o'er this watery waste from above."

And the Frenchman raised his eyes on high and sighed as he gazed afar,
Where the buffalo grunted and roared on the plain, and the dun-colored prong-horns are.
And he swore an oath, it was round and long, to protect this land for France,
By hook and crook, by sword and book, by pike and silvery lance.

"La Salle! La Salle! O brave La Salle!"
Sang the bird on the waving branch,
"La Salle! La Salle! O good La Salle!
You're a soldier true and staunch.
O take this land, with its silvery sand, for the King and Queen you serve;
And bring us peace; make the redskins cease,
From warfare make them swerve."

So the Frenchman stayed, and his men were afraid to leave the land he'd found,
Yet they hated their leader bold and brave, and determined to have him downed.
And they hatched a plot, the bloodthirsty lot, to shoot the bold and good,
Alas! 'twas sad that men were so bad, for they killed him where he stood.

And the Mississippi gurgled on; it romped, it waved, it ran,
It pushed by silvery beaches, and it curled by the homes of man,
While the mocker sat on the whispery branch, it sang and caroled away:

"La Salle! La Salle! O brave La Salle!
Too bad! Too bad! Good day!"

Chapter 16

ROBERT EDWIN PEARY

DISCOVERER OF THE NORTH POLE, (1856-)

Where the green bergs go careening past,
And the white bears gambol and fight,
Where the little auks whimper and whisper a tale
Of the Ice King's palace of white.
Where the musk-oxen frisk and frolic,
Where the walrus fondles his mate,
'Tis there that a man, who was built on a plan

Of steel, went forth to his fate.
O'er the glittering hills of the ice-pack,
O'er the floe and the treacherous lead,
The brown dogs hauled the loaded sledge
With courage and quickening speed.
With Eskimos tried and trusted,
With a negro of steadfast soul,
He shook out the flag of the U. S. A.
And placed it on top of the Pole.

Imagine the sensation which was caused when there suddenly appeared in the newspapers the following telegram:

"April the 6th, 1909. Stars and Stripes nailed to the Pole. Peary."

People were astonished and looked amazed. Could it be possible that the North Pole had at last been discovered, after hundreds of years of effort upon the part of numerous adventurers, many of whom had never come back to tell the tale? Was it true that, after twenty-three years of effort, Commander Peary had at last reached the most northern point upon the earth's surface? Yes, it seemed to be the fact. At last the North Pole had been trod upon by the foot of a white man. Instantly the news was scattered from St. John's, New Brunswick, and from New York, to the four corners of the globe, and a great shout of enthusiastic congratulation went up from every place where civilized men were gathered together, for all the world had been watching the plucky commander of the United States Navy, who, for twenty-three years, had been working upon the problem of how to reach the North Pole. "Hurrah! Hurrah for Peary!" was heard on every side. "He has been victorious where hundreds have failed. Again Hurrah!"

Those who disbelieved the first telegram were soon assured by others that the Pole had really been reached, for Mr. Herbert L. Bridgman, Secretary of the Peary Arctic Club, was telegraphed to as follows:

"Pole reached. Roosevelt safe. Peary."

And, still later, the Commander's devoted wife at South Harpswell, Maine, received the message:

"Have made good at last. I have the old Pole. Am well. Love. Will wire again from Chateau. Bert."

Now there could be no doubt that the great feat had really been accomplished and soon a wireless message from Indian Harbor, Labrador, told that the good ship Roosevelt was there with all safe on board, and was steaming southward as fast as she was able.

At length she arrived at New York. A throng of newspapermen and citizens gathered immediately around the bold explorer, who, with his companions, was given a royal welcome home. This was as it should have been, for Peary was the only man who had really stood upon the very top of this sphere upon which we live.

Robert Edwin Peary, who "nailed the Stars and Stripes to the North Pole," was born in Cresson, Pennsylvania, May 6th, 1856. When still a mere lad he moved to Portland, Maine, and, after studying in private schools and an academy in North Bridgton, Maine, he entered Bowdoin College, graduating in 1877. He now became a draughtsman in the U. S. Coast and Geodetic Survey, then passed a stiff examination and entered the United States Navy as a Civil Engineer, ranking as a Lieutenant. In 1884, or three years later, he was an assistant government engineer in the surveys for the proposed route for the Nicaragua Canal, inventing several rolling locks for the use of the workmen. He became engineer-in-chief of the Nicaragua Survey.

About this time he began to have ideas connected with the search for the North Pole, and, obtaining a short leave of absence, made a trip into Greenland, accompanied by a Dane called Margaard. A faithful Negro, named Matthew Henson, who had served with him in Nicaragua, followed him to the Arctic on this trip, and continued to be with him upon all his subsequent expeditions.

Upon his return to civilization, the explorer immediately began to spend his spare time in preparing for another expedition to the north. He married, meanwhile, Miss Josephine Diebitsch whom he had met in Maine when a young man.

In 1891-92 he again made a trip into the frozen fastnesses of the polar region, which was financed by the Academy of Natural Sciences in Philadelphia. The Expedition was thoroughly organized before the men started north, and supplies were left at convenient points, so that starvation would not kill off the adventurers as it had done to so many other explorers.

Establishing headquarters at McCormick Bay, on the western coast of Greenland, Peary and his men made sledge excursions along Whale Sound, Inglefield Gulf, and Humboldt Glacier, proving that the coasts of Greenland converged at the northern portion, doubtless forming an island of what was thought to be a peninsula. Although his leg was broken when crossing Melville Bay, the brave explorer persisted in his work, and returned in September, 1892, with a brilliant record of results accomplished.

Figure 16. Robert Edwin Peary.

With one companion, Astrup, he had ascended to the summit of the great ice cap which covers the interior of Greenland, 5,000 to 8,000 feet in elevation, and had pushed northward for 500 miles over a region where no white man had ever been before. The temperature was from 10 degrees to 50 degrees below zero. On July 4th, 1892, he discovered Independence Bay, and found a valley nearby, which was radiant with gorgeous flowers and was alive with murmuring bees. Here also were many musk-oxen, browsing lazily upon the long, rank grasses.

The explorer now determined to spend his life in an attempt to reach the Pole, which lay 396 geographical miles farther north than any man had yet penetrated on the western hemisphere. He was convinced that the only way to eventually reach his goal was by adopting the manner of life, the food, the snowhouses, and the clothing of the Eskimos, who had learned how to combat the rigors of Arctic weather by centuries of experience. He must also utilize the game of the northland, the walrus, the musk-oxen, and the reindeer, in order to keep his men in fit condition and of good temper when the long winter night came upon them. Lastly he must train the Eskimos so that they should become his sledging crew.

The first north polar expedition lasted for four years, from 1898 to 1902, and Peary failed to get nearer than 343 miles of the Pole. Each year dense packs of ice blocked his passage to the polar ocean and he was compelled to make his base 700 miles from the Pole, or 200 miles south of the headquarters of Nares, from which point he could reach the Pole in one season. But during this period, he explored and mapped hundreds of miles of the coastline of Greenland and of the islands to the west and north.

The navigator and explorer now designed and constructed the Roosevelt, a boat built to withstand the crush of the masses of ice, and with this he battled a way to the desired haven upon the shores of the polar sea. From this place he made a wonderful march to the point 87° 6′, or nearer to the Pole than any man had ever been. He would have reached the Pole, this time, but winds of excessive fury opened great leads and robbed him of the prize and nearly of his own life. This was in 1906.

Commander Peary was now resolved to make his next advance upon the Pole by the same route as he had just used. His previous efforts had been financed by Mr. Morris K. Jessup, whose interest in Polar explorations, and faith in Peary, made him willing at all times to furnish whatever money the Commander required. But the kind Mr. Jessup was now dead and the explorer knew that he would have a difficult time to raise the funds to equip another expedition.

Commander Peary had established a training school for the Eskimos and their dogs at Etah, and he now learned of the departure of Dr. Frederick A. Cook, who had served with him upon a previous expedition, and Mr. John R. Bradley, a noted sportsman, to this point. He knew that these men might use his Eskimo friends, with their dogs, for a "dash" to the Pole, while he was held behind a prisoner in New York, because of the lack of funds. Yet, what could he do without the money?

The Roosevelt was in bad shape and needed overhauling. She was built in Maine by the Peary Arctic Club for the expedition of 1905 and was designed by the explorer himself. She was a three- masted, fore-and-aft schooner-rigged steamship, built entirely of white oak with treble frames close together, double planked. Her walls were 24 to 30 inches thick. Her heavy bow was backed by 12 feet of solid deadwood. Her keel was 16 inches thick and was reënforced with false keels and a keelson. Her stern, reënforced by iron, had a long overhang to protect the rudder from the ice, and the rudder itself was so arranged that it could be lifted out of the water, when jammed or entangled.

It was out of the question to go in 1907, but, by the next season a great deal of work had been done and sufficient funds had been secured to make the good, old ship strong and ready again, and to fill her with necessary stores. A crew was secured, presents for the Eskimos were on board, and material for sledges, dog harness, guns, ammunition, and scientific instruments. The ship's sides were strengthened, her machinery was made as good as new, and so, at last, she steamed up the East River, outward bound.

On July 7th., 1908, she stopped near Sagamore Hill, Long Island, the home of the then President Roosevelt, and the chief Executive grasped the explorer by the hand, bidding him: "Good luck and God speed!"

The voyager replied that he had never before felt so confident of winning the Pole and would reach it, this time, or "bust."

Mr. Roosevelt laughed and waved "good-bye," as the staunch craft, which bore his name, plowed forth into the Atlantic.

Reaching Etah in safety, a number of Eskimos were taken on board, and, pointing her nose toward the north, the Roosevelt disappeared into a murky fog. A ship called the Erik was nearby, and soon returned to civilization with the last words from Peary and his men. This was in August, 1908.

Meanwhile, the Roosevelt was steadily pushed northward, through the defiles of Kennedy and Robeson channels, where the moving ice opened here and there and allowed the vessel to steal between the floes. Three weeks later the Arctic Ocean came in sight. Entering it, the steamer was turned to the left and was pushed along the coast as rapidly as could be done against the ice pack. Commander Peary meant, if possible, to reach Cape Columbia, a headland well to the west and on the north coast of Grant Land. Yet he could not do this, for the ice, which pressed against the promontory of Cape Sheridan, shut off any progress beyond that point. Thus, on the first day of September, the Roosevelt was laid to in a snug harbor under the protection of Cape Sheridan, and the crew went into winter quarters.

The men amused themselves hunting polar bears, musk-oxen, and caribou during the long months which had to be passed before the "dash" could be attempted. The continuous night at length wore itself to a close, and, in February, the first gray light of the approaching Arctic dawn began to dispel the darkness.

Upon the fifteenth of that month, 1909, a sledging expedition left the ship in the direction of Cape Columbia, which was to be the base camp in the "dash" for the goal of Peary's ambition. This overland trip consumed a fortnight, Cape Columbia being reached on March 1st. Here the adventurers were 420 miles from the North Pole in a straight line, and, with parties to support him and leave food, the daring Peary now started towards the top of the earth. In order to get away from open water he had gone far westward in the effort to avoid the usual eastward drift of the polar ice and open water, which would defeat his efforts.

At last he was off. Open leads—cracks in the ice filled with water—delayed him greatly during the first ten days of the expedition, so that by March the eleventh the party had only reached the 84th. parallel. He kept on, found the ice more even, and by the seventeenth, had reached the eighty- sixth. On the twenty-third of that month he outdistanced the best record of a Norwegian, that of Nansen. Here his last supporting party was sent back, the leader of which, Professor Ross G. Marvin of Cornell University, lost his life by drowning in an open lead, April the tenth.

The chosen few, gaunt, hollow-eyed, and energetic, pressed towards their goal, and, on March the 24th, the best Italian record was distanced. On, on, they crept over the ice-pack, the dogs trotting along briskly, and pulling the little sledges slowly but surely towards the apex of the earth. Living on pemmican (dried meat, sugar, and raisins) and tea, the leader and his companions kept up both their strength and their spirits. On March 27th, the 87th. parallel was passed, and on the 28th. Peary's own record of "farthest north" was distanced. The goal was near and confidence increased with every mile of the advance.

When traveling in this region, heretofore, the gallant explorer had been often hindered by leads of open water and massive hummocks of ice. Fate was now propitious and the ice seemed to be more flat and solid than Peary had ever experienced before. On April 2nd, the 88th. parallel was crossed. Two days later the 89th. parallel was left behind, and in two days more, on April the sixth, the little party reached the center of the northern hemisphere, and Commander Peary stood at the North Pole. Hurray! Hurray! The goal had been reached!

With the explorer were four trusted Eskimos and the Negro Henson, who had been with him on every expedition. The Eskimos were Ooqueah, Ootah, Seeglo, and Egingwah. Each of them placed a different flag upon an ice cap at the uttermost end of the earth. These were the banners of the Navy League, the D. K. E. Fraternity, the Red Cross Flag, the D. A. R. Peace Flag, and the flag of the United States carried by the explorer for fifteen years. All cheered for the Pole and for the flag, and then had a right merry feast upon the very apex of the earth. No ice was needed in the water which they drank!

The explorer had been so exhausted when he arrived at the Pole that he had to seek a few hours' sleep. Then he arose and wrote the following words in his diary:

"The Pole at last. The prize of three centuries. My dream and goal for twenty years. Mine at last! I cannot bring myself to realize it. It seems all so simple and commonplace!"

Yet, here he was, and he shook hands with all the Eskimos, who seemed to be childishly pleased at the feat which they had accomplished. Again they gave "three times three," with a vim, for the North Pole.

The Commander had good reason to be delighted, for, as he says: "For more than a score of years that point on the earth's surface had been the object of my every effort. To its attainment my whole being, physical, mental and moral, had been dedicated. Many times my own life and the lives of those with me had been risked. My own material and forces and those of my friends had been devoted to this object. This journey was my eighth into the Arctic wilderness. In that wilderness I had spent nearly twelve years out of the twenty-three between my thirtieth and my fifty-third year, and the intervening time spent in civilized communities during that period had been mainly occupied with preparations for returning to the wilderness. The determination to reach the Pole had become so much a part of my being, that, strange as it may seem, I long ago ceased to think of myself, save as an instrument for the attainment of that end. To the layman this may seem strange, but an inventor can understand it, or an artist, or any one who has devoted himself for years upon years to the service of an idea."

At about four o'clock on the afternoon of April 7th, the explorers turned their backs on the Pole, leaving with a sense of sadness, for this was certainly a scene which their "eye would never see again." The journey home was fraught with danger. Would they make it?

The extraordinary speed which they had made in reaching the Pole was exceeded in the journey home. In sixteen days Cape Columbia had been reached, for the dogs were good ones, and they averaged twenty-six miles of travel a day. On April the 23rd, Peary entered his "igloo," or ice-house, at "Crane City," Cape Columbia.

In one march of forty-five miles, Cape Hecla was reached, and the Roosevelt in another of equal length. The Commander's heart thrilled, as, rounding the point of the cape, he saw the little black ship lying there in her icy berth, with her sturdy nose pointing straight to the Pole. His dreadful trip was over and Victory perched upon the masts of the intrepid vessel.

The ship was soon made ready for the homeward voyage. In ten days' time she was prepared to sail, and, on July 18th, with only the tragic memory of the lost and lamented Marvin to lessen the high spirits of all, the Roosevelt pulled slowly out from the cape and turned her nose again to the south. On September 25th, she steamed into Indian Harbor, in Labrador, and the first dispatch went on the wires: "Have made good at last, I have the Pole."

Yet, much of the glory of Peary's Arctic discovery had been spoiled by Dr. Frederick A. Cook, an impostor, who had come from the north, some months before, had stated that he had reached the Pole, and had spread the news broadcast over the civilized world. Many had believed him, and he was given receptions, balls, the freedom of cities, until his records were found to be worthless and his story finally discredited. His advent into the arena at this time was most unfortunate for the gallant Peary, to whom belongs all the glory and honor which is due a brave man who did a big deed.

The Roosevelt at last reached the little town of Sydney, Cape Breton, where Mrs. Peary and the children were to meet the explorer. As the vessel neared the city, the entire water-front was alive with people. The seaport to which the adventurous navigator had returned so many times, unsuccessful, gave him a royal welcome as the Roosevelt steamed into view, flying at her masthead a flag which had never before entered any port in history,—the North Pole flag.

The success of the expedition was due to the experience, the courage, endurance, and devotion of its members, who put all that there was in them into the work; and to the unswerving faith and loyalty of the Peary Arctic Club, which furnished the funds without which nothing could have been accomplished. Again, three cheers for Peary! He is a hero of whom all may be proud.

THE MISTY MAID

Away up North, in the frozen sea, where the booby walrus breed,
There lives a Maid, dressed all in white, who rides a snowy steed.
Her eyes are blue and her tresses gold, she has cheeks of a crimson stain,
On her head a helmet of dazzling hue, on her bosom a breastplate plain.

Oh! hear the penguins laffin, saying, "Baffin! Baffin! Baffin!"
Oh! Hear the penguins laffin, while the cutting blizzards sigh,
Oh! Hear the penguins laffin, saying, "Baffin! Baffin! Baffin!"
The little penguins all bob low as the Misty Maid goes by.

She's seen the trail of Nansen, and she's hovered o'er Peary's head,
She's cried at the fate of Hudson, at the boat of a hundred dead,

She's watched the fires of Davis, she's fastened the anchors of Kane,
And she's been near the tents of Franklin, by the icy wind-ripped lane.

Oh! hear the penguins laffin, saying, "Baffin! Baffin! Baffin!"
Oh! Hear the penguins laffin, while the cutting blizzards sigh,
Oh! Hear the penguins laffin, saying, "Baffin! Baffin! Baffin!"
The little penguins all bob low as the Misty Maid goes by.

Yes, the Maid is a Maid of sorrow, her cheeks with tears are dim;
For the skeletons of a thousand men she's seen on the North Pole rim.
As she prances on her snow white steed she beckons to stay away,
For her home is a home of frozen death—yea! pain and death alway.

But hear the penguins laffin, saying, "Baffin! Baffin! Baffin!"

The penguins still are laffin while the cutting blizzards sigh;
You can hear them always laffin, saying, "Baffin! Baffin! Baffin!"
The little penguins all bob low as the Misty Maid goes by.

The Maid is a girl of sadness, and the Maid is a girl of woe,
For she's Mistress of the Polar Sea, of the ice and the darkling floe;
The Maid has seen the starving crew, she has viewed the drowning boat,
And her eyes are dim, and her face is cold, for she hears the rattling throat.

But hear the penguins laffin, saying, "Baffin! Baffin! Baffin!"
You can always hear them laffin, while the cutting blizzards sigh.
Oh! Hear the penguins laffin, saying, "Baffin! Baffin! Baffin!"
The little penguins all bob low as the Misty Maid goes by.

And the snowy owl, with his wintry cowl, sighs a song of bitter woe,
While the narwhal swims, and the musk-ox grins, at the crushing ice-pack flow,
For the great white bear sneaks to his lair, where the little seals are lying,
And out of the mist, with the moonlight kissed, a great weird song comes sighing:

Don't follow the Maid of the Northland; don't gaze at her laughing eyes;
For the Maid knows naught but sorrow, and naught but the ice king's lies;
Don't look at the Maid of the Polar Seas, her wand is a witch's staff,
Just stay away from the North Sea gray. Don't go where the penguins laugh!

Epilogue

The history of these adventurous men shows that the human mind, ever curious and ever anxious to discover new and unknown facts, will stimulate the endeavors of staunch physical beings to do feats of daring and energy which those of more contented and passive mentality will never feel either willing or able to accomplish.

Leif Ericson, Hudson, Pizarro, Peary, all were propelled onward upon their missions of discovery and of adventure by that curious spark of daring and love of adventure which has stimulated a Roosevelt and a Dillon Wallace.

It is the mind that drives onward the body; it is the bump of curiosity which propels the adventurer to take the risks and the hazards which are necessary for exploration of unmapped countries. Restless, dare-devilish souls will always exist, and, now that there are no parts of the North American continent which are unknown to the geographer and the man of scientific bent, those who are prompted onward by the spirit of hazardous adventure must search for the unknown in the unmapped and untouched regions of Africa or of South America. Here vast wildernesses call to those of adventurous blood to come and to admire; to struggle with the elements and to battle with the currents of their water-courses and the unmarked trails of their mountains. But no treasure of the Montezumas, nor gold of the Incas, lie where the restless grasp of the invader can reach out and appropriate as in the days of the dauntless Cortés and the avaricious Pizarro.

So, live on! O Spirit of Adventure, without which there would be no sparkle to life, no zest to the journey into the wilderness, no tang to the canoe trip through the unknown chain of lakes, or the beaver-dammed water course. Live on! and may you ever exist in the minds of young America, so that, when the great call shall go up for those of Viking soul and de Soto daring to rise and press onward for the honor of the flag, there will be thousands of adventurers who have been trained to the hazard of the camp, the slap of the paddle, and the gleam of the rifle-barrel.

They, like the intrepid Peary, will "nail the good, old flag" to the very ends of the earth, for it represents "liberty, equality, fraternity"—three glorious qualities for the maintenance of which every true-minded boy, when he grows to be a man, will be willing to give his time, his energy, and, if necessary—his life.

INDEX

A

Albuquerque, 128
Almagro, Diego, 151, 152, 153, 154, 155, 156, 168, 169
Almedo, Father, 88, 107, 116
Alvarado, Lieutenant, 108
Alvarado, Moscoso de, 184
ambassadors, 82, 83, 86, 91, 98
Anastase, Father, 278, 279
annihilation, 147
Antonio, Father, 47, 50, 52, 53
Asia, 15, 17, 20, 21, 30, 39, 140, 212, 214, 218, 227
Astrup, 286
Atamara, 42, 43, 45

B

Balboa, Vasco Nuñez de, vii, xi, xvi, 57, 58, 59, 60, 61, 62, 63, 64, 65, 66, 67, 68, 69, 70, 133, 149, 150
banks, xv, 3, 9, 23, 154, 184, 191, 192, 210, 215, 222, 251, 255, 265, 266, 276, 280
Barentz, William, 214
Bartola, 52
Bayard, 118, 202
Belgium, 37
Berardi, 30
beverages, 78
bible, 163, 164, 228
birds, 17, 18, 20, 35, 38, 45, 50, 53, 82, 84, 97, 141, 154, 163, 213, 214, 254
bison, 255
Bjarni, 3, 4
boat, 3, 7, 19, 22, 55, 75, 77, 79, 106, 133, 141, 142, 143, 145, 192, 210, 211, 214, 216, 217, 219, 220, 221, 222, 223, 224, 225, 228, 229, 230, 236, 240, 267, 271, 287, 293, 294
Bonaparte, Napoleon, 156
bones, 7, 36, 55, 138, 247, 265
Bradley, John R., 288
Brazil, 35, 39, 129
Bridgman, Herbert L., 284
Brittany, 141
brothers, 8, 16, 28, 55, 112, 158, 166, 171, 199, 220, 244, 253, 256, 261
brutality, 121
buffalo, xv, 183, 255, 266, 270, 276, 277, 278, 280

C

Cacama, 97, 105, 106, 116
Cæsar, Julius, 156
Candia, Pedro de, 156
Capac, Huascar, 159, 161, 165, 166
Capac, Huayna, 159
Capac, Manco, 159
Carthagena, Juan de, 131
Cartier, Jacques, xiii, xvi, 190
Catholics, 131
Cempoalla, 83, 87
Champlain, Samuel de, vii, xi, xvi, 187, 188, 189, 190, 191, 192, 193, 195, 196, 197, 198, 199, 200, 201, 202, 203, 204, 205, 206, 207, 236, 237, 238, 239, 247
charm, 53, 262
Chastes, Seigneur Aymar de, 188, 189
cheese, 228
China, 21, 192, 212, 266
Christianity, 88, 106, 251, 260
Christians, 33, 100, 254
Cilapulapu, 135, 136
civil war, 189
civilization, 102, 285, 289
cocoa, 134
Colman, John, 219
Columbus, Christopher, vii, xi, 7, 9, 11, 12, 13, 14, 15, 16, 17, 18, 19, 20, 21, 22, 23, 24, 25, 26, 27, 30, 37, 39, 58, 63, 74, 124, 131
conflagration, 110
conflict, 135
Cook, Dr. Frederick A., 288, 292
copper, 120, 145, 216, 219
Cortés, Hernando, vii, xi, xvi, 73, 74, 75, 76, 77, 78, 79, 80, 81, 82, 83, 84, 85, 86, 87, 88, 89, 90, 91, 92, 93, 94, 95, 96, 97, 98, 99, 100, 101, 102, 103, 104, 105, 106, 107, 108, 109, 110, 111, 113, 114, 115, 117, 118, 119, 120, 121, 122, 123, 124, 125, 139, 140, 150, 189, 296
cotton, 21, 59, 68, 78, 82, 84, 85, 88, 91, 92, 97, 99, 100, 108, 155, 159
crabs, 16
creditors, 58, 60, 269, 272
crocodile, 277
crown, 15, 19, 30, 68, 70, 86, 96, 129, 203
crystalline, 9
Cuba, 21, 24, 26, 30, 55, 68, 73, 75, 78, 79, 86, 87, 108, 123, 173, 174, 177, 178, 181, 184
Cuilahua, 98

D

dance, 109, 128, 193, 197, 202, 205, 207, 236, 237, 280
danger, 28, 35, 63, 75, 78, 93, 156, 169, 189, 191, 235, 239, 240, 275, 291
Dautray, Sieur, 274
Davis, Richard Harding, 37
Diebitsch, Josephine, 285
dignity, 103
disaster, 85, 94, 154, 209
dogs, 110, 215, 244, 246, 250, 283, 288, 290, 291
Dolores, Doña, 44
drawing, 35, 132
dream, 5, 25, 35, 185, 189, 244, 280, 291
drinking water, 68
Drulettes, Father, 250
Duhaut, 277, 278, 279

E

Easter, 260
Egingwah, 290
Encisco, 59, 60, 61, 67
endurance, 279, 292

Index

enemies, 34, 69, 91, 110, 120, 123, 165, 169, 192, 193, 194, 195, 201, 205, 235, 242, 256, 268, 269
England, 74, 203, 211, 213, 214, 226, 228, 230
Enriquez, Carlo, 180
Eric the Red, 3, 4, 7
Ericson, Freydis, 8
Ericson, Leif, vii, xi, xvi, 1, 2, 3, 4, 5, 6, 7, 8, 9, 230, 295
Ericson, Thorstein, 3, 7
Escobar, 113
Escovedo, Rodrigo de, 23
Esequera, Perez de, 45
Europe, 38, 45, 203, 212, 215
execution, 14, 31, 105, 131, 229
exposure, 155, 184, 276

F

Falero, Roy, 129
famine, 123, 157
favorite son, 89
fear, 28, 50, 51, 100, 154, 161, 199, 202, 205, 223, 240, 241, 249, 253, 255, 266
Ferdinand V, 15, 17, 22, 46, 61, 63
Fernandez, Garcia, 12
fever, 55, 66, 68, 151, 152, 154, 184, 252, 254, 258, 259
Finnibogi, 8
firearms, 95, 96, 199, 239, 273
fires, 78, 129, 141, 143, 200, 293
fish, 5, 7, 8, 16, 44, 48, 77, 132, 141, 178, 197, 200, 210, 213, 215, 216, 222, 228, 255, 257
fishing, 2, 5, 33, 132, 199, 210, 215, 224, 229, 243, 273
Florida, xi, 39, 45, 46, 47, 48, 50, 54, 172, 173, 174, 176, 180, 184, 185
Florin, Juan, 139
flowers, 25, 42, 44, 84, 93, 154, 219, 287

food, 34, 36, 38, 59, 66, 68, 90, 112, 133, 141, 151, 152, 177, 199, 222, 227, 228, 242, 244, 250, 252, 270, 273, 278, 287, 289
force, 46, 54, 70, 80, 87, 90, 94, 97, 99, 102, 103, 104, 111, 118, 121, 155, 157, 182, 190, 239
France, 14, 15, 139, 140, 144, 145, 146, 187, 188, 189, 190, 191, 192, 197, 199, 200, 202, 203, 243, 245, 247, 249, 250, 252, 255, 266, 267, 273, 274, 275, 276, 280
Francis I, 144
fraud, 131
free will, 50
freedom, 66, 165, 166, 292
friendship, 31, 85, 91, 130, 268
Frontenac, Count de, 268, 275
frost, 227
fruits, 36, 44, 84, 98

G

Gama, Vasco da, 211
geography, 29, 30
geometry, 38
Georgia, 177, 178, 179
Germany, 39, 147
God, 12, 19, 24, 28, 47, 52, 54, 78, 129, 131, 137, 158, 164, 213, 249, 252, 253, 254, 255, 256, 259, 260, 261, 262, 273, 288
good behavior, 220
goose, 249, 262
Gosnold, Bartholomew, 217
governor, 60, 82, 103
Grijalva, 76, 78, 79
Groseillers, 246, 247
Guacanagari, 22
Guatemozin, 120, 121, 122, 123
Guinea, 129

Guitierrez, Pedro, 19
Gulf of Mexico, 77, 184, 266, 275, 276
gunpowder, 119

H

harbors, 38, 211, 214, 260, 275
Helgi, 8
Hennepin, Father, 271
Henson, Matthew, 285, 290
Herjulf, 3
Hiens, 277, 278
Holguin, Garci, 121
horses, 50, 51, 77, 80, 81, 87, 90, 113, 117, 153, 157, 158, 159, 177, 179, 180, 181, 182, 183, 278
hospitality, 88, 159
hostility, 52, 268
Hudson, Henry, vii, xi, 209, 210, 211, 212, 214, 218, 219, 221, 229
Hudson, John, 212
human, 26, 45, 96, 100, 107, 114, 124, 129, 130, 152, 237, 295
humidity, 66
hunting, 127, 132, 181, 194, 199, 235, 236, 238, 239, 267, 273, 289
husband, 15, 241

I

Iceland, 1, 3
Idona, 42
Ilacomilo, 39
India, 16, 21, 38, 133, 215
Indians, 7, 20, 23, 25, 26, 31, 33, 34, 37, 44, 46, 47, 52, 53, 58, 59, 61, 62, 63, 66, 76, 80, 81, 83, 85, 88, 90, 91, 93, 96, 111, 114, 119, 120, 121, 122, 131, 141, 142, 143, 144, 145, 146, 157, 158, 164, 165, 168, 174, 175, 177, 178, 179, 181, 182, 183, 191, 193, 197, 198, 199, 200, 203, 216, 217, 220, 221, 222, 223, 224, 226, 230, 234, 235, 236, 245, 250, 251, 254, 255, 258, 259, 261, 266, 268, 273, 276, 277
indolent, 37
intoxication, 230
Iowa, 246
Ireland, 227, 229
iron, 43, 69, 87, 130, 150, 159, 160, 184, 185, 192, 193, 195, 202, 224, 225, 259, 265, 288
Isabella, 13, 14, 19, 22, 23, 24, 25, 26, 30, 129
islands, 5, 7, 21, 24, 25, 28, 34, 36, 38, 43, 45, 52, 55, 65, 129, 132, 133, 134, 136, 145, 194, 211, 222, 236, 239, 287
Italy, 12, 29, 31, 39

J

Japan, 212, 266
Jessup, Morris K., 287
Joliet, Father, xi, 252, 253, 255, 259, 266
Jontel, 278

L

La Motte, Sieur de, 267
La Salle, Robert de, viii, xi, 247, 265, 266, 267, 268, 269, 270, 271, 272, 273, 274, 275, 276, 277, 278, 279, 280, 281
lakes, 98, 141, 202, 247, 251, 267, 268, 272, 296
Lamudio, 60, 61, 65
Larcheveque, 278, 279
leadership, 34
legs, 11, 20, 53, 132, 178, 210, 257
Leon, Juan Ponce de, vii, xi, 41, 42, 43, 44, 45, 46, 47, 48, 49, 50, 51, 52, 53, 54, 115
Leon, Velasquez de, 104
Leonora, 127

Index

liberty, 238, 296
light, 12, 14, 18, 70, 80, 87, 139, 253, 289
Liolot, 277, 278
Lothair, 2, 3
Louisiana, 184, 275
Luque, Hernando de, 151

M

Magarino, 115
Magellan, Ferdinand, vii, xi, xvi, 30, 127, 130, 131, 132, 133, 134, 135, 136, 137
malaria, 26, 184
Margaard, 285
Marina, 80, 84, 93, 94, 100, 104, 107, 114, 122, 123
Marquette, Father, viii, 249, 250, 251, 252, 258, 260, 261, 265, 279
marriage, 68, 103, 223
marsh, 33, 233, 235, 270
Martin, Alonzo, 65
Marvin, Professor Ross G., 231, 290, 292
Maryland, xiii, 217
meat, 134, 236, 238, 244, 247, 270, 278, 290
Medici, 30
Mendoza, Luis de, 131, 132
metals, 92
Mexico, xi, 73, 76, 77, 83, 85, 86, 89, 91, 92, 94, 97, 100, 106, 108, 112, 122, 124, 125, 140, 150, 171, 173, 183, 185, 189, 275, 276
Miami, 254, 269, 272, 273, 275
military, 13, 43, 99, 128
mission, 48, 87, 201, 203, 250, 252, 254, 259, 260, 261, 268, 295
Mississippi River, xi, 171, 253, 274, 277
monks, 14
monopoly, 268
Montana, 246
Montaño, Francio, 119

Monteleone, Duke of, 124
Montezuma, 73, 80, 81, 82, 83, 84, 85, 86, 89, 90, 91, 92, 93, 94, 95, 96, 97, 98, 99, 100, 101, 102, 103, 104, 105, 106, 107, 109, 111, 112, 114, 115, 116, 120, 121, 139
Monts, Sieur de, 190, 191
Moon, 211, 215, 216, 217, 219, 220, 221, 222, 223, 224, 225, 226
Moraquet, 278, 279
mosquitoes, 154, 156, 171, 184, 241
mountain ranges, 61
Moya, Marchioness, 13
Murat, Joachim, 118
murder, 8, 96, 166, 277, 278

N

Nansen, Fridtjof, 290, 293
Nares, 287
Narváez, 108, 110, 115, 174, 177
Native Americans, 142
Navarre, 188, 274
New England, 7
Nicaragua, 285
Nika, 278
no voice, 261
nobility, 161
Nomi, 42
North America, xiii, 39, 140, 195, 212, 216, 249, 295
Norway, 3, 4

O

Ojeda, 31, 35, 36
Olatheta, 51, 52, 53, 54
Olid, 120
Ooqueah, 290
Ootah, 290
Ortiz, Juan, 174

Index

oysters, 221

P

pain, 100, 225, 231, 293
Panama, 36, 59, 66, 67, 68, 133, 139, 149, 150, 151, 152, 153, 154, 155, 156, 157, 158, 159, 171, 189
peace, 3, 10, 31, 45, 48, 49, 50, 55, 77, 92, 97, 121, 133, 159, 189, 193, 200, 220, 237, 241, 247, 255, 256, 257, 258, 260, 262, 277, 280
Peary, Robert Edwin, viii, xi, xvi, 191, 212, 231, 283, 284, 285, 286, 287, 288, 289, 290, 291, 292, 293, 295, 296
Pedrarias, 67, 68, 69, 70
Perez, Juan, 11, 12, 13, 14, 24
perseverance, 27, 69, 279
Peru, xi, 66, 70, 149, 150, 151, 153, 156, 157, 158, 159, 160, 168, 169, 173, 174, 177, 181
pests, 154
Pinzon, Martin Alonzo, 13, 16, 23
Pizarro, Francisco, vii, xvi, 66, 70, 149, 150, 151, 152, 153, 154, 155, 156, 157, 158, 159, 160, 161, 162, 163, 164, 165, 166, 167, 168, 169, 171, 174, 295, 296
Pocahontas, 174
poison, 136, 184
polar, 214, 287, 289
Pontgrave, 191, 192
Portugal, 24, 30, 37, 38, 44, 127, 128, 135, 211
poverty, 27, 156
prisoners, 32, 33, 76, 78, 85, 99, 116, 197, 199, 237, 241, 250
private schools, 285
privation, 63, 154
Puerto Rico, 55

Q

Quanhpopoca, 103, 105
Quetzalcoatl, 77, 81, 82, 86, 92
Quito, 149, 159

R

race, 6, 21, 76, 152, 178, 219, 242, 263
Radisson, Pierre-Esprit, viii, 233, 234, 235, 236, 237, 238, 239, 240, 241, 242, 243, 244, 245, 246, 247
rash, 109
religion, 52, 135, 158, 163, 188
Richelieu, Cardinal, 203
Rodriguez, Sebastian, 13
Rolfe, John, 174
Ruiz, 153, 154, 156

S

Saget, 278
Salamanca, Juan de, 119
salmon, xv, 5, 6, 9, 209
San Salvador, 20, 24
sanctuaries, 107, 114
Sandoval, Captain, 108, 115, 120, 122
Sannatowah, 48, 49, 50
sapphire, xv
savannah, 63
scent, 9, 146, 204
scientific knowledge, 197
security, 15, 173
Seeglo, 290
Senate, 29
settlements, 59, 242, 247, 272, 277
shores, xv, 7, 8, 9, 39, 58, 76, 98, 140, 141, 145, 158, 190, 212, 217, 225, 227, 233, 251, 266, 267, 270, 271, 274, 287

Index

signs, 17, 21, 31, 52, 134, 141, 142, 152, 228
silk, 163
silver, xv, 9, 16, 44, 53, 67, 78, 82, 102, 139, 154, 157, 158, 160, 163, 166, 169, 181, 204, 216
skeleton, 200
skin, 1, 9, 28, 77, 130, 133, 136, 193
slaves, 21, 37, 41, 80, 81, 82, 91, 96, 134, 183
Smith, Captain John, 211, 215, 217
smoking, 180, 193, 194, 219, 237
snakes, 154
Soto, Hernando de, vii, xi, 43, 58, 171, 172, 176, 179, 180, 181, 183, 184, 185, 296
South America, xiii, 31, 32, 34, 35, 36, 37, 38, 39, 61, 131, 154, 172, 295
South Dakota, 246
South Pacific, 217
sovereignty, 111
Spain, xi, 11, 12, 13, 14, 15, 21, 22, 23, 24, 25, 26, 28, 30, 33, 34, 37, 39, 41, 43, 46, 47, 54, 58, 60, 61, 64, 65, 66, 67, 68, 69, 70, 74, 82, 85, 86, 91, 97, 106, 108, 110, 123, 124, 128, 129, 131, 132, 135, 137, 139, 140, 150, 157, 158, 159, 160, 163, 164, 167, 169, 172, 173, 183, 185, 211
starvation, 121, 154, 155, 227
state, 99, 108, 123, 146, 151, 180
steel, 8, 51, 62, 133, 135, 136, 178, 180, 182, 193, 195, 204, 205, 209, 210, 224, 259, 283
storms, 38, 133, 141, 151, 213, 215
sulphur, 119
Sun, 157, 167
surging, 4, 23, 46, 128, 183, 202, 214
survivors, 8, 136, 155, 192

T

Tafur, Captain, 155, 156
Talavera, 14
teeth, 103, 258
Tegesta, 49, 50
Teissier, 278
Tenhtlile, 80, 81, 82
territory, 19, 22, 49, 51, 59, 62, 65, 67, 76, 86, 89, 135, 159, 177, 246
Tezcuco, 76, 82, 89, 105, 106, 120, 124
Thorwald, 8
tin, 210, 236
Tlacopan, 76, 82, 116, 117, 120
tobacco, 21, 194, 219, 220, 221, 222, 224, 241, 255, 257
Tonty, Chevalier de, 267, 270, 271, 272, 273, 274, 275, 277
Totonac(s), 83, 84, 85, 86, 88
trade, 14, 129, 145, 191, 211, 216, 220, 221, 225, 242, 251, 266, 271
training, 43, 288
transport, 69, 94, 115, 120, 146, 158, 184
Triana, Rodrigo de, 19
tribesmen, 83, 88
Trinidad, 79
tropical forests, 61
Tryggbesson, Olaf, 4
Tual, 135
Tubanama, 66, 68
Tuscaloosa, 178, 180, 183

U

United States, 26, 41, 189, 272, 284, 285, 290

V

Valencia, 44
Valverde, Father, 163, 164
vegetables, 192
vegetation, 17, 62, 154
Velasquez, Diego, 75, 76, 79, 86, 104

Index

Venezuela, xi, 31, 32
Verrazano, Giovanni, vii, xi, 139, 140, 141, 142, 143, 144, 146
Vespucci, Amerigo, vii, ix, xi, 29, 30, 32, 33, 34, 35, 36, 37, 38, 39
vessels, 17, 18, 19, 20, 21, 23, 30, 31, 33, 34, 35, 38, 44, 45, 46, 48, 61, 67, 69, 70, 79, 84, 85, 97, 120, 129, 132, 139, 140, 141, 150, 153, 155, 174, 178, 184, 188, 190, 212, 229, 267, 268, 275, 276
victims, 68, 77, 78, 94, 101, 102, 111, 278
Viking, 1, 2, 3, 4, 5, 7, 8, 296
violence, 88, 96, 130, 152
vision, 45, 46, 48, 55, 58, 160, 218, 266

W

war, 17, 30, 33, 36, 49, 51, 73, 76, 77, 93, 99, 101, 107, 110, 111, 113, 116, 117, 118, 120, 121, 124, 135, 139, 173, 177, 181, 188, 189, 193, 194, 195, 197, 199, 202, 205, 206, 220, 230, 236, 237, 238, 242, 246, 267
water, xv, 1, 4, 17, 18, 20, 21, 22, 31, 36, 38, 42, 43, 45, 46, 47, 48, 52, 53, 54, 58, 61, 63, 65, 75, 86, 102, 114, 120, 121, 129, 132, 133, 134, 139, 141, 142, 151, 154, 156, 173, 174, 175, 190, 194, 195, 196, 207, 210, 214, 215, 216, 217, 219, 220, 221, 222, 223, 224, 227, 234, 235, 236, 239, 240, 251, 252, 253, 255, 258, 268, 272, 273, 274, 277, 288, 289, 290, 292, 295, 296
wealth, 21, 35, 67, 79, 82, 150, 156, 157, 188, 212
weapons, 6, 81, 110, 197
West Indies, 14, 21, 25, 26, 30, 31, 74, 140, 188
whales, 212, 213, 214, 227
white oak, 288
wilderness, 50, 62, 83, 184, 185, 189, 192, 193, 202, 203, 221, 243, 247, 249, 250, 251, 252, 253, 268, 270, 271, 272, 276, 277, 279, 291, 296
wires, 292
Wisconsin, 246, 251, 254
wood, 1, 9, 39, 78, 98, 131, 154, 195, 201, 214, 222, 233, 237, 242, 276
woodland, 194, 202, 207, 235, 238
wool, 154, 166

X

Xuarez, Catalina, 76

Y

yellow fever, 26